Contents

Foreword

You can't teach an old dog new tricks. Regardless of age, as change washes over us, we can easily view ourselves as old dogs, washed up, left behind, obsolete, out of the game. Unfortunately, the older you get, the less time you feel is left to change. You have worked hard to gain a lifetime of useful awareness and experience, then the Internet comes along, changing everything. Lifestyle, workstyle, competition, even the words we use are changing. Do you "get it"? What the heck does that mean anyway? Suddenly you are an old dog needing to learn new tricks. The more you read about the success stories, instant wealth, and high paying jobs all around us, the more depressing the prospects become.

Let's face it. You are doomed. The other guys and gals who "get it" have won. It's over. Get ready to file bankruptcy and go to work flipping hamburgers.

So much for the stay awake at night failure fantasies. You get the point. So here is the good news: Research has shown that old dogs can learn new tricks, especially if their survival depends upon it. Your economic survival is at stake. You are smarter than a dog. So what do you do about it?

Well of course, finish reading Frank Fiore's book. I have known Frank for many years. He uses everyday language to help people understand change, how it affects what they are doing and what they need to do about it. Frank has combined this style with his in-depth knowledge of emerging Internet commerce to provide a roadmap of how business is changing in the New Economy and what you should do about it.

Okay, what should you do about it? How about trying to get lucky? Not the win the lottery type of luck, but the luck that happens when opportunity meets preparation.

Opportunity comes from your awareness of what's happening around you. It is often very selective. Buy that unique one-of-a-kind automobile you have been wanting for months and suddenly you see that model everywhere. They were there before, you saw them, but you were not aware of them. Awareness is learned over time, a lifetime.

Likewise, preparation comes from experience. Experience happens a day at a time and builds over a lifetime. No help here? If it takes a lifetime to gather awareness and experience, does it take a lifetime to change it? The younger you are the quicker your capacity to change. Well, maybe, however there is more to awareness and experience than the passage of time.

Since we are smarter than dogs and have bigger brains, we do a much better job of describing things and understanding how they work. Even if you feel you are an "older dog" you can quickly change how you see and understand the world around you. Your vision, how you describe the world, and what you "see" leverages your awareness. Think back to something that excited you, like buying that new car. You changed how you saw your world. Likewise, once you change your vision you become aware of new opportunities all around you.

You can also quickly change your understanding of how the world works, your reality map. Try this obvious but often overlooked approach. When you get frustrated because something does not work for you, read the manual. Understand how it should work then apply your experience to have it work for you. If you really are motivated, you will learn why it works and change that part of your reality map. Your experience is applied in the context of how you believe the world works. Change your reality map and your experience can be applied in a whole new way.

The great news is that you can change your vision and reality map in the time it takes for you to read this book—if you are motivated. Excitement, frustration, almost any emotion will do. Changing your vision leverages your awareness to see new opportunities. Changing your reality map leverages your experience so you are prepared to act on new opportunities. Changing your vision and reality map together is how you can get lucky.

Even old dogs get lucky in the New Economy.

Read Frank's book. It's an easy to use manual for how Internet commerce works.

Alan P. Hald

Co-founder, MicroAge

www.microage.com

About the Author

Frank Fiore is an e-commerce expert and consultant, and author of e-commerce books titled *Dr. Livingston's Online Shopping Safari Guidebook* published by Maximum Press and *The Complete Idiot's Guide to Starting an Online Business* published by Macmillan. He has been involved with e-commerce from its inception on the Net and with his experience as an e-commerce expert and direct marketer of products, he knows e-commerce from both sides of the transaction. He is currently president and co-founder of Concurrent Commerce Technologies, a cutting-edge dynamic pricing technology company in Phoenix, Arizona, and the official online shopping guide for About. He has been interviewed for numerous TV and radio talk shows and print media on the subject of e-commerce and online shopping.

Dedication

To my son Christopher who'll be living, working, and playing in the New Economy. Thriving in the New Economy will not be simple. That's why I didn't handicap you by making your life too easy—keeping you long on hugs and short on pocket money.

Acknowledgments

This book was quite a challenge. As one of the first in Macmillan's new series on e-business, there were no prior examples to draw upon. The subject matter itself is very forward thinking and took a leap of faith and much support from my acquisitions editor, Angelina Ward, and my development editor, Nick Goetz, to complete a book that was easy to understand, useful, and professional in nature. So, to Angelina and Nick—hat's off!—and thanks for all your help and support.

Tell Us What You Think!

As the reader of this book, *you* are our most important critic and commentator. We value your opinion and want to know what we're doing right, what we could do better, what areas you'd like to see us publish in, and any other words of wisdom you're willing to pass our way.

As an associate publisher for Que, I welcome your comments. You can fax, email, or write me directly to let me know what you did or didn't like about this book—as well as what we can do to make our books stronger.

Please note that I cannot help you with technical problems related to the topic of this book, and that due to the high volume of mail I receive, I might not be able to reply to every message.

When you write, please be sure to include this book's title and author as well as your name and phone or fax number. I will carefully review your comments and share them with the author and editors who worked on the book.

Fax: 317-581-4666

Email: consumer@mcp.com

Mail: Greg Wiegand
          Que
          201 West 103rd Street
          Indianapolis, IN 46290 USA

Dear e-marketer,

Today's e-commerce is just a rehash of brick-and-mortar stores—with a few interactive tweaks here and there. Banner ads, animated or static, and Web storefronts are just carryovers from the Industrial Age we've left behind. Concepts like fixed pricing on a fixed site, take-it-or leave-it offers, the need for old fashioned middlemen, accessing the Net only from PCs, disregard for customer privacy—even the need for dot-coms themselves—are so last century.

Advancements in personal software agents such as shopping bots and selling bots will radically change the landscape of e-commerce and as the Internet permeates our society, the wireless Web will allow transactions and interactions to happen anywhere—the home, office, in the car, on the cell phone, the TV, the microwave—even our refrigerators!

Fixed pricing will be history. Flexible pricing schemes that give consumers more control over the prices they pay for products are already in place. Name your price auctions, supply and demand pricing, and aggregated buying already exist, soon to be replaced by new forms of dynamic pricing that combine them all and add even newer applications.

The bottom line?

Selling anything, anywhere, any time, any way, and at any price will be the norm of doing business on the Net. To do that, e-businesses will have to understand the new Rules of the Road that apply to e-marketing. This book will give you, the person responsible for creating marketing strategies for your e-business, an understanding of how to position, price, and promote your company to online consumers within the changing nature of the Internet.

So, come with me and I'll show you how your e-business can survive and thrive in the New Economy.

Sincerely,

Frank Fiore

Conventions Used in This Book

Throughout this book you will find a variety of special elements designed to give you additional information. These margin notes explain the icons you will encounter.

Buzzwords

These margin notes will bring you quickly up to speed on technical terminology used in the book.

Heads Up

On the Net you never know where your competition is coming from—nor when the next big thing will arrive. These margin notes will give you a 'heads up' on what's coming down the information superhighway.

Trend Setter

The Net has a surprising way of making tomorrow today. These margin notes will cite examples of businesses that are setting the trend for the Internet.

CASE STUDY

CASE STUDIES

Throughout the book you'll find a series of brief case studies of real companies. These case studies are intended to give real-life examples of the subjects presented in this book.

Rules of the Road: Sell Any Where, Any Thing, Any Time, Any Way, at Any Price

As the U.S. aircraft carrier *Enterprise* steamed out of port one evening, it encountered a strange light up ahead—dead in its path. What follows is the radio conversation between the *Enterprise* and the strange light.

Enterprise: Please divert your course 15 degrees to the North to avoid collision.

Civilian: Recommend you divert YOUR course 15 degrees to the South to avoid collision.

Enterprise: This is the Captain of a U.S. Navy ship. I say again, divert YOUR course.

Civilian: No. I say again, divert YOUR course.

Enterprise: This is the aircraft carrier *Enterprise*. We are a large warship of the U.S. Navy. Divert your course NOW!

Civilian: This is a lighthouse. Your call.

Whether true or not this story is a good example of what's happening in today's economy. Businesses are playing the *Enterprise* and the Internet is playing the lighthouse—and this scene is being acted out on a new economic playing field called the Digital Economy. This New Economy makes clear that the Internet is not a new business tool—but a whole new toolbox. And this toolbox is requiring businesses to change how they do business now and in the near future. Over the last couple of years, more and more companies have been realizing that they're not up to speed on emerging e-business strategies or on many of the key issues that their own e-businesses are creating, such as privacy concerns, intellectual property rights, and taxation and market positioning. To believe the current Internet hype, most of the winners in the e-commerce turf war have been identified and their business strategies have won. If you're a Johnny-come-lately to this party, you're told you've already lost. But on the other hand, if you listen to the gloom-and-doom crowd of late (in most cases, the very same people who hyped e-commerce just a year or so ago), pure e-commerce companies have seen their day and the Big Dogs of the Old Economy are reasserting their dominance.

So who's right? Neither. As usual, the truth is somewhere in the middle.

As we enter the next millennium, we're only now seeing through the haze of hype and the din of the doomsayers to make out in the distance the emergence of e-business soon to come. Or as one wag has said, "We're in the black and white stage of the Internet and we have no idea what color looks like." The next wave of e-business will create the next stage of buying and selling that is uniquely suited to the power of the World Wide Web.

The Internet, like all new technologies, has a common problem. New technologies are not fully understood and used to their full potential until later in their development. Take television for example. When TV first appeared, the commercials acted more like radio ads than the sophisticated advertisements we see today. In the beginning, commercials on TV were just fixed billboards with a product picture and a voice-over pitching the item. Ad agencies just borrowed on what came before and applied it to the new medium. No attempt was made at using the abilities of the new technology—the pictures could *move*! It wasn't until later that ad agencies saw the potential of the new technology and exploited its full potential.

It's the same with the Internet today. Banner ads—animated or static—and Web storefronts are just carryovers from the Industrial Age we've left behind. And current e-business strategies fare no better. Most e-commerce is just a rehash of brick-and-mortar stores—with a few interactive tweaks here and there. Concepts like "fixed pricing on a fixed site," "take-it-or leave-it" offers, the need for old-fashioned middlemen, accessing the Net only from PCs, disregard for customer privacy—even the need for dot-coms themselves—are so last century!

If that's not enough of a change, the Internet is also facilitating a different set of interactions that could never take place in the real world. Buyers can communicate with sellers, buyers with other buyers, and sellers with other sellers. Information on both buyer and seller is easily and quickly accumulated for each other's use in the purchasing process. Both buyers and sellers can tap into virtual communities on the Web to critique merchants, evaluate products—even ask sellers for personal offers—anywhere and at any time. On one side, e-businesses can ask and collect information on buyers to personalize their shopping experience. On the other, buyers can choose to remain anonymous until the time they want to identify themselves to sellers.

But that's not all. Advancements in personal software agents like shopping *bots* (robots) and selling bots will radically change the landscape of e-commerce. Shopping bots will seek out and purchase products at the best price, and selling bots will make offers to shopping bots suggesting colors, sizes, and other selling features that match the shoppers' preferences and requirements. And as the Internet permeates our society, the wireless Web will allow transactions and interactions to happen anywhere—the home, office, in the car, on the cell phone, the TV, the microwave—even our refrigerators!

Fixed pricing will be history. Flexible pricing schemes that give consumers more control over the prices they pay for products are already in place. "Name your price" auctions, supply-and-demand pricing, and aggregated buying already exist—soon to be replaced by new forms of dynamic pricing that combine them all and add even newer applications. Product pricing will parallel the stock market with bid and ask, market orders, and futures contracts. All this and more will transform our current business models into true e-business strategies. But it won't be easy. The challenges for e-business today are to make buying simple, easy, and fast while giving consumers good pricing, good availability, good service, and a fun shopping experience.

Yes. The die has been cast, the gauntlet thrown down. From here on out, selling anywhere, anything, any time, any way, and at any price will be the norm of doing business on the Net. To do that, businesses will have to understand new marketing strategies, and captains of industry will have to listen to the lighthouse.

And that's what this book is all about.

PART I

Positioning Your Business for the New Economy

Next Generation e-Business

Dot-coms are dead. At least, the way we've defined them so far. The Internet is its own medium and e-businesses will have to learn how to use this new technology in ways that could never be used in real world businesses. The power has gone to the buyer and because the Net offers more choices, they will be more and more in control of both the transaction and sales. What's critical for an e-business now and in the future is access to the buyer—how, where, when, and what he or she buys and, whenever possible, owning the relationship with them. One of the threats to face is the Net's power to disintermediate a business—in other words, cutting out the middleman—and the question an e-business must ask itself today is this: "Is my industry slated next for disintermediation and if so, how do I deal with this threat?" An e-business must also understand that what is valued most in any economy is what is scarcest. In today's economy, that is consumer attention. You can't buy a consumer's attention—it's earned! The size of your business or your site has little to do with it. To capture the attention of a buyer, e-businesses will need to understand how to market through all channels of contact—not just through a Web site, a brick and motor storefront, printed catalogs, or a telemarketing call center. For the Internet's days of being English-centric, U.S.-centric, and PC-centric are numbered.

To paraphrase an old investment quote—"If you want to make a small fortune in e-commerce—start with a large one." At least that's the way it seemed during the first few months of the new millennium.

After months of unbridled optimism and Internet hoopla, the dot-com magic evaporated. Investors abandoned the dot-coms in droves, driving e-commerce stocks down to IPO levels or below. Even industry analysts who were previously e-commerce boosters said it was curtain time for e-tailers. StrategyWeek.com (www.strategyweek.com) declared that 80% of e-commerce sites will fail by 2005. Not to be outdone, Gartner Group (www.gartner.com) predicted that 95% to 98% of all dot-coms will fail over the next 24 months!

Dot-coms are dead. At least, the way we've defined them so far. Going from bricks to clicks has been just a rehash of what came before—a new channel for doing old things. So, it's no surprise that the carryover of Old Economy marketing concepts to the Internet wouldn't work. The Internet is its own medium and e-businesses will have to learn how to use this new technology in ways that could never be used in real world businesses.

The first generation of e-commerce is coming to an end. The next generation has begun. Companies must now move from claiming territories to defending and capturing them.

Storm Warnings

Over the last few years, the Internet has kept many a businessperson awake at night. First it was the fear that their business would be "Amazoned" by free wheeling dot-coms flush with millions of dollars in venture capital and billions of dollars in IPO money. Then, after making the dive into e-commerce, real world businesses had to worry about channel conflicts with their existing distributors and their own retail stores. If they sold the same products on the Net that they sold in their stores, they feared they would cannibalize their own existing retail sales.

And what about pricing? The new generation of e-consumers expected lower prices and instant service when buying from *e-tailers*

New Economy Index

To keep up on the newest happenings in the New Economy, check out the New Economy Index (www.neweconomyindex.org). This site provides a set of economic indicators specifically geared to the New Economy gathered from both private and public sources.

What Is an e-Tailer?

An e-tailer—or electronic retailer—is a company that has opened a storefront on the Net.

What Is Brochureware?

Some companies on the Net create a Web site that is a mere reproduction of a company's existing print materials—or brochures. This is called brochureware. Another name for it is shovel-ware because the company just shovels their existing marketing communications materials onto Web pages with no regard to how it's presented or read by online consumers.

on the Net. Should businesses sell at one price online and another offline? Is it superior business models or superior technology that rules the roost in the New Economy? Who's to call the shots? The CIO or the CEO? Who should decide the rules of engagement in this new competitive environment?

At first, technology ruled. After all, wasn't the Internet all about technology? Just get some hotshot programmers, graphic artists, and IT engineers, and then turn them loose to project your business strategy on the Net. Many Webmasters had a field day with the new technology and added every new whistle and bell that came down the Information Highway. Complex graphics, animation, plug-ins to view content, and hard to navigate sites led to the slow download of Web pages, lost visitors, and frustrated consumers. Boo.com (www.boo.com) is a very good example of a site designed by engineers not by marketers. It's filled with cumbersome programming tricks, requires a software plug-in, and at least a 56K modem to fully utilize the site. At launch only 40% of the users were able to access the site. After investors sank hundreds of millions of dollars into Boo.com, it recently filed for bankruptcy.

Businesses that didn't take the technology route turned their e-commerce site over to the Marketing Communications Department who promptly turned the site into electronic *brochureware*. Finally, e-commerce companies woke up and came to the realization that *"It's the customer"* and turned its attention to selling on the Net (which too many online businesses have failed to do).

Power to the Customer

An important shift has happened to retailing. The power has gone to the buyer. Because the Net gives buyers more choices—more e-tailers to choose from, more ways to buy, and more access to information—they are more and more in control of both the transaction and the sales. Where there once was scarcity of choices, there is now an overabundance of options. Companies must now formulate marketing strategies to achieve a competitive advantage—and the battlefield where competitive advantage is won or lost is not on best price but in access.

What's critical now is access to the customer—how, where, when, and what he or she buys and, most importantly, owning the relationship with them. New Internet enabled business models and the emerging marketing strategies that follow give e-businesses the tools to reach the consumers whenever and wherever they buy. Peter Drucker, consulting for Ford Motor Company many years ago, asked top management, "What business are you in?" They said, "Making cars." He replied, "No you're not. You're in the business of making money." If that same question was asked today, that question would not be "What business are you in?" but, as Adrian J. Slywotzky, vice president at Mercer Management Consulting says, "What's the next-generation business model that we should be running?"

Companies that are the first to recognize and act on the strategic changes in their industries will be the winners in the New Economy. One word of warning, though. There are dangers in being the one ahead of the curve in your industry. Clayton Christensen, professor of business administration at the Harvard Business School, calls it the "innovator's dilemma." The dilemma is that the more accurate your description of the future, the more likely you're describing the present. If you're successful at predicting what's ahead, you might harm your present business by charging ahead too soon.

Still, today's e-business has little choice. The pace of innovation in today's business environment demands that companies take the risks.

Disintermediation—Cutting Out the Middleman

Disintermediation. Such a mouthful for a simple idea, disintermediation means creating shortcuts. Or in other words, removing links from a trading chain, or what is called in more colloquial language, "cutting out the middleman."

Disintermediation puts the producer of goods or services directly in touch with the customer. As the Internet connects everybody to everybody else, the opportunities for shortcuts increase. If you can connect directly to a stock exchange, your bank account, a music

What Is Disintermediation?

Disintermediation is used to describe the "disintegration" or extinction of the middlemen in the trading chain as we know it today, that is the distributors, wholesalers, and retailers.

artist, author, or airline, then stockbrokers, bank tellers, record companies, publishers, or travel agents start to look like overpriced terminals.

Strangely enough, disintermediation didn't start with the Internet. It was your conservative local bank that was one of the first to usher it in. ATMs, or Automated Teller Machines, disintermediated many a human teller since its inception. The Internet just accelerated the disintermediation process and affected many more industries.

One of the first to go were the stockbrokers. New investment Web sites such as E*Trade (www.etrade.com) gave the common investor the tools to buy stocks directly without going through a traditional stockbroker. Other companies soon followed E*Trade's lead. Insurance and mortgage companies started offering quotes directly to the consumer bypassing the traditional mortgage and insurance brokers. Then companies such as mp3.com (www.mp3.com) raised the ante by cutting out the music publishers by letting the artists sell their music directly to consumers. All the consumer had to do was download a song onto their computer and play it through their computer speakers or load it into their portable MP3 player.

Who's next to be disintermediated? How about the movie industry? Studio moguls are looking over their shoulders as the ability to make movie videos using a PC and offer them to the consumer over the Net is becoming a reality. And book publishers are soon to follow. New authors who couldn't get the time of day from established publishing houses are taking their manuscripts to the Web and selling their books directly to consumers. And just recently, the idea of buying and downloading a book from the Web has been greatly validated by Stephen King. More than 100,000 copies of his new novella were purchased and downloaded in a matter of hours.

Disintermediation is the definite trend of the future because the Net is shifting the balance of power to the buyer. The question a company must ask itself today is "Is my industry slated next for disintermediation?" And the next one after that is, "How do I organize my company to deal with this threat?" The answer is to become a new type of *intermediary*, one that focuses on personalized, individualized customer service and targeted after-marketing.

The middleman will not go away—just change its stripes. Sure, the Net allows sellers and buyers to interact directly. Problem is, it's not that efficient. Even for simple transactions, the Net still needs intermediaries. Let's say you want to buy Madonna's latest CD on the Web. You go to Yahoo! (www.yahoo.com) or some other search engine, type in Madonna's name and her new CD and get dozens of links—some about the CD, some about Madonna, some on where to buy it.

You can whittle down your choices by using a comparison-shopping agent such as mySimon (www.mysimon.com) or DealTime (www.dealtime.com). When you do that, you're using an intermediary.

The challenge to e-businesses today is to add value to the consumer's shopping experience by building better and stronger customer relationships and connecting with them through all channels of contact. That's how you win the disintermediation game.

What Is an Intermediary?

In an e-business, an intermediary is a company that adds value to a purchasing process and makes it easier to find, decide, and buy a product or service a consumer is looking for.

The Attention Economy

What's valued most in the New Economy? Money? Products? Information? No. What's valued most is always what's scarcest. And in today's information-overloaded world, the scarcest commodity of all is a consumer's attention.

Consumer attention is scarce because there is only so much of it to give. Today's consumers divide their limited attention between work, home, family, friends, TV, books, listening to music, reading newspapers (remember newspapers?), email, and the Internet. As the Internet permeates more and more of the consumer's lives, it becomes more difficult to get their attention. Not only are dot-coms proliferating at an enormous rate but new forms of e-commerce are emerging that will demand more consumer attention. With the approaching opportunity of buying anytime and anywhere, the challenge to today's e-business is how to capture and keep a consumer's attention, a consumer who at the same time defines freedom as having *not* to pay attention when they don't want to.

Over the next several years the Internet will provide a widening range of media such as streaming media, multicasting, two-way video, mobile commerce, always-on information appliances—even virtual reality. These technologies will become a major part of life for everyone on the planet and will challenge the marketing departments of every company on the Net.

Yahoo! is a good example of keeping a consumer's attention. Here's a company that doesn't sell anything to consumers and gives away information for free yet has made millionaires of its founders by finding a way to get consumer's attention. Over the years they added valuable free services and got the lion's share of attention on the Net. They translated this consumer attention—millions of visitors a day to their Web site—into money by selling the consumer's attention to advertisers.

Because Yahoo! is a Web directory and searchable database, Yahoo! is able to deliver to its advertisers not just any old consumer's attention—but a targeted one. For example, the kind of people who search for information about dogs or dog breeding in Yahoo! are exactly the people that dog food retailers want to pitch to. People looking for Web sites about travel are shown ads from travel agencies. And because Yahoo! lists everything under the sun, that's a lot of targeted attention. Companies on the Web that offer free Web pages or email work the same way. They get consumer's attention and sell that attention to advertisers or sponsors.

CASE STUDY

CYBERGOLD

Cybergold, at www.cybergold.com, was one of the first online marketing incentive companies to allow individuals to earn and spend money on the Internet. Nat Goldhaber founded Cybergold in 1995 with backing from marketing legends Jay Chiat, Regis McKenna, and Peter Sealey. Cybergold rewards online consumers in a variety of ways. Consumers earn actual cash, typically starting at 50 cents, when making online purchases, downloading free software, registering for online services, or simply visiting a Web site. More than 200 online merchants, including Disney, AOL, E*Trade, Autobytel, and MBNA have used Cybergold's incentives program to acquire new customers cheaply and efficiently.

Cybergold delivers measurable, pay-for-performance results for its clients' online advertising campaigns that can result in a reduction of the cost of customer acquisition by up to 50% for its merchant clients. These same merchants enjoy no-risk advertising with Cybergold, paying only when a Cybergold member completes a transaction.

As Michael Goldhaber, the person who coined the phrase "Attention Economy" said, "Money flows to attention." Big companies don't automatically get attention on the Web just because they have a lot of money. With lots of money you can hire a lot of engineers, copywriters, and graphic artists to create a Web site. With lots of money you can spend truckloads of it promoting your site— but without an engaging offer it will not win a consumer's attention. In other words, you can't buy attention—it's earned!

Create enticing content or an engaging experience that demands attention; consumers and money will follow. The size of your business or your site or the type of business model you have has little to do with it. Take WebPagesThatSuck (www.WebPagesThatSuck.com), for example. It grabbed loads of attention from Web surfers through Web sites that linked to it, email referrals, newsgroups, and ordinary conversation. Word quickly spread about a site where you could learn good design by looking at bad design. WebPagesThatSuck got so much attention that it could sell adverting on its site—turning attention in money.

The lesson to be learned by an e-business is clear. CIOs and other IT leaders at companies know how to provide information, and they know how to connect their organizations and people within them. What they're not skilled at is winning consumer attention. That's the mission of the marketing and sales professional. Michael Goldhaber says that there are two players in the Attention

Cybergold's member can have the cash they earn transferred to a VISA credit card, into their bank account, or spend it with participating merchants on the Web.

In exchange for some personal information, including what types of ads a consumer is interested in, he or she receives email updates that inform him of discounts being offered at Cybergold clients' Web sites. In addition, through Cybergold's micropayment system, consumers can conduct online transactions involving amounts as low as a few cents. This allows them to spend the cash they earn on MP3 music, software, and other digital content. Consumers can also donate any amount of their Cybergold to a number of nonprofit organizations directly via the Internet.

The company has received a United States patent for "Attention Brokerage and Orthogonal Sponsorship," giving Cybergold broad protection over the distribution of online incentives to consumers interacting with Internet advertisements.

Economy—Stars, who gather a great deal of attention, and Fans, who pay their attention to Stars. Your e-business has to be a Star that's popular enough to draw Fans—that is buyers—to your product or service offer.

So, can your company be an e-business Star? And what's the best way of gathering lots of Fans? By getting your message out through all channels of communications.

Integrating All Channels of Contact

In the movie *Sleepless in Seattle*, Rob Reiner was commenting on how a series of unrelated events came together to give Tom Hanks' character a chance for a date. Reiner said, "She's an interior decorator. You're an architect. You're both unattached. What do you call it when many different things intersect?"

Hanks responded, "The Bermuda Triangle."

The *convergence* spoken about here will not be as bad as Hanks remarks. But it could be scary for your e-business. The convergence of the digital and analog world and the integrating of all channels of contact whether in customer service, between business models, or through digital devices will soon be the norm. e-Businesses will compete not only for attention but access to that attention as well. e-Businesses will need to understand how to market through all channels of contact—not just through a Web site, a brick and mortar storefront, printed catalogs, or a telemarketing call center.

Take the digitizing of information for example. The translation of everything from Ally McBeal to our kid's homework into digitized ones and zeros is well on its way. Although it's not going to be as bad as Hanks remarks, the convergence of voice, data, wireless, and optical is a revolution that's coming, and those companies that aren't ready for it will put their competitive position at risk.

In digital convergence, bits are bits, and those bits can be made available to anyone, anywhere, and at any time via the Internet. That means that you can reach buyers on any digital device that is connected to the Net that you have or carry. How connected? In just a few short years the Net will be ubiquitous. It will be

What Is Convergence?

Convergence is the coming together of two or more separate technologies. For example, the convergence of the Net with TV or cell phones where you can access the Web from either device is a good example.

everywhere. In every TV, telephone, cell phone, PDA—even our refrigerators, microwaves, and washing machines.

Customer service will feel the effects of convergence, too. It will give companies a leg up on their competition and a jump on meeting their customers' needs through the integration of call centers, instant and integrated messaging, fax access, email, and live chat. Customer service will lead to customer care, giving customers the ability to communicate with you in real-time via multiple channels of contact. The result is a quality experience with little delay and fewer complications and this gives your customers the ability to control their own service needs.

Finally, there's the convergence of business models.

On the one hand we see consolidations in almost every market shrinking the number of players. Yet, on the other we have new competitors entering the very same markets with new business models acting as something completely different. Take grocery stores for instance. In the real world, drug stores are expanding their food-related offerings competing with the traditional grocery store. Costco now carries perishable groceries. On the other hand, grocery stores are approaching restaurants by offering prepared meals. Fast food restaurants such as Boston Market are going upscale and supplementing their menu with traditional grocery offerings.

Manufacturers such as Hewlett-Packard (www.hp.com) and Sony (www.sony.com) are behaving like retailers selling their products direct to consumers, e-tailers such as Dell (www.dell.com) and Gateway (www.gateway.com) are manufacturers acting like e-tailers, and Amazon (www.amazon.com) wants to be everything to everybody. The boundaries between retailers, manufacturers, distributors, entertainment, financial services, news, and information are blurring more and more every day. The competitive threat for companies today can come not only from their own market space but from anywhere at any time.

So what's the game plan? What are the new rules of engagement? Today's New Economy e-business must compete on reach, affiliation, and rich information and, at the same time, it must connect with consumers and adapt to their needs.

Scanning for Price Drops

ReverseAuction.com (www.reverseauction.com) and BarPoint.com (www.barpoint.com) have joined forces to help consumers discover if a certain product is at auction at ReverseAuction.com. Consumers find a product in a store, note the bar code, enter it into BarPoint.com's site, and see if there is a ReverseAuction for it.

The large booksellers on the Web have a greater reach than any physical bookstore could ever have. While the largest of the brick and mortar bookstores carry about 250,000 titles, e-tailers such as Amazon offer more than five million books and are located on more than 25 million PCs. The same goes for CDs, videos, and a variety of other commodity products sold on the Web.

And you don't have to be an Amazon to have reach. A company can also extend its reach through affiliation by establishing joint ventures with other companies. An online automobile e-tailer such as Autobytel (www.autobytel.com) not only will sell you a car, but through affiliations with more than 100 banks, will help you finance it as well. They also offer one-stop auto insurance quotes from the nation's top insurance companies. By extending their reach through affiliation, Autobytel can offer its customers a one-stop shop for their car buying needs.

As for richness, manufacturers and suppliers have deeper and more up-to-date information on products while retailers have a large amount of information on consumers. Putting these two types of information together correctly can offer a richer shopping experience than can be supplied by either one alone. The richer the shopping experience, the more the chance a shopper can be converted into a buyer.

Finally, if you think the arrival a few years ago of AOL newbies to the Net was fraught with problems, wait until the next wave of billions of consumers hits the Net who will be accessing it not

FINGERHUT

In the early 1990s Fingerhut launched its own home-shopping channel on TV. Or at least it tried to. They were going to be one of the 500 cable channels that were projected to appear by the end of the decade. They knew that shopping channels were a big hit then and were well prepared for the onslaught of orders that they expected to receive from theirs. Unfortunately, the 500 channels of cable TV never materialized and

neither did the orders. Instead, Fingerhut was left holding four million square feet of warehouse space and a sophisticated fulfillment system.

So, what does a company do with all this excess warehouse space and a state-of-the-art fulfillment system? Become a fulfillment house!

A few years later, a new opportunity became apparent—e-commerce. Fingerhut looked around and saw that there was a real need for through PCs, but cell phones, telephones, TVs, and other noncomputing devices. And that's not all. Hundreds of millions of these newbies will not speak English! Connecting with them through Internet appliances—not PCs—and dealing with their cultural differences will be quite a challenge for e-businesses to come.

The Internet's days of being English-centric, U.S.-centric, and PC-centric are numbered.

Beyond PCs and Web Sites

Don't look now but the always-on, always-connected Internet is just around the corner. Perpetual access and consumers being connected at all times, no matter where they are will drastically impact your e-business. We can already access our email and certain Web sites through our Palm Pilots and cell phones. But newer and more powerful *Net Appliances* are making their appearance and they will be much more affordable and easier to use than PCs for the masses of consumers who will hit the Web over the next few years.

At Netpliance (www.netpliance.com) for $99 and a small monthly service fee, consumers can have a Web and email browser that's always on whenever they need it. They can check their email or surf the Web without the need of a PC. WebTV (www.webtv.com) is another inexpensive Net Appliance that hooks up to a television. Consumers can check email and surf the Web between commercials, and even play along and interact with their favorite game shows such as "Jeopardy" or "Who Wants to Be a Millionaire?"

What Is a Net Appliance?

A Net Appliance is a wired or wireless device that is specifically designed to connect to the Internet. They could be used to retrieve email, surf the Web, or shop for products and services.

a third-party fulfillment service for e-tailers on the Net—and that need was only going to grow larger. So, they optimized their system for third-party fulfillment and now their warehouses are hopping 24 hours a day fulfilling orders from eToys, Wal-Mart, and other clients such as TurboTax and Pier One.

Why would a company such as Wal-Mart have Fingerhut do their Web site fulfillment? After all, Wal-Mart is a well known logistics innovator. Why don't they do their own Web site fulfillment? The reason is simple. Outsourcing is less expensive than building new distribution centers to handle the influx of their online business and it doesn't require a large up-front investment. So for Wal-Mart it was a simple decision to build or buy. They bought. And they bought the state-of-the-art fulfillment system that Fingerhut provided.

Fingerhut saw and acted on the strategic changes in their industry and are well on their way to becoming one of the winners in the New Economy.

The market for these and other Net Appliances will be large. International Data Corporation (IDC) (www.idc.com) reported that Net Appliances are expected to represent more than one third of total Internet access device shipments by 2003. These Net Appliances will compete with, and take market share away from, PCs—and in turn—the traditional Web site.

These new Net Appliances and application software are challenging the traditional Web site business model. New marketing channels and sales methods will enter the encyclopedia of e-business such as m-commerce (mobile commerce), d-commerce (distributed selling across a network), dy-commerce (dynamic-pricing commerce), d-mail (direct-selling email), and c-mail (commerce-enabled email).

What does this mean for your e-business?

Well, you've put a lot of work into your e-commerce Web site. It's up and running and functioning well. You're taking orders, providing customer order status, your site is secure, and your page views are climbing. Your advertising and sponsorship deals are in place and are starting to pay off.

Too bad that business model is obsolete.

Up until now the predominant e-business model has been the e-commerce Web site. Companies have invested huge amounts of money to make their sites content heavy, attractive, and "sticky." But new Net Appliances and applications are about to shoot holes in this Web site dominant business model. Like in the physical world, the virtual world will have multiple channels of distribution where the Web as we know it today filled with hundreds of thousands of e-commerce Web sites will become just another channel of distribution—and not necessarily the most important one.

Companies, such as Napster (www.napster.com), that search Napster subscribers' hard drives for MP3 music titles; OnePage (www.onepage.com), that lets you create a tailored Web page pieced together from many other Web sites; FireDrop (www.zaplet.com), whose Zaplets translate email messages into a format for commerce engines and commerce-enabled wireless devices such as Palm IVs and Nokia cell phones, will make the current e-commerce Web site an evolutionary has-been.

Shop the Web from a Telephone

NetByTel (www.netbytel.com) enables companies to open up a whole new market and bring their online products and services to any consumer using any telephone, anywhere. Companies using NetByTel's technology can speech-enable their Web site so a customer can call from anywhere and transact business over any wire line or wireless telephone.

All these companies have one thing in common. They are all technologies that will transform the Internet from, as Will Chen, the CEO of OnePage puts it, "a clumsy, page-by-page experience" to a customized experience controlled by the consumer. And they are not alone. More powerful applications are on the way that will force companies to change their e-business marketing and sales strategies as the control of the experience shifts from the site operator to the consumer.

There are more than 200 million computers in the world today. It's estimated that by the year 2002 that number will grow to 500 million (see Table 1.1). Yet the number of noncomputer chips now operating in the world is 6 billion! Where are they? They're embedded in our cars, stereos, TVs, household appliances—even our rice cookers! All these devices will be connected to the Net at all times via wire and wireless devices communicating with each other and networked throughout our homes and communication appliances.

Table 1.1

Multiple Net Access Devices Will Grow Dramatically by 2003			
	1999	2001	2003
Net Appliances	14 Million	237 Million	755 Million
Net Population	14 Million	240 Million	602 Million
Devices Per Surfer	1.02	0.98	1.25

Source International Data Corporation (IDC)

The result? In the coming months and over the next few years, more and more e-commerce will be conducted offsite—that is, off Web sites—and if your marketing strategy is focused on only one channel of distribution, you will be left far behind.

Learning the Rules of the New Economy

The New Economy has new rules, and companies that follow the new rules will prosper in the New Economy. Those that don't, will not. Space and time will shrink causing markets to expand. Market share will yield to mind share. New intermediaries will appear replacing the old, and market growth will run on Internet time. Power will move to the consumer, mass customization will be the rule, and companies will have the ability—and challenge—to sell anything, anywhere, any way, anytime, and at any price.

On the Net your business can sell as easily to a customer around the world as around the block. The entire world is your market, connecting with customers instantly anywhere around the globe. But the world is also your competitor. The infomediary will be the new middleman in the information distribution chain of the New Economy. It will manipulate information to extract higher value from it by reselling it, reusing it, repackaging it, or giving it away. e-Businesses will have to rethink the way they price their products and services and how they present their offer.

Consumers will be given an infinite number of purchasing choices with the ability to buy what they want the moment they hear about it.

To paraphrase the Golden Rule—"He who has the gold makes the rules." At least that's the way it seemed in the Old Economy—not so anymore. Case in point: Microsoft and the computer era.

Other than Intel, Microsoft has contributed more to the advancement of the personal computer revolution than any other company—and grown wealthy in the process. But the computer era, which had its heyday with the creation and spread of the personal computer, lasted only a few short decades. It's now over. Like Microsoft, the personal computer has feasted on most, if not all, of the innovations it has created.

The big story now is what's happening between computers and other computer chip-based devices. They're talking to each other.

Now, it's connections, not computations, that are creating a networked economy—the New Economy. Peter Drucker spoke of the New Economy back in 1969 when he predicted the rise of the knowledge worker. To him, the acquisition, manipulation, and application of information—not material resources or capital—is the engine that generates wealth in the New Economy. Today, the PCs that we've used to crunch spreadsheets and produce documents have been utilized instead to network our PCs and connect everything together. The networking process is still in its infancy but it has profoundly changed the rules of how businesses will do business now and in the decades to come.

In early 1998, a new magazine by the name of Business 2.0 noticed these developments and forged them into a new set of rules. They named them the "Ten Driving Principles of the New Economy" and predicted that those companies that follow the new rules will prosper in the New Economy. Those that don't, will not.

Principle 1: Matter Doesn't Matter

Remember the marketing hype a few years back around the movie *Godzilla*? It screamed from every billboard, TV ad, and movie trailer—"Size does matter!"

Not in the New Economy.

Look at Microsoft. Their legal troubles with the Federal Government aside, Microsoft is more a creature of the Old Economy than the new. Sure, the product that Microsoft creates is more digital than say, an automobile. But Microsoft had more in common with General Motors than it did with Netscape. It produced software (disks, manuals, packaging) or what they say in the New Economy—"matter." The irony of it all is that just when the Federal Government is about to break up Microsoft for being a threat to innovation and competition, the "matter"—PC software—it produces, doesn't matter.

If a company produces products that are bigger, heavier, and more solid, it doesn't mean that they have more value. Per pound, automobiles have less value than computers and computers less value than software (see Table 2.1). Look at today's Internet and you'll begin to see that value is in the information, services, knowledge, and entertainment it provides. The value of the heavy metal of the Net—the computers, servers, and the like—decreases in cost year by year, while the information on the Net increases in value. Look at the top 100 Internet properties that make up the New Economy. The vast majority of them practice their trade in information—not products.

Table 2.1

Value Per Pound	
Product	Dollar Value Per Pound
Taurus	$5.22
Jeep	$6.59
iMac	$31.47
PC	$76.41
Laptop	$396.23

Source: Ernst & Young Center for Business Innovation

That doesn't mean that hard goods such as books, CDs, furniture, apparel, gifts, and the like will not be sold online. Far from it. Every product has a certain amount of information tied to it, and this information can be used to market and sell that product more efficiently and effectively on the Net.

In e-business, it's people, ideas, and strategic relationships that are of value today. Matter matters less. Information is the new product to be transported. Electrons not atoms are to be moved. Computer chips and circuit boards are the transportation highways of today and they, not railroads and trucking companies, carry the heavy freight of information goods. Information has another unique characteristic unlike any matter around. You can give it away, and yet still possess it.

Take the revolution in downloadable software. You don't create matter-intensive disks, manuals, or packaging; you just post the software on the Net and supply and charge as many copies as necessary. No inventory problems and no production delays. The Net is also ready made for the service industry. Service can be performed over the network from anywhere at anytime extending the information resources of service providers far and wide.

Which brings us to the second driving principle: Space.

Principle 2: The Shrinkage of Space

First the good news:

On the Net, your business can sell as easily to a customer around the world as around the block. Where your business is physically located is no longer important. The entire world is your market connecting with customers instantly anywhere around the globe.

Now the bad news:

The world is not only your customer—but your competitor too. Where once companies had to compete with others in the same city or region, now they have to compete with companies around the world. With the limitations of geography eliminated, competitors that you never dreamed possible are suddenly competing for customers in your market space. Amazon not only competes with bookstores in this country, but with bookstores all around the world. National telephone companies are seeing competition from telephony startups from the other side of the globe that seek to provide telephone access over the Net.

The integration of Web services and wireless technologies have extended the reach of companies to sell to anyone, anywhere at anytime. When it's as easy to buy a product or service from a cell phone as it is from a PC, then your e-business will face a whole new crop of competitors. And when companies like Dell, Gateway, eToys, or CDNow can sell directly to customers around the world using DHL and FedEx to deliver the product, we can quickly see both the promises and challenges your e-business faces today.

But the collapse of space in the New Economy can just as quickly work against an e-business. Instant communications between consumers is the flip side of instant contact with customers. Consumers can quickly and effectively communicate to each other their experiences with your company—good or bad. Using the technologies of the Web, they can easily compare one product against another and one offer against another to find the best deal. If they feel a company mistreated them in any way, they can quickly make their complaints heard far and wide in newsgroups, discussion lists, chat rooms, and bulletin boards on the Net. The collapse of space not only threatens your e-business with new competition, but with assaults on your brand.

Just as the space between an e-business and its customers is shrinking, time is collapsing.

Principle 3: The Collapsing of Time

Dell Computers is the number one direct marketing catalog company in the world. With more than $15 billion sales in 1999 it has proven that it knows how to ride the acceleration curve of the New Economy. Dell Computer (see Figure 2.1) understood the concept of interactivity. It didn't sell computers based on what it thought the market wanted, it built computers based on what the customer wanted. By tracking and adapting to order trends from customers, it was able to build a quick inventory and purchase cycle that both pleased its customers and threatened its competitors.

The Net Is Calling

The Internet has spawned a number of new competitors in the telephony market space. Using the technology of the Net, consumers can download software that allows them to make long-distance calls to any phone in the world—free of charge. One such company that supplies this software is InternetPhone at www.eurocall.com/e/ip5.htm.

Instant interactivity is accelerating change, and companies that can adapt quickly to changes in their market space will be the ones that succeed. Time is money, and if a company can save a consumer time, that will quickly equate to money in their cash registers. Companies that can accelerate consumer convenience factors like product search capabilities and comparisons, multiple channels of contact, and various ways to purchase will attract more customers and more sales.

As time collapses on the Net, the bar is being raised higher and higher by the consumer. And as time accelerates in the New Economy, so does the competition. Consumers expect instant response, instant service, and instant satisfaction, or as Jay Walker, the founder of Priceline.com said, "Consumers want Wal-Mart prices with Nordstrom service and 7-Eleven convenience." And if they don't get it, the ease of finding your competitor is just a mouse click away.

If you think that setting up barriers to competition will keep the competitive wolf at bay—it won't. After you're on the Net, "You open your kimono" exposing your business model and marketing strategy for the entire world to see. The only competitive barrier in the New Economy is speed. Speed to market and the immediacy of products and services to the consumer when and where he or she wants them is what consumers want. You get this kind of speed from brains, not brawn. The kind of brains that can see beyond the e-commerce horizon and act on it with innovative marketing strategies that give consumers what they want, when they want it, and how they want it.

Which brings us to the fourth principle: people.

Principle 4: It's People That Matter

In the New Economy, intellectual capital is more valuable than cash. To succeed in the New Economy, companies need to cultivate two types of intellectual capital—their employees and their customers.

As Peter Drucker predicted and whom the Macintosh computer targeted, the "knowledge worker" has come of age and has become a key component to the success of New Economy companies. At Net time, learning faster than your competitor is the only thing that will keep you ahead of the pack. In the New Economy, the only assets that count are intellectual assets and a company obtains these assets from people—not programs.

A good example of this need for intellectual capital is Microsoft.

Soon after Netscape went public and the Internet seemed no longer a fad, Microsoft was close to missing the Internet boat. Many in top management clung to the idea that the PC and PC software was still the dominant market for the company. Microsoft could have poured millions of dollars into the market promoting PC software and its position as a PC company. They had the capital to do it. But it was intellectual capital that saved the company. Microsoft, because of the relationship it had with its employees, was able to see the light and turn the company on a dime, repositioning it as an Internet company.

Why?

Outside investors (institutions and non-Microsoft employees) own half of Microsoft stock. But Microsoft employees own the other half. It's these employees with a large stake in the company's future that convinced management to take the Internet seriously and that a shift in strategy was necessary. For your e-business, it is imperative that you understand the value of your intellectual assets and how easy it is to lose them to competitors. As a CEO of a consulting company once said, "Our assets leave the building in the elevator every night."

But there's another form of intellectual capital that must be romanced. The kind consumers can give. The more you know about Net consumers, the better the chance of selling to them. Consumers are getting smart to the value of their personal information. Expect potential customers to begin demanding compensation for this information—be it points, air miles, free products, or even cash.

Marketing doesn't stop at just a company's product or service. In the New Economy, an e-business must market itself to both its employees and, just as importantly—the customer. The customer is an important part of your marketing equation. Not just as a consumer of your product, but also as an evangelist of your business.

Principle 5: Turning Customers into Salespeople

"Build it and they will come." This is not the case on the Net. Getting attention in the New Economy is no easy task and it's getting more difficult day by day. Rising above the digital din of the network is getting harder and harder to do. On the one hand the immensity of network is the problem. On the other—it's a solution.

A network has a hidden resource, one waiting to be tapped by those that understand its particular power—the power to accelerate growth. The growth of good news—and bad—replicates itself across an online network at the speed of the Internet. This speed of replication can be harnessed by your e-business to spread your message to potential customers far and wide. And because the Internet connects everybody to everything, every customer can be

Paying Customers to Surf the Web

If you can't convince consumers to come to your site with ads, try bribing them. That's the strategy of myPoints (www.mypoints.com). Consumers can earn Points that can be used to purchase rewards such as simply reading email, shopping online, or visiting Web sites. Consumers can exchange their points for air miles, dinners, and merchandise from retailers such as Barnes & Noble, Hilton Hotels, Macy's, JCPenney, Sprint, and Red Lobster. A similar site is Beenz (www.beenz.com). By just surfing the Web and visiting sites you earn beenz—what they call the "New Internet Currency." You can spend beenz for actual products and services at participating online merchants.

turned into a sales person—all your customers into a sales force. Communication is so easy on the Net that product awareness can spread like wildfire.

This speed of replication can be called *viral*, and viral marketing is one of the e-merging strategies of digital marketing. Understand that the snowballing effect of viral marketing can make a company grow far faster than spending money. Take the free email service of Hotmail (www.hotmail.com) for example. A viral marketing strategy should offer customers something free in exchange for spreading your company word. In free email, the customer gets a free email account and at the bottom of every message that he or she sends is an invite to the recipient to get their free email address from the same service.

This same viral strategy can be applied to a host of other free services. For example, Homestead (www.homestead.com) offers a free Web page to affinity groups, which lets users broadcast their recruitment messages to family, friends, and colleagues—attracting them to the service. Those using a free personal calendar service can invite others to join the service by asking them to add their upcoming events to the calendar—and in turn setting up their own. But viral marketing can also pay the customer for being your salesperson. Netcentives (www.netcentives.com) offers customers frequent flyer miles for spreading the word of its service or generating new sales.

The effect of viral marketing and the power of the network can quickly increase your share of market in your particular market space. And with the increase in market share comes an increase in value.

Principle 6: Value Rises with Market Share

Several years ago, before the Internet appeared on the radar screens of Venture Capitalists, I was at a dinner party of a close colleague of mine. There was a Venture Capitalist there who I struck up a conversation with. I told him that the Internet was going to be the next big thing and asked if his firm was investing money in Net companies. He said no because he could not see how an Internet company could make money.

I could empathize with him.

Venture Capitalists were used to seeing plans that asked for money to first develop a product, then test it, then market it, then sell it—and get a return on their investment. Now take an Internet company. They need money to develop a product or service, test, it, market it—then give it away for free!

"If you don't sell it," puzzled the Venture Capitalist, "how do I get my return on investment?" What Venture Capitalists finally realized was that the Internet was a different animal. The key to success on the Net was market share and in cyberspace the fastest way to build

into its sales department by including a simple tag at the end of each email a user sent that read "Get Your Private, Free Email at http://www.hotmail.com." The word of free Web-based email was spread far and wide across the Net every time a Hotmail user sent a message. Each email sent was not only an advertisement but also an implied endorsement by its sender. After all, the person who sent it believes it's a good service or else he wouldn't use it. The beauty of this is that Hotmail required no marketing dollars. Its customers did the selling.

And here's the best part of Hotmail's business model. Every Hotmail subscriber, without exception, had to fill out a profile filled with personal information that could be sold to advertisers. Hotmail used the power of the network combined with the power of Viral Marketing to become the hands down leader in its category. It would be close to impossible to duplicate Hotmail's subscriber reach and push it from its position as the leading Web-based email provider—that's why Microsoft bought it.

market share was to use the Yoda Principle—give, then take. That proved to be the successful marketing strategy Netscape and other market leaders used to quickly claim market share and become the dominant players in their space.

Why does it make sense for companies to give away their product or service? The greater the network of people who use it, the more valuable it is to the network and the more likely it will become the standard in a particular market space. After a product or service becomes a standard, its value grows exponentially. Take Mirabilis ICQ (www.mirabilis.com) as an example. It gave away its service—instant messaging—free to anyone who would download it. But like the telephone, it takes at least two people to use it.

So, the first thing a new user does after installing it on his or her machine is to email their friends, family, and associates telling them about ICQ and to download a free copy so they can talk to each other. By giving away the product, ICQ grew its subscriber base faster than any company in history. ICQ soon became the standard of instant messaging.

But ICQ was more than just an instant messaging service. It also was a community. ICQ knew how to create this community by getting users to talk to one another. The network of consumers on the Net that used ICQ and its future enhancements created a stickiness that kept its users coming back again and again using its service. This community of users caught the eye of AOL who already had their own instant messaging service for its members. AOL saw the value built by the ICQ network and the potential of turning the attention and community of ICQ users into advertising dollars. In the New Economy attention equates to dollars. AOL with its near 20 million members knew this all too well and quickly bought ICQ.

Creating value for your e-business isn't difficult—just different. Your company must be able to build value fast through a network because the more plentiful users become, the more essential each individual consumer is to the network. Companies need to reach consumers and build a network not just through PCs, but over their cell phones, PDAs, pagers, and other Internet appliances as well. They must also build loyalty and personalization programs that keep customers coming back for more.

Principle 7: Value Rises with Information

As the Net disintermediates one set of middlemen, it creates another. A new type of middleman—the infomediary—is replacing traditional middlemen like stockbrokers and travel agents. As the amount of information on the Net grows and becomes more unwieldy, infomediaries are needed to turn data into usable information.

Infomediaries create digital value out of the bits and bytes of information on the Net. Their job is to take information on buyers, their needs, preferences, criteria, and profiles, as well as information about sellers such as inventories, products, services, and terms and conditions and provide new aggregate services for both buyers and sellers. Infomediaries manipulate information to extract higher value from it by reselling it, reusing it, repackaging it, or giving it away.

Examples of infomediaries include comparison-shopping services like mySimon (www.mysimon.com), referral services like My Wish List (www.mywishlist.com), and electronic audience brokers like DoubleClick (www.doubleclick.com). These companies help consumers through the maze of buying and selling on the Web and make informed purchasing decisions. But any company that has access to and collects information can become an infomediary. In fact, by just being in business, an e-business collects different types of information that can be reused, repackaged, and resold to others.

The infomediary is the new middleman in the information distribution chain of the New Economy. With infomediaries, new markets are opening for both seller and buyer.

Principle 8: Buyers Are Gaining Power and Sellers Opportunities

Take-it-or-leave-it pricing has seen its day. Fixed pricing is relinquishing its crown to dynamic pricing schemes where prices change based on supply and demand. On the other hand, sellers using the same dynamic pricing methods are able to quickly find

To Disintermediate

The process of cutting out the middleman in the distribution channel from manufacturer to customer.

A Wedding Infomediary

The Knot at www.theknot.com is one stop shopping for a wedding. At The Knot you can plan and schedule your nuptials, send out invitations, register your china, silverware and other wedding gifts, and find and book your honeymoon.

Buying Turned on Its Head

With MyGeek (www.mygeek.com), consumers tell merchants what they want to buy, merchants respond with bids, and the consumer picks the best deal. With MyGeek, the buyer is in control of what he or she wants to pay.

what price a product will clear the market at and personalize offers to the needs and demands of individual consumers.

As the physical barriers to competition fall, infomediaries, new technologies, and intelligent software will help buyers find the best deal that meets their personal requirements. At the same time these breakthroughs give sellers that offer unique services or better pricing visibility to discriminating buyers. Dynamic pricing technologies like auctions from eBay (www.ebay.com), name your price from Priceline.com, aggregate buying from Mercata (www.mercata.com), and bid pricing from MyGeek (www.mygeek.com) are putting the customer in control of what he or she will pay for a product or service.

The annoying haggling process of purchasing a car has been all but eliminated by online shopping services such as Autobytel (www.autobytel.com), which allows consumers to research the car they want based on model, features, and price. After a consumer has decided on a car, within 24 hours, he or she will be contacted with quotes from nearby dealers.

Dynamic pricing is infiltrating the buying equation and will soon be part and parcel of almost all transactions in the future. e-Businesses will have to rethink not only the way they price their products and services but also how they will present their offer. The arrival of more sophisticated shopping comparison agents—or shopping bots—that scour Web pages for their owners looking for the best deal that meets their master's requirements, will force sellers to realize that their traditional Web-based catalog of pages will have to be either overhauled or abandoned completely. Web sites cannot be adequately displayed on mobile commerce devices like cell phones and PDAs. Web pages, likewise, are not the best way to present offers to shopping bots. Shopping bots will soon compete with selling bots that can locate, gain the attention of, and negotiate with consumer shopping bots.

While these developments are challenges, they also present tremendous opportunities. The Net is opening up. The networked economy with access to both the wired and wireless world will give your e-business the tools to reach individual consumers where and when they are ready to buy. All this will lead to more personal transactions and more of a one-to-one consumer marketing game.

Which brings us to Principle 9: winning customers one at a time.

Principle 9: Value Rises with Mass Customization

Information is easier to customize than hard goods. Luckily, customizing information is ready made for the Net. An e-business—if done right—can collect enough information on its shoppers to personalize their shopping experience, bringing them back again and again, and keeping them as a customer.

Take the office-supplier site of Staples (www.staples.com) (refer to Figure 2.2). It uses personalization to the advantage of its large number of online customers. Staples can create a customized supply catalog that contains only those items and prices negotiated in contracts with the customer by keeping lists of previously ordered items. In addition, armed with this information, Staples uses it to make customized special offers.

What Is WAP?

Wireless Application Protocol is the leading global open standard for applications over wireless networks. WAP provides a uniform technology platform with consistent content formats for delivering Internet- and intranet-based information and services to digital mobile phones and other wireless devices.

To establish a one-to-one relationship with customers, your company will need to find ways to have consumers volunteer their personal information and shopping preferences. With privacy concerns right up there with credit card fears, it's not easy for an e-business to collect the information it needs to personalize offers to its customers. Companies must first gain the trust of its customers, then create incentives as reasons to release their personal information. And customization doesn't end with personalized information. The rush toward a global wireless environment will put a premium on self-contained, highly efficient, stylized interfaces to size-constrained devices.

Short multivaried media presentations customized for different Net appliances will replace the Web pages we see today. So, an understanding of streaming audio and video and multimedia technologies will be critical for your e-business. In addition, interactions with the customer must be both ways. A useful and effective media presentation can deliver an offer but it must also be simple enough for customers to interact with an offer in return. Nokia (`www.nokia.com`) is committed to the *Wireless Application Protocol (WAP)* revolution that is changing the way consumers surf the Web.

They are one of the founders of the WAP Forum, a nonprofit industry association open to all companies. The WAP Forum is made up of more than 200 members and has developed the defacto world standard for wireless information and telephony services on digital mobile phones and other wireless terminals. WAP Forum members represent over 95% of the global handset market. It has published a global wireless protocol specification based on existing Internet standards. Their mission is to create new business opportunities for companies by providing a new channel for their existing services and the possibility for totally new services that can reach customers 24 hours a day, wherever they are.

Your e-business needs to work with organizations like the WAP Forum and others like it that are delivering the next wave of interconnectivity on the Net, where every product is available everywhere, all the time.

Principle 10: Every Product Is Available Everywhere, All the Time

Shelf space on the Net is unlimited. Look at Amazon.com. It claims to be the world's biggest bookstore simply by listing almost every book in print for sale on their site. On the Net, a company can offer an infinite amount of its products to the consumer giving them the ability to find the product that suits their needs.

The impulse to buy and the purchase itself used to be separated by place and time. If you saw an ad for a CD or heard a song on the radio, you needed to go to store to buy it. The Net changes that. Consumers will be given an infinite number of purchasing choices, customized to their needs and with the ability to buy what they want the moment they hear about it.

For example, you can hear a song on MP3.com, pay for it, and download it to your computer within minutes. No delayed gratification. No need to go to a store. Just hit the buy button and it's yours. The Net has taken buying on impulse to a high art. Yet, that's just the Net of today. Tomorrow, the process of marketing, sales, and fulfillment will merge into one process. One way to do this is through distributed selling.

By using a distributed selling strategy, companies can offer their products to consumers across the entire Internet. Known originally as affiliate selling, Amazon.com created the concept in July of 1996 and it has turned out to be one of most powerful means for impulse buying on the Net. Basically, any Web site can make sales from its site by joining an online merchant's affiliate program and sell their products or services without having to build warehouses, handle inventory, enter the order-fulfillment business, or do customer service. An affiliate site simply embeds hyperlinked banners or text to the merchant's Web site on their site of the product or service it wants to sell. Then, any visitor who wants to buy the product on the affiliate site clicks on the merchant's link and is sent off to the merchant's order page.

What's Next in Affiliate Programs

Vstore (www.vstore.com) gives any Web site the capability to have their own online store—right on their Web site. Vstore provides the products, design, marketing tools, and technology—all for free. And they do all the fulfillment and customer service.

Here's another example: Visitors to a Web site that review children's software titles and are eToys affiliates can make additional money by selling children's software from eToys. This type of selling "in context" helps the affiliate site earn additional revenue without having to create and manage an online store on their site. eToys gets the order and the affiliate site gets a commission for the sale.

Distributed selling strategies—affiliate selling being one of them—come in all shapes and sizes and is one of the important emerging marketing strategies for e-business in the future.

Restructuring the Value Chain

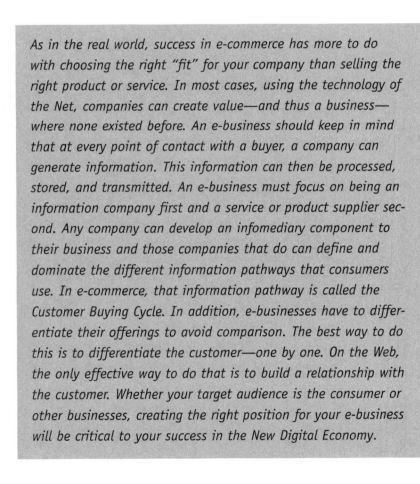

As in the real world, success in e-commerce has more to do with choosing the right "fit" for your company than selling the right product or service. In most cases, using the technology of the Net, companies can create value—and thus a business—where none existed before. An e-business should keep in mind that at every point of contact with a buyer, a company can generate information. This information can then be processed, stored, and transmitted. An e-business must focus on being an information company first and a service or product supplier second. Any company can develop an infomediary component to their business and those companies that do can define and dominate the different information pathways that consumers use. In e-commerce, that information pathway is called the Customer Buying Cycle. In addition, e-businesses have to differentiate their offerings to avoid comparison. The best way to do this is to differentiate the customer—one by one. On the Web, the only effective way to do that is to build a relationship with the customer. Whether your target audience is the consumer or other businesses, creating the right position for your e-business will be critical to your success in the New Digital Economy.

Several years ago, Jack-in-the-Box differentiated themselves from McDonald's by showing a boardroom full of McDonald executives happily singing the praise of "billions and billions" of hamburgers sold. The commercial then went on to show that Jack-in-the-Box had a more varied menu of meal offerings thus differentiating them from the other burger competitors.

As in the real world, success in e-commerce has more to do with choosing the right fit for your company than selling the right product or service. Like the old saying about trying to sell refrigerators to Eskimos, your e-business needs to position itself properly on the playing field of the New Economy. The Net has opened many opportunities providing unique services to consumers and businesses alike that cannot be replicated in the real world. The old distribution channels that delivered products and services to consumers are being reborn on the Net and with them the value to the buyer.

In most cases, using the technology of the Net, companies can create value—and thus a business—where none existed before. The trick for your company is to find these new opportunities, add value where there was none before, and then exploit them for profit.

Information is the engine that generates wealth in the New Economy. e-Commerce means selling products, services, and information over the Net—but not necessarily inventorying or shipping them. Every e-business not only can capture information at each point of customer contact, but also provide it.

The old approach to providing information was the Web site. It either provided content at the site—information, products, or services—or linked to other resource sites on the Web. And the new technologies of the New Digital Economy will provide even more ways to provide information. At every point of contact with a buyer, a company can generate information. This information can then be processed, stored, and transmitted. When a sale is made, a company captures a certain amount of information about the buyer.

Companies can even generate information on a potential buyer before they make a purchase through newsletter sign-ups, free downloads, and so on. This information can then be processed, stored, and used to market to the buyer or potential buyer at some time in the future. With a focus on being first an information company and second a service or product supplier, selling products and services becomes easier and more efficient.

A well positioned e-business must not only find the right market fit but also provide consumers with the information they need to make a purchase at every—and any—point in the buying cycle. With proper positioning, a company can differentiate itself from the competition and create a brand. And brand recognition is what makes business a success in any kind of economy—old or new.

The Three IPs

During the atomic age the distribution channel for products was from manufacturer to distributor to retailer to consumer. In the Information Age it is electrons that are moved—not atoms. The new distribution channel of the New Digital Economy is what I call the three IPs—the Information Producer, the Information Provider, and the Information Packager.

Several decades ago there was a little company that carried no inventory and manufactured no products, as we know them today. What it did was collect, organize, and publish a well-packaged listing of television schedules. These scattered bits of information were available to anyone from a number of different sources but a small publication pulled all these bits of information together and created a new business.

That publication was sold in 1987 for $2 billion, a market valuation higher than any one of the major broadcast networks—ABC, CBS, or NBC—whose schedule they listed at the time. The publication was *TV Guide* and it was one of the first examples of an infomediary and an excellent example of an Information Packager. *TV Guide* packaged and sold the information from the producers—the TV and film production studios—and the information from the providers—the three major TV broadcast networks, and built a thriving company.

TV Guide knew that the TV networks had the schedule of their own shows but would not create a method of information dissemination to TV viewers. Why help their competitors by listing theirs? The studios made the sitcoms, dramas, and movies but could not provide a schedule of when they would be broadcast—nor did they want to. It wasn't their business. This situation opened the door to *TV Guide* to become an infomediary between the Information Producers and Providers and the TV viewer, building a value in the company that exceeded any individual TV network.

The *Official Airlines Guide* or *(OAG)* is a monthly listing of flight schedules. OAG, like *TV Guide*, simply aggregated existing flight schedules that the airlines provided and made it available to the flying public. It sold for almost a billion dollars—almost triple the value of Eastern Shuttle at the time and slightly less than the market valuation of US Air. AOG was another successful infomediary.

These businesses owned no inventory nor sold any product and the information they used didn't even belong to them. They merely took the information that the producers and providers created, repackaged it, and sold it to the end user.

Think of the movie *Miracle on 34th Street*.

When a mother complained that Macy's doesn't stock a toy that Santa promised the child, he tells her the name of a rival department store—Gimbals—that does have it. The mother is shocked that the Macy's Santa would recommend Gimbals. So Santa says to her, "The only important thing is to make the children happy. Right? It doesn't make any difference if Macy's or someone else sells the toy."

This new merchandising concept does not endear Santa to the Macy's VP of Sales. The VP plans on firing him but has second thoughts when customers start expressing their undying loyalty to Macy's because of the gimmick. Seeing the public relations, Mr. Macy decides to promote it storewide and in their advertising. In the end, Santa Claus performs a miracle of commerce. Both Gimbals and Macy's compete to make the customer happy and both gained more sales and customer loyalty than ever before.

Other than the meaning of Christmas, you can learn a lesson here from e-businesses. Understanding what their customers' needs and

Quotron as an Infomediary

Quotron (www.turnaround.com/ww_done/clients/citicorp/) is another example of an infomediary. Quotron provided information about security prices to brokers. It had no proprietary access to this information. Quotron merely captured the security transaction information and recycled it back to the brokerage houses that generated it in the first place.

Taking a Leaf Out of Dell's Book

Hewlett-Packard followed Dell and Gateway Computers by selling personalized custom PCs with its HP Village Store (www.hp.com/country/us/eng/buy.htm).

The Value Proposition

The value proposition of an offer includes not only the price of the product or service but shipping and handling costs, warranties or guarantees, rebates, liberal return policies, customer support, and any other elements that add value to the offer above just price.

wants are going to become more and more important to the survival of companies—online or off. Once known, an e-business can either fill that need themselves or pass the customer on to someone that can. Now, the Internet is perfectly suited to the "pile them high and sell them cheap" strategy, interacting with a consumer only when he or she is ready to buy. But that's about to change.

As I said before, most companies on the Net today are mere reflections of the brick and mortar world. The Net, with its new technologies and distributed nature, will radically change both online and offline ways of doing business. If shopping agents can query catalogs of products online returning the best prices on a product or service, then what's left to differentiate merchants from one another other than price? If more and more manufacturers are taking a leaf out of Dell and Gateway's book and selling direct to the consumer, what will be the role of the e-tailer in the future?

Sure there are issues involved in both of these developments. Shopping agents are getting more and more sophisticated as time goes on and will return more of the *value proposition* of a merchant to the consumer—that is, their complete selling position—and not just the price. And manufacturers that want to sell direct to consumers have the challenge of selling products one at a time to customers. Compaq and IBM are struggling with that issue now to compete with Dell and Gateway.

Still, e-businesses have to differentiate their offerings to avoid comparison. What's the best differentiator? How about differentiating on the customer—one by one? And on the Web, the only effective way to do that is to build a relationship with them.

Price is a concern to consumers. But consumers are looking for more than just price—they're looking for value. They want a relationship with a brand, one that understands them and meets their needs. The unique nature of the Web gives companies the ability to segment markets down to a market of one, then develop products and services to reach these individual market niches. And thanks to the Web, consumers now have a quick and easy way to tell you what they want and what personal information they are willing to share to get it.

This will open up a whole new opportunity for e-business besides selling products and services. Companies will increasingly become personal agents for their customers, know them intimately, and recommend products and services for each individual. The end result will be e-businesses looking and operating more like infomediaries.

This is important because infomediaries *own* the customer. Owning the customer means that a business has developed a strong relationship with a customer. And this is done by building a profile of a customer from his or her personal information gathered by the business. This profile is used to better target and serve the customer's wants and needs. Every e-business today must have as its primary strategy the capability to build a close relationship with its customers. The tighter the relationship the less likely a company will be disintermediated by some unexpected competitor and the less likely that the manufacturers it represents will bypass it and own the customer. By developing an infomediary component, e-businesses can protect themselves by being infomediaries for consumers and a service to buyers.

And becoming an infomediary is not hard. Any company can develop an infomediary component to its business and those companies that do can define and dominate the different information pathways that consumers use. In e-commerce, that information pathway is called the Customer Buying Cycle.

The Customer Buying Cycle

A lot goes into a consumer's decision to buy. In fact, it can be looked at as a process. According to MIT Media laboratories, the Consumer Buying Process consists of five elements: Need Identification, Product Brokering, Merchant Brokering, Negotiation and Purchase, Product Service and Evaluation.

> **Need Identification**—In the first stage of the buying process, the consumer becomes aware of some unmet need. This need could be realized either through passive or active means. The passive means would be an advertisement—TV, radio, or direct mail—aimed at him or her personally. The active means would be if he or she has asked to be notified about an upcoming or periodic event.

Product Brokering—After a need is realized, the consumer embarks on a process of retrieving information to help determine what to buy. This includes the evaluation and comparison of products based on manufacturer, institutional, and consumer provided information. The result is a *consideration set* of products. A consideration set for a product would include its price, delivery options, any warranties or guarantees, return policies, customer support, color or size, and so on.

Merchant Brokering—At this stage in the process, the consumer compares the consideration set with merchant-specific information to help determine whom to buy from. This includes the evaluation of the merchants themselves—price, convenience, availability, service, warranty, delivery time, reputation, security, and other factors. Some of this information will undoubtedly come from the merchant. Other information will come from the consumer community and independent organizations that provide information on merchants.

Negotiation and Purchase—At this stage in the process, the terms of the purchasing transaction are discussed and finalized. The purchase of the product signals the end of the negotiations stage and then delivery options are discussed. This stage of the process might or might not be included in the negotiation stage. Shipping and handling costs could influence the final purchasing price.

Product Service and Evaluation—The last stage in the process involves product service, customer service, and a self-evaluation of the satisfaction of the overall buying experience. This experience can be communicated to the merchant, consumer-oriented organizations, other shoppers, and the shopping community.

A company has the opportunity to collect information on the consumer during this entire process. That information can be used to differentiate the company and provide the information service to the consumer. Let's take a look at what kinds of information can be collected and then offered to consumers to help them through the Customer Buying Process that an e-business can use to position itself in a market niche and differentiate itself from the competition.

Need Identification and Product Recommendation

Any purchase of a product or service starts with a consumer's perception of a need. This gives a company its first opportunity to build a relationship with a potential customer by either anticipating or stimulating a consumer need. By helping a consumer fill a product or service need, a company can collect—voluntarily—information on a potential customer.

A reminder service is a good example. This kind of service reminds a consumer to purchase a product or service for an important event. A consumer might want to be reminded about a family member's birthday, his or her wedding anniversary, or Mother's or Father's Day. There are several dozen reminder services on the Net today where consumers can list their important dates and be reminded via email about an upcoming event. Candor's Birthday and Anniversary Reminder Service (www.candor.com/reminder/) is an example of a service that reminds you about upcoming birthdays via email.

The value to the consumer is the timely reminder—the value to the e-business is the collection of specific information on the consumer and a potential sale. An e-business can add a reminder service to any product or service it sells. A simple example is an online florist. When a consumer registers with its reminder service, a predetermined bouquet of flowers is sent out automatically for birthdays, Mother's Day, and the like.

Another way to collect consumer information is to offer a wish-list service. My Wish List (www.mywishlist.com) enables consumers to create a shopping list of products that they want and direct friends and family to the site to view their list. Another such service is gift registries such as Your Registry (www.yourweddingregistry.com) that create a custom gift-list registry for any occasion, then offer to purchase the gift from a variety of stores.

Your Registry directs consumers to other stores. But an e-business could also provide registries on their site, such as Target (www.target.com) (see Figure 3.1) does for weddings and baby showers, and sell its own products to gift registrants.

Novator's Reminder Service (www.novator.com/Remind/Remind.html) Partner Program offers a tailored version of its Reminder Service for your Web site. It offers online registration and reminder editing; calendar-based reminders; and multiple reminders per event.

Finally, a company can collect targeted consumer information by a recommendation-engine based on personal tastes and lifestyle indicators. Several sites on the Net will let you choose a gift based on profession, lifestyle, age, or sex. The Perfect Present Picker (www.presentpicker.com) is a good example of this type of service.

All these services offer the e-business two things: The capability to sell a product or service to a targeted customer and the opportunity to create a strong relationship with them.

Product Brokering

After the consumer has realized a need for a product, he or she needs to locate information on what to buy. The consumer needs to not only locate the product or service but also evaluate the different product or service options available to create a consideration set.

In this case, the primary function of the e-business is to provide the information that the consumer needs and in the process to build a stronger relationship with the potential customer. Like in the case of Macy's Santa Claus, the better the service, the stronger the loyalty to the business.

Web sites such as Deja.com (`www.deja.com`) offer consumers reviews and recommendations on any number of products in a variety of categories. Deja.com helps consumers find precisely the product that they want then directs them to merchants armed with competitive pricing information who have that exact product in stock. In this way, Deja.com collects consumer information to further personalize their shopping experience. That can bring consumers back again to use their service—in effect, creating a very "sticky" site to attract and keep shoppers.

Another way to create stickiness is to create a sense of community among consumers. Discussion boards, chat rooms, discussion lists, and electronic newsletters are great ways to create shopping communities at your e-business. Monitoring these community-building activities gives a company the opportunity to collect information on its users to build a better shopping experience.

Merchant Brokering

After finding the right product or service, the consideration set moves from what to buy to where to buy it. At this stage, the consumer starts the process of evaluating the merchant itself. Price, convenience, availability, service, warranty, delivery time, reputation, security, and other factors all enter the merchant choice equation.

Comparison shopping agents such as mySimon (`www.mysimon.com`) that compare prices from hundreds of different merchants; and Frictionless Commerce (`www.frictionless.com`), which gives consumers the ability to search, select, and negotiate products; are two examples of merchant brokering.

Consumers can also get comparison information on merchants and their reputation. BizRate (`www.bizrate.com`) rates merchants based on surveys that actual customers have supplied at the time of purchase. These merchant brokers are examples of another type of infomediary.

Negotiation and Purchase

Every customer wants a good deal. But what's considered a good deal is different from buyer to buyer. Most everyone would admit that they got a good deal when they purchased their last car. Yet, the chances of any two buyers paying the same price for the same car are slight. Another example is an airline ticket. The odds are not good that two travelers sitting next to each other paid the same price for their airline tickets. Still, both probably felt they got a good deal on their tickets at the time.

The car and airline game of different pricing for different people will pale in comparison to the dynamic pricing schemes that are hatching on the Net. Over the last few years, companies such as Priceline (www.priceline.com), uBid (www.ubid.com), MobShop (www.mobshop.com), and Respond.com (www.respond.com) have given consumers the power to negotiate the price they pay for products and services.

Companies using these types of dynamic pricing schemes and new ones to follow will add value to the shopping experience and command more loyalty from consumers than their traditional fixed-price cousins. Information gathered here can tell an e-business what kinds of products or services a consumer wants and what price they're willing to pay for it—information that both e-tailers

CASE STUDY

MYSIMON

Founded in early 1998, mySimon (www.mysimon.com) came late to the comparison shopping game. Comparison shopping agents—or shopping bots—such as Jango, Junglee, and B2C were already in existence and even they weren't the first. Anderson Consulting created a prototype of a shopping bot that searches for the best prices on CDs a few years before mySimon.

The other established comparison-shopping sites would recruit and charge merchants to be in their database of sites to shop. This limited the number of e-tailers that their bots could shop. In the comparison-shopping game, the more merchants in your database, the more price comparisons you can return to the shopper, and thus, the more valuable the service. mySimon's proprietary technology allowed it to add more merchants faster than any of its competitors—even those that were well established before mySimon came to town.

Within just over a year, mySimon was shopping more than a thousand merchants, comparing prices on tens of thousands of products, and became the number one destination site for comparison shopping. Today, mySimon's shopping service offers unbiased information on products and merchants,

and manufacturers will find valuable for their pricing strategies and production forecasts.

Until this point in the Customer Buying Cycle, a company went a long way toward creating a personal profile of the customer. The closing of the deal offers an opportunity for the e-business to apply this knowledge of the customer either to up-sell him or her or offer an add-on sale at the time of purchase.

Product Service and Evaluation

After the product or service is delivered, a buyer then evaluates the entire purchasing experience. This experience can be communicated to the merchant in the form of a compliment or complaint—or no comment at all. The buyer can relate his or her experience to consumer-oriented organizations such as BizRate, other shoppers on community bulletin boards, or can file a complaint with one of the complaint services on the Net.

For when an e-tailer has failed to satisfy its customers, a number of complaint services have sprung up on the Net where not only can consumers air their grievance, but the service will actually take up their cause and seek to resolve the customer complaint with the merchant. Companies such as Digisolve (www.cemptor.com) provide free complaint resolution services and statistical information on

iShip Puts the Consumer in Control

iShip (www.iship.com) lets consumers price, compare, track, and manage shipments over the Internet. Consumers can see what kind of deal they received on shipping or do their research ahead of time to make sure they're charged a reasonable shipping rate by the e-tailer.

including price comparisons, product availability, and other merchant information. As a one-stop resource for smart shopping, mySimon helps shoppers find the best values on millions of products, saving visitors time and money.

mySimon also understood the concept of Information Packaging. They were one of the first shopping services to offer Shopping Guides to consumers starting out with Holiday Shopping Guides, moving on to Event Shopping Guides, then individual Product Category Guides. They were even the first to understand the power of providing their shopping service not only on a PC but also on Net appliances as well, such as the Palm Pilot VII. By downloading and installing the mySimon-to-Go software, shoppers can compare products and prices while they walk down the aisles of their favorite brick-and-mortar stores. They can comparison shop online and offline merchants, without leaving the store.

All this earned the attention of CNET (www.cnet.com) which purchased mySimon in January of 2000 for $700 million. mySimon is continuing its development of innovative features that will further simplify and enhance the Web shopping experience.

e-tailers such as the number of complaints logged against a company along with the average time of resolution.

The question is where can your e-business fit in the Customer Buying Cycle? Do you need to become one or all these information companies to succeed?

The answer is no.

By understanding that valuable information can be collected on customers and potential customers, and seeing the importance of this collected information in developing a company in the New Economy, you can add an infomediary component to any e-business and position it to sell anything, anywhere, anyway, anytime and at any price to a targeted niche of buyers.

And buyers are not just consumers. They can be other businesses as well.

Business-to-Business

B2B and B2C

B2B is short for selling business-to-business and B2C is short for selling business-to-consumer.

It's official: Business-to-business e-commerce is where the money is, or at least will be soon. When the strong e-commerce stock correction hit the charts in early 2000, pundits and analysts declared that business-to-consumer (B2C) companies on the Net had seen better days. So they went looking for the next big thing and what they found was business-to-business (B2B). Analysts like the Boston Consulting Group predicted that one-fourth of all US business-to-business e-commerce will be done online by 2003 and reach $2.8 trillion in transactions.

With predictions like these, it seemed that it was B2B's time to shine and within a few short months, anything that hinted at being B2B got the lion's share of attention and funding. In the rush to distance themselves from the out-of-favor B2C label, many B2C companies even recast themselves as B2Bs. There's no doubt that the B2B marketplace is full of opportunities for e-business. However, a company still has the challenge of positioning itself in that market.

B2Bs are similar to B2Cs in one respect. The majority of them bring together many buyers and sellers at a single site. Some serve several industries at a time while others serve a specific niche.

Revenue is generated from most B2B companies by charging fees for making introductions or handling the transaction and payment.

Basically, the B2B universe consists of four types:

- **B2B Product and Service Suppliers**—The most typical and the simplest B2B commerce is the one most similar to B2C companies. Let's say a business manufactures computer cases. Another business uses computer cases for the PCs it manufactures. The PC maker visits the manufacturer's Web site, chooses the cases it wants and the quantity, and places an order. Done deal.

  But these types of transactions are not limited to products alone. Let's suppose that a manufacturer needs to ship its products to distributors around the country. It visits the Web site of a trucking company and schedules a pickup and delivery. A simple service transaction between businesses done over the Net.

  This one-to-one business model works best as long as products are standardized and prices are normally stable. Computer makers are just one example of who uses this kind of B2B e-commerce, as are companies that sell the hardware for the Internet.

- **B2B Non-industry Exchanges**—There are many products that almost every industry needs, such as office supplies, advertising services, cleaning supplies, industrial glues, and so on—anything that can sell across more than one industry—but do not include the actual material to manufacture a product.

  MRO.com (www.mro.com) is good example of these kinds of exchanges that supply businesses with products for maintenance, repair, and operations. iMark (www.imark.com) is another. It focuses on selling used industrial equipment in an auction format between businesses while iProcure (www.iprocure.com) provides instant access to millions of industrial parts and supplies.

UPS Starts Tracking

Through an alliance with two Internet payment companies, United Parcel Service (UPS) will allow businesses to track the status of their invoices and make payment adjustments. With this service, companies can cut administrative costs and streamline business transactions through online dispute resolution, payment scheduling, and payment automation.

Some B2B Markets Hit Resistance

The promise of B2B success for super-exchanges such as PlasticsNet is fading as key players balk at paying transaction fees to do business with their existing partners. Super-exchanges need to offer additional value above and beyond just duplicating a B2B process that already exists for companies.

- **B2B Industry Exchanges**—Unlike Non-industry Exchanges, Industry Exchanges focus on one specific industry. They cater to a single market like steel for cars or paper for boxes. They're often called vertical markets because they offer everything within a single industry, from raw materials to finished products. Flush with cash from venture capitalists, independently owned online exchanges are being formed for every conceivable product. While these exchanges are diverse, most of them will accommodate only one exchange. In this game, it's winner take all.

  These types of exchanges work best for commodity type products like metals, paper, or plastics. ChemConnect (www.chemconnect.com) connects buyers and sellers worldwide on everything from raw chemicals to finished plastics and resins. Another Industry Exchange is PaperExchange (www.paperexchange.com), which offers a marketplace for everything from cardboard to fine office paper.

- **B2B Trading Hubs**—When General Motors needs to purchase the necessary parts to make its automobiles, it puts out its request for bid and the many different businesses that make the hundreds of items that go into a new car bid for GM's business. Batteries, radios, seats, paint, and hundreds of other products that go into a new automobile are bought and sold on the Trading Hubs.

  General Motors became a classic example of this type of B2B play when it put its procurement process online. Other automakers soon followed and joined GM's Trading Hub, choosing to share the benefits of a centralized purchasing process and the economies of scale it provided.

  While this type of exchange is forming on the ground, another has formed in the air. Six major airlines including Air France, American Airlines, and British Airways have formed an exchange to link sellers of airline-related goods and services such as fuel and fuel services; airframe, avionics and engine components; and maintenance services.

Automakers Create B2B Exchange

Five major automakers—General Motors, Ford Motor, DaimlerChrysler, Renault, and Nissan Motor formed an automotive Internet Exchange called Covisint. Covisint is an outgrowth of an exchange that GM, Ford, and DaimlerChrysler formed in the early part of 2000. Covisint (www.covisint.com/) is touted by the automakers as the largest Internet business ever created. The marketplace will create a single automotive-parts exchange for the companies' thousands of suppliers and dealers.

B-ing in the Middle

Over the last several months some B2C Internet companies have been switching their focus to B2B by applying the technologies developed and the lessons learned in their B2C marketplace. Their strategy is to sell products, services, and technologies to other businesses to increase their consumer sales.

With revenues from advertising, product margins, and consumer sales slowing down on their B2C sites, these newly focused B2B2C e-businesses hope to derive revenue from custom program development, licensing fees, and charging for services. In short, the B2B2C company earns revenues from a business, not the consumer.

Take Beyond.com (www.beyond.com) as an example. It has created a new revenue stream for its e-business by partnering with companies such as Compaq Computer, Symantec, and Hewlett-Packard's Shopping Village. Beyond earns revenues and transaction fees by building and operating software stores for these business partners. Businesses can also use Beyond's technology. Using Beyond's software download service allows independent software companies to sell directly to their users—something they couldn't do before because of their agreements with distributors and retailers.

Ask Jeeves (www.ask.com) is another example of a B2B2C configuration. Ask Jeeves provides its natural language search technology to other Web sites and companies such as Wal-Mart and Chrysler. In Chrysler's case, it lets the automaker provide better responses to online customer inquiries.

But B2B2C is only one application of being the *B* in the middle. Companies can refocus their technology and products to help one business serve another (B2B2B), a business serve its employees (B2B2E), and even the government serve its constituents (G2B2C). With some thought, almost any e-business can focus its technology, products, and services, and position itself as the *B* in the middle as a business services supplier in the New Economy.

Whether your target audience is the consumer or other businesses, creating the right position for your e-business will be critical to your success in the New Digital Economy.

ASK JEEVES

Ask Jeeves is an example of a company that has made a successful transition from a business-to-consumer (B2C) company to a business-to-business-to-consumer (B2B2C) company.

Ask Jeeves began as a consumer search engine in 1997. It soon craved out a niche in the search engine market by offering Web surfers a way to search the Net using natural language queries. Consumers didn't have to provide keywords or Boolean search strings. Consumers just entered a natural language question like "Where can I find Nike shoes?" and Jeeves—the cartoon mascot—searched the Net finding Web sites that had the answer.

The Jeeves underlying database incorporates an artificial intelligence technology and tags the question and answer for faster response with similar questions in the future. Ask Jeeves combines a unique natural language engine with a proprietary knowledge base. Taken together, this mechanism processes the meaning and grammar of real questions in plain English; links directly to relevant, high-quality answers; and gets smarter over time, as its knowledge base expands with each question asked and each answer delivered.

By the time the first year of operations was over, Jeeves had answered millions of questions and was one smart fellow. This is when management realized that Jeeves could help improve customer interaction at other Web sites. Ask Jeeves has converted its core business from B2C to B2B2C, helping companies like Chrysler provide better responses to their online customer inquiries by customizing their search technology. Ask Jeeves charges monthly licensing fees based on the number of consumer queries answered that adds to the revenue stream it gets from its two Web sites.

CHAPTER 4

Staying Up to Date in e-Business

The Internet can help keep your e-business on top of what's happening in the e-commerce world with current market intelligence from a variety of sources. The Net can also help you gather important marketing information direct from consumers without ever leaving your PC. Over the last few years a number of different Web resources have come into being where your e-business can gather market intelligence. These Web resources include market research Web sites, online government sources, private research agencies, online focus groups, and survey companies. It's important to understand that there is a whole new way to perceive the Internet. Not as a centralized location where buyers go to make purchases, and not where the personal computer is the only way—nor the dominant way—to access the Net. Instead of having a Web site that you have to drive traffic to, your offering, whether to consumers or other businesses, will be distributed across the network, served on demand by your buyers. Whether that offer is content, community, or commerce related makes no difference. In other words, the Internet—not a Web site—is the database. As the customers—consumers or businesses—gain more and more control over their buying experience, they can choose to buy whenever, wherever, whatever, at any price and in any way they choose.

When I ran my own direct marketing company selling computer hardware and software, my management team and I would travel from one end of the country to the other silently observing focus groups in Atlanta, Los Angeles, and New York. We would sit in a dimly lit room behind a glass wall and observe and videotape a handful of carefully selected consumers giving us their opinion of our company, the products we sold, and how we sold them. We would then take these hours and hours of videotape, review them, and hope we would find some nugget or two of wisdom that would direct our future marketing plans.

Back then, the acceleration of change in the personal computer industry made it one of the fastest changing sectors around. Being a PC retailer, we had to stay in front of this accelerating curve of change if we wanted to stay competitive. We had to constantly stay up-to-date on new product trends and market opportunities. Before the onset of the Net, the different ways to stay on top of one's market space was through research reports from PC industry analysts, articles in the industry publications, and face-to-face focus groups.

But the Net is changing all that.

Industry analysts still exist and industry publications still churn out the latest news on a sector and their sage opinions on where it's going. But because of the interactive nature of the Net and its capability to collect information at the source, companies today can more easily stay up to date on consumer wants and market trends.

e-Scouting—Marketing Intelligence Resources

In today's fast paced digital business world, a company has to keep its ear to the ground gathering the essential market intelligence necessary to effectively compete and strategically grow a business. All companies need to have continuous updates on the customers they're targeting, the markets they're competing in, and the competitors they're competing with. Before the advent of the Net, this was a slow and expensive process. Hiring consultants, listening to long-winded research reports, and doing face-to-face focus groups were the prime ways that a company gathered market intelligence.

All this was both expensive and time consuming.

With the Internet, an e-business can stay on top of what's happening with current market intelligence from a variety of sources and gather important marketing information directly from consumers themselves—and without ever leaving your PC. Not only is information available for study at these Web sites but also market intelligence—both on your customers and your competition.

In 1999, companies began to accept the Internet as a valid means for conducting marketing research. Online market research revenue will hit $230 million by the end of 2000, up from $96 million in 1999. This shows that using the Net as a market research tool is becoming one of the dominant ways to gather market intelligence on consumers, your marketplace, and the competition (see Table 4.1).

Table 4.1

Online Research Revenues					
	1996	1997	1998	1999	2000
Revenue in Millions	$3.5	$10.2	$29.2	$96.2	$229.9
Percent Change	N/A	+189%	+189%	+230%	+139%

Source: Industry Newsletter Inside Research

As with most businesses, research companies have moved many of their reports and publications to the Net. Over the last few years many different Web resources have sprung up where any e-business can gather market intelligence. These Web resources include market research Web sites, industry analysts, online government sources, private research companies, online focus groups, and survey companies.

Industry Analysts

The sages of market intelligence are the industry analysts. The prognosticators read the entrails of each sector of the Internet industry and publish reports on the status of the Net and where each of its sectors are heading. There are two well-known industry

The Intelligence Store

The Standard Intelligence Store (www.thestandard.com/research/store/) enables us to browse a variety of research reports all in one place. Report topics range from e-commerce and marketing to Web usage and auctions.

analysts that focus primarily on Internet commerce. They're the 500-pound gorillas of e-commerce research and they are Jupiter Communications and Forrester Research. Both are subscription services and charge a yearly fee to companies who use their services.

Established in 1986, Jupiter Communications (www.jup.com) focuses entirely on the Internet economy. Jupiter provides its business-to-business and business-to-consumer clients with comprehensive views of industry trends, accurate forecasts, and today's best practices, all backed by their proprietary data. Clients have access to both their research reports and their analysts for private discussions for a yearly subscription fee. Jupiter also produces a wide range of conferences that offer senior executives the opportunity to hear firsthand the insights of its analysts and the leading decision-makers in the Internet and technology industries.

They offer expert analysis of Internet strategies (focused on broad business issues) and market strategies (focused on industry and region-specific issues). Their research provides clients with information to

- Assess market trends.

- Identify revenue models.

- Evaluate success criteria.

- Develop data-driven strategies.

- Analyze competitive landscapes.

- Assess the value of partnerships and acquisitions.

- Prioritize new product development initiatives.

- Analyze industry adoption trends.

- Benchmark against key players.

- Anticipate customer demand.

The other large Internet research company is Forrester Research.

Founded in 1983, Forrester Research (www.forrester.com) is also a subscription service and covers many of the same areas as Jupiter, such as research and analysis on the impact of the Internet and

Capitalize on Disgruntled Customers

Some of the best sources of inexpensive, on-target market research are people who give your product a free trial—then turn it down. Disappointed customers provide invaluable feedback. If they don't buy after the free trial, don't write them off. Contact them and find out why they didn't purchase you product or service. It'll pay off.

emerging technologies on business strategy, consumer behavior, and society. Their research spans consumer, business-to-business, and technology marketplaces. In addition, Forrester offers comprehensive analysis of the global Internet Economy and its impact on society and business. They call this their whole view of Internet commerce. The company's whole view approach helps companies develop their business models and infrastructure to embrace broader online markets and to scale their Internet operations.

Forrester focuses on four major research areas:

- **Internet Commerce**—Leveraging the Internet for sales, trade, marketing, and content delivery.

- **Corporate Technology**—Developing and managing corporate technology infrastructures, products, and applications.

- **Technographics Data Analysis**—Quantitative research on how today's technologies impact consumer attitudes and behaviors.

- **Baseline Research**—Small business research packages that are designed for emerging companies.

While the services of these companies seem pricey and their research reports cost in the thousands of dollars, subscribing to one or the other is an important way to stay up-to-date on e-business trends. In addition, the information and assistance from these companies can help immensely in designing and executing the marketing plans of your company. Access to the analysts alone is worth the price of admission for two reasons.

With private one-on-one discussions of your company's marketing strategies and the visibility of your company with the industry analysts, you can help promote your company in the eyes of your marketplace. This visibility can help differentiate your e-business from your competitors and position your company in a particular market niche, as a new technology solution, or carving out an entirely new marketplace.

What you hope to do for your company is to be used as one of the examples—if not *the* example—of a company in your market space. mySimon is a good example. Although mySimon was a

Johnny-come-lately to the comparison shopping space (there were three others before it), mySimon succeeded in the eyes of the analysts at becoming the standard example of comparison shopping agents on the Net. When Jupiter or Forrester generate a report on comparison shopping, mySimon, more often than not, is mentioned as a successful example.

This kind of coverage from analysts does not come easy. You need to constantly stay on their radar screens through a combination of PR, advertising, and media mentions. However, if your company can be seen as a standard example of your marketplace, the credibility in the eyes of your customers, vendors, and investors rises dramatically.

Web Sites

Today, more and more companies are gathering market intelligence from the comfort of their keyboards. Not only can your e-business do research on your particular market space right from your PC, but you can also gather market intelligence about your competitors.

Although not as proprietary or in depth as analysts like Jupiter and Forrester, Web sites such as eMarketer (`www.e-land.com`) are a comprehensive, objective, and easy to use resource for any business interested in the Internet. And the information on their site is free to all. eMarketer provide statistics, news, and information on all aspects of the Internet. eMarketer aggregates, filters, organizes, and analyzes data from hundreds of leading research sources and puts the information into handy, easy-to-read tables, charts, and graphs and provides analysis, statistical estimates, projections, and long-term trends for the evolving Internet marketplace. Their e-reports offer a comprehensive and accurate picture of the Internet marketplace, giving mission critical information to e-businesses.

Another free information source for market research is WebCMO research (`www.webcmo.com`). The marketing information they offer is not about what people have bought, but why people choose a product and the different market segments they belong to. Their research is not only about the past market activities but also about future market changes and explores winning Web-marketing

Demographic Reports

Get up-to-date demographic data to target your market from the Right Site (`www.easidemographics.com`). Use their search interface to narrow your search by geography (ZIP codes, regions, and so on) and type of data (quality of life, income, and so on) for detailed market-specific statistics and reports.

strategies. Your company can also subscribe to their free *Journal of Web Marketing Research,* a weekly publication about Web-marketing research and strategy. Topics included are online branding, effectiveness of Web business promotion, targeting demographically online, one-to-one marketing, market segmentation, advertisers' preferences, and other subjects relating to market research and strategy.

WebCMO was the first to study the comparative effectiveness of Web business promotion methods, advertisers' preferences, and even the first to question the reliability of online research projections. Don't be put off by the statistical semantics of these topics. The Journal reports are all in plain English.

There are many other Web sites that provide valuable resources too. They include

> **Cyber Atlas** (cyberatlas.Internet.com)—Gathers online research from the best data resources to provide a complete review of the latest surveys and technologies available.
>
> **NUA** (www.nua.ie)—Offers a compendium of news articles, reports, and surveys on all facets of the online world.
>
> **Deep Canyon** (www.deepcanyon.com)—Provides market research to help companies on the Net make informed strategic decisions.

And what about your competition? Where on the Net can you conduct competitive-intelligence research on your competitors?

The first place to start, of course, is the search engines. Just type in your competitor's name and visit their site. There's much that can be gleaned about their business model by just perusing their Web site. Next, financial data on public companies has always been available but now is even more accessible on the World Wide Web. At Hoover's Online (www.hoovers.com) you can find the income statements and balance sheets of nearly 2,500 public companies. The service is not free but Hoover's Online lets anyone download free half-page profiles of 10,000 (mostly public) companies.

Inc. Magazine's own Inc. Top 500 database (www.inc.com/500) lists the fastest-growing companies in the country and provides information on thousands of privately held companies that have made

Search Company Data

You can access more than 11,000 public, private, and international companies from Inc.com (www.inc.com/research/details/0,3470, AGD1_CNT49_RSC15654,00.html). Using their search facility, you can find basic company information, financials, key executives, key competitors, and home page addresses.

the list in the past eight years. This information includes revenue information, profit-and-loss percentages, number of employees, and Web links. You can find the latest news on your competitors at NewsDirectory.com (`www.ecola.com`). This site lists more than 2,000 newspapers, business journals, magazines, and computer publications. You can search any number of periodicals to locate news stories on your competitors. Some of the periodicals are more easily searched than others, and some charge fees.

Then there's the online grapevine.

The Net can give your e-business a good opportunity to listen in on conversations about you or your competitors. This might represent one of the best market research values on the Net. The grapevine I'm referring to are the newsgroups and discussion groups around the Net. Net consumers are always talking about products, services, and the companies that provide them in these community gabfests. One the best places to listen in on these conversations is Deja.com's Usenet Discussion Service (`www.deja.com`). At Deja.com, you can search keywords such as the name of your competitor or the product or service that you offer and see what the Net community is saying about them.

Other places to check out include Remarq (`www.remarq.com`) and Liszt (`www.liszt.com`), a searchable directory of email discussion groups.

Finally, are you contemplating filing a patent or want to know if your proposed business methodology has already been tied up? Then check out the Patent and Trademark Office Web site (`www.uspto.gov`). There you can get a good idea on whether or not someone has filed a patent on a product or business methodology that your company is considering.

Online Focus Groups

On the market research scale of value, nothing comes closer to good market intelligence than talking to actual consumers. By going right to the source, you can get feedback on your marketing plans right from the horse's mouth—so to speak. Although not as quantitative as a broad research study involving thousands or even tens of thousands of respondents, a comparatively small focus

A Caveat

When reading posts on any discussion board or newsgroup, keep in mind that what's posted there may or may not be accurate. After all, these are posts from people whose credibility and motivation is unknown to you. So a good caveat is to check the information posted when you can.

group can give more qualitative results. And if you increase the reach of this marketing tool using the Net, a company can increase the results as well.

Each year more and more companies are appearing on the Net offering virtual focus group programs to e-businesses that want to tap directly into the minds and hearts of real consumers. Instead of crowding 8–10 people into a stuffy room, using the technology of the Net, online focus groups can be easily formed and reports quickly sent to client companies.

SurveySite (www.surveysite.com) is one such company. SurveySite invites 8–10 people from around the Net or from a client's customer base for a specified period of time (90 minutes to two hours) to a specialized chat room. The controlled chat room environment allows participants to view text, graphics, sounds, jingles, video, or multimedia for evaluation and testing. On the evening of the focus groups, your company can watch the group in action and send private messages to the co-moderators as the group is progressing. Unlike traditional focus groups, complete transcripts of the session are available minutes after the conclusion of the group and a complete qualitative report is then written by a SurveySite professional analyst and provided to your company in less than a week.

Another online focus-group company is Strategic Focus (www.sfionline.com). They've been doing online focus groups since 1997 and offer companies an extensive screening and identification process. All screening specifications are established and approved in advance by your company. Similar to SurveySite, online groups are usually conducted with an average group of 6–8 respondents, each group lasting between 80 and 90 minutes.

Strategic Focus's Web-based process provides separate chat windows for the moderator, client, and participant to ensure confidentiality. Upon conclusion of the sessions, a set of transcripts is produced and delivered to the client, available via facsimile, email, or traditional mail services.

Online focus groups are a cost effective alternative to conventional face-to-face focus groups. But keep in mind that these online focus groups provide value, but cannot replace the real thing. Right now, online focus groups can not replace traditional real world testing where a company can gauge how intensely a user feels about a particular feature and ask follow-up questions face-to-face. There are benefits of online testing, but for now at least, it can not replace face-to-face human interaction.

Surveys

Although not as personal as an online focus group, market surveys of consumer opinions can expand your company's reach to thousands of consumers on the Net. A new breed of Web-based survey companies has emerged that can give your company the capability to poll tens of thousands of consumers across the Net on subjects like your Web site design, advertising campaigns, special product offers, and customer service opinions.

Vividence (`www.vividence.com`) is one of a new breed of Web-based survey groups that evaluates Web sites through online user testing. Vividence has a stable of nearly 100,000 online testers to view and comment on a company's Web site. These testers are grouped by specific demographics that allow companies to cross-tabulate results. For example, your company can see how your site is received by respondents of certain age groups, household income, or gender, and in particular, to see if your site or your product or service offer is favorably received and being used easily and effectively by your target audience.

Another online survey company is Active Research. Their service is called ActiveFlash (`www.activeresearch.com/products/ara_4c.htm`) and is a custom Web survey service available for companies offering products or services within a large number of categories such as consumer electronics, home appliances, sporting goods, and so on. It allows companies to ask their panel of interested shoppers any question, or a variety of questions, on any subject. Using ActiveFlash, companies can present new ideas, get feedback on advertising copy, test a proposed product or services, and gather the opinions of consumer segments.

Damage Control

Like many businesses, Professional Exhibits & Graphics, in Sunnyvale, California, sends its customers follow-up letters that include customer survey response cards asking them to rate the level of service and the clarity of training they received and whether or not they would refer other customers to the company. One of the most valuable questions, according to president Dick Wheeler, is the one at the bottom, asking customers whether or not they would like to receive a call from Wheeler himself. In addition to fostering more loyal customers, the practice gives Professional Exhibits the opportunity to fine-tune its systems. "If you can salvage a dissatisfied client and get them happy again," he says, "that pays huge dividends in the end."

For a different, more targeted, real-time approach to surveying a site visitor, OnlineOpinion (www.opinionlab.com) fills that requirement. Companies that subscribe to OnlineOpinion's survey service place a small OnlineOpinion icon on any page of their Web site, which invites consumers to voice their opinion on what they see or read. The icon is in the form of a small plus (+) or minus (-) sign. Consumers simply roll over the icon, click the appropriate response on the five-point pop-up scale, and their opinion of that page is delivered to the company. This is a good way to get accurate feedback from users at the very time they experience a Web site page.

Finally, Insight Express (www.insightexpress.com) lets you create an online survey in minutes, choose your target audience, and receive feedback in hours. Through strategic relationships with Web sites and database companies, they can provide your company with access to more than 70% of the entire Internet. You can build a survey based on a product or service category, age, household income, geographical location, or by an individual's attributes. You can even target your own database of online consumers, your employees, or visitors to your Web site.

Your company need not be kept in the dark about your customers, market space, and competition. With the market research and

CASE STUDY

EXCITE@HOME

Competing in the portal world is tough. Providing useful content and community services is not enough. To attract continuous traffic to their site, the major portals had to transform surfers into settlers. One of the best ways to do this was to create a set of exclusive member services.

Excite@Home (corp.excite.com) already went the standard user-testing route, placing Excite@Home users into rooms and looking over their shoulders as they clicked away. But traditional focus group services didn't come cheap. A typical session, involving 10 subjects over two days, ran $10,000 to $12,000. The costs mount up fast. Each focus group session includes the expense of equipment

rental, the facility in which to hold the focus group, payment to the testers, the cost of a moderator, and the expense of a summary of the results.

And, if you did these sessions 10–15 times a year like Excite@Home did, it got to be quite costly. The bad news was that this costly service did not result in a direct increase in customer satisfaction. So, the company looked elsewhere for a solution.

They found Vividence, an online user-testing company.

Based in San Mateo, California, Vividence has almost 100,000 testers that it can recruit to test a client's site. A typical test employs 200 test subjects and costs clients $20,000. For that fee, clients receive a large amount of intelligence gathering resources available to you on the Net, you can keep your company up-to-date on e-business.

The New Rules of the Road

Over the last several years, billions of dollars have been spent by companies building sophisticated Web sites, online stores, community sites, and portals—all in an attempt to gain a competitive edge or to lock out their competition. Huge content, community sites, and commerce sites are just throwbacks to an economy long past. What we're talking about here is a whole new way to perceive the Internet. Not as a centralized location where buyers go to make purchases, and not where the personal computer is the only way— nor the dominant way—to access the Net. Nor will fixed prices be the only way products and services will be purchased.

In other words, the Internet—not a Web site—is the database.

The Net is a decentralized medium. And, up to now, many e-businesses have not been using it that way. e-Business today has a site-centric mentality. But there's a new trend called Distributed Networks. Instead of having a Web site that you have to drive traffic to (and spend a lot of time and money to maintain), your offering, whether to consumers or other businesses, will be distributed

valuable data that they can parse and cross-tab in a number of ways. While the the testers are looking at a company's site, Vividence watches everything they do and see, and are asked questions via instant messaging such as "Why did you click that particular offer? When you went to the company's About Page, were your questions answered? Can you find help with your order easily on the site?"

The Vividence tasks to the testers can be specific or general. Users could be asked to find a certain product, asked if the special promo is enticing to buy, or asked to briefly surf a site and relate their impressions.

Excite@Home was impressed. The Vividence testing gave them more accurate and actionable feedback than the traditional focus group. After reviewing the Vividence user feedback, Excite@Home realized that they were losing members because they had trouble recovering lost passwords from the site. Members would start the construction of their home page, stop halfway, and then return later to complete it. If members lost their passwords they were forced to re-create the whole page again. So they abandoned half-completed personal homepages and Excite@Home lost a member.

Excite@Home's solution based on the Vividence results? Move a button on the password page to a more obvious location. The change took only an hour and led to a 40% improvement in password recovery.

Vividence's service paid off for Excite@Home.

A Community Without a Web Site

Third Voice (www.thirdvoice.com) offers a browser companion application that lets you annotate any Web page you visit with both private notes and public comments. To read other people's posts, all you need to do is download the Third Voice client. The beauty of this is that the community that forms around annotated Web sites does not exist on a Web site at all.

across the network, served on demand to your buyers. Whether that offer is content, community, or commerce related makes no difference.

As the customers—consumers or businesses—gain more and more control over their buying experience, they can choose to buy whenever, wherever, whatever, at any price, and in any way they choose. How, where, when and at what price a purchase is made is quickly shifting from the seller to the buyer.

The business rules have changed and these are the New Rules of the Road for the Information Highway:

> Rule #1—Sell Anywhere
>
> Rule #2—Sell Anything
>
> Rule #3—Sell Anytime
>
> Rule #4—Sell Any Way
>
> Rule #5—Sell at Any Price

Follow these five rules and incorporate them into your marketing strategy and your e-business will be well prepared to face the challenges of the New Digital Economy.

Finally, there's one last rule—the most important one. Like the old joke about the 11th Commandment—obey the previous 10—there is an overriding Rule of the Road that takes precedence over all five.

It's the customer that counts.

The wild and woolly Web can be a dangerous place for both consumers and businesses. Over the last several years, the media has presented the Net as a wild, buyer-beware commerce environment, loaded with unscrupulous Web operators who imitate legitimate businesses, steal credit card numbers, or peddle substandard goods.

But e-businesses are at risk too. Deliberate fraud, theft of intellectual property, and damages to brand are real problems that can hurt or even cause irreparable damage to your e-business. Unfortunately, the technology of the Net is an easy tool to use for disgruntled customers, hackers, and competitors to damage or invade your company. The resources and energy spent on building and marketing a strong company brand can be quickly and easily damaged on the Net if you don't take proper precautions. Through newsgroups and chat rooms, customers and potential customers are comparing your business to the competition and telling stories about you according to their experiences. Monitoring these discussions is a must. In addition, your company's intellectual property is one of its most important assets for competing in the New Digital Economy. Diligent security is of prime importance. But there is a more insidious threat to your brand that has arisen over the last year or so. One that is practically invisible and one you should be aware of—the screen scrapers.

When you do business on the Internet you open your kimono.

Just about everything an e-business does on the Net is visible to one and all. And those parts that are not directly visible are vulnerable to security breaches both from outside and inside the company. The Net is unique. There's no other business environment in the world that subjects a company to threats to its operational security, brand, and company reputation as the Net does.

Threats to your e-business come in many forms—credit card fraud, theft of intellectual property, irate consumers, and deliberate attacks from those who want to soil your company reputation. And the Net makes it so easy to do. Your competitors and dissatisfied customers have access to an electronic soapbox with an audience ready to listen to any news about your company. In addition, hackers regularly break into sensitive areas of company servers through security walls thought adequate, while thieves use fraudulent credit card procedures to steal goods and services you have so effectively marketed.

All the time, resources and energy spent on building and marketing a strong brand can be quickly and easily damaged on the Net if you don't take proper precautions.

New Economy—New Dangers

Over the last few years, the media has had a field day writing about unscrupulous Web operators who imitate legitimate businesses, steal credit card numbers, or peddle substandard goods. But legitimate, online merchants are also fooled every day by smooth operators who use stolen credit card numbers. No matter what the media says, the Internet is a pretty safe place for consumers to shop thanks to SSL, SET, and other security technologies.

But how safe is it to sell?

A fraud survey conducted by CyberSource (www.cybersource.com), a provider of e-commerce transaction services and an early pioneer in the area of Internet fraud detection, delivered some disturbing statistics. Although most e-merchants acknowledge that credit card

What Is SSL and SET?

SSL stands for *Secure Socket Layer* and *SET* stands for *Secure Electronic Transaction*. SET is a new standard that will enable secure credit card transactions on the Internet. SET has been endorsed by virtually all the major players in the electronic commerce arena including, Microsoft, Netscape, Visa, and MasterCard. SSL is a protocol designed by Netscape Communications Corporation to enable encrypted information to be transmitted over the Internet.

fraud is a concern, 41% did not know that merchants are often financially liable for online fraud. The survey reported that 4.6% to 7.8% of attempted transactions for physical products, like books, CDs, and clothing, are fraudulent, while 14.4% to 23.5% of transactions for digital products, like downloadable software or music, are fraudulent.

Credit Card Fraud

Every credit card holder has up to 120 days to dispute a charge on his or her credit card statement. This is in place to protect the credit card holder. If a cardholder sees a charge on his statement that he doesn't recognize or that he wants to refute, he just contacts his credit card company and the charge is reversed. This is called a *chargeback*. Chargebacks are deducted automatically from a merchant's account and there's little the merchant can do about it.

Those who are deliberately stealing from an online merchant abuse the chargeback privilege. The customer can easily contact his credit card company, claim he never got the goods, and request a chargeback. The charge is reversed, the merchant's account is hit for an equivalent sum, along with a hefty $25 chargeback fee, and the customer walks away with the goods.

Scammers also use stolen credit card numbers or have goods shipped to a mail drop box. Other common tricks include identity fraud, card generators (using fraudulent credit card numbers generated via software), and post-purchase *ship to* changes, where a thief requests a change in the ship to address on someone else's legitimate transaction, diverting the package from its rightful destination.

Contrary to popular belief, the customer is not always right. Sometimes the customer is a crook. The trick is knowing when. Companies such as CyberSource can help.

CyberSource offers the CyberSource Internet Fraud Screen to online merchants that use their services to clear credit cards. The Screen is an automated service that calculates the risk associated with every order, and returns a score to the merchant in about five seconds. The service examines more than 150 different risk factors associated with a given online purchase. For example, CyberSource uses a "pure Internet" transaction history database comprised of millions of Internet transactions. This extensive database tracks and profiles every transaction serviced by CyberSource, making it possible to compare one order against another across the Internet looking for common fraud elements. CyberSource is able to detect unusually expensive purchases and their number from an individual account within the same site and across the base of merchants served.

Other examples of their screening include indicating whether a previous merchant has incurred a chargeback with no return of product; the comparison between the customer's phone number, billing address, shipping address, and other factors determined to be suspicious; and whether the customer is attempting to purchase a particular product more frequently than the merchant desires or would normally expect .

Another useful service is No Chargebacks (www.nochargebacks.com), which has a system that provides merchants access to a database of credit card numbers that have charged back transactions to mail order or Internet businesses.

Finally, don't overlook services provided by your bank. You can request that all card transactions be cleared first through Address Verification Service (AVS), which can tell you if the address provided by the buyer matches what's on record at the issuing bank. Such verification is a handy way to spot some, but not necessarily all fraudulent transactions. Other security checks that are easy to apply include requiring a signature upon receipt to avoid claims that the goods were never shipped; not accepting an order that doesn't have a complete name, address, and phone number; and being suspicious of orders coming from free email addresses, such as Hotmail, because they are anonymous.

Affiliate Fraud

Remember that great affiliate marketing program that you put in place to increase the visibility and sales of your goods and services—for which you pay your affiliate Web sites only upon performance? That is a potential source of fraud, too.

What's Affiliate Marketing?

Affiliate Marketing, or Performance Marketing, allows online marketers to increase sales, drive traffic, generate qualified leads, and extend brand reach while paying only for results. Web sites participating in an affiliate program place banners, text, or images on their site and get commissions or fees from merchants when their site visitors buy by clicking a merchant's banner.

So how do you know? Joel Gehman, the affiliate marketing manager for Infonautics, points out the red flags.

The first tip off he points to is the unexpected success of a new affiliate. It goes like this: A new affiliate signs up for your program and in less than a week, he becomes a super affiliate and immediately begins generating significant volume. They typically have high click-through rates and conversion rates—even higher than your best affiliates.

He advises that anytime you get a new affiliate such as this, get involved quickly. First check out his site. Make sure you investigate all the referring URLs. Referral URLs that don't match the site's profile are a sure warning sign. The same goes for any referral URLs that bring up 404 errors (page not found). When you do successfully find your links and banners on the affiliate site, you will probably find that he is using programming tricks to artificially inflate the hits to your banners.

If you're not sure of fraud, another technique he recommends is to send the affiliate a personal nonconfrontational email asking about where the affiliate's traffic comes from, how long the site's been running, why the site joined the program, and so on. If you get no response from your email after a few business days, you should flag the affiliate and watch his logs carefully. Also, look for inconsistent patterns in an affiliate's traffic—several days of low volume followed by a day with a significant increase, and so forth. Inconsistent traffic patterns could mean that their pages were down for some reason. Ask and find out. If you are dissatisfied with their reply, keep a close eye on their transactions for possible fraud.

The Threat to Your Intellectual Property

The most obvious threat to intellectual property is from outside your company. Cases of hackers breaking into computer systems to steal credit card numbers and company secrets are well documented. But there is a real danger from your own employees, too.

A recent study released by Elron Software of Burlington, Massachusetts (www.elronsw.com)—a supplier of monitoring software for corporate email and Internet accounts—interviewed 576 employees who have Web and email access at work. It found that the number of respondents who reported receiving confidential email leaks more than doubled since 1999.

Another survey by the American Society for Industrial Security and PricewaterhouseCoopers found that Fortune 1,000 companies lost more than $45 billion from thefts of proprietary information during 1999, with high-tech firms reporting the most number of incidents (530). The study also found that anywhere from 50% to 70% of the value of a company today is derived from its proprietary data and trade secrets, and 90% of those secrets can be found in digital form. The survey also shows that companies are most concerned with the threat from within their own company.

The problem, it seems, is people, not technology. Hacking into a network is only one piece of the security puzzle. Robert Steele, a former CIA officer and CEO of Open Source Solutions, says the biggest threat to e-businesses comes from within. "Most losses…come from disgruntled or dishonest insiders using authorized access to do unauthorized things."

"Another potential for espionage is the contracted worker. Smaller businesses often are forced to rely upon contracted skills, such as software development, which makes them particularly vulnerable," says George Smith, a cybersecurity specialist and editor of the online CryptNewsletter (www.soci.niu.edu/~crypt). "Often, the people they commission or hire to do some programming or proprietary business function through the Net will also be doing the same work for a competitor or competitors," he claims.

Your company's intellectual property is one of its most important assets for competing in the New Digital Economy. Diligent security is a must.

Protecting Your Brand Reputation

Whether you're an e-business with a well-established consumer or business-to-business brand or are in the process of establishing a consumer or business-to-business brand, your company and its products have a good chance of being talked about in conversations on the Web. And it's happening right now.

Protecting Your Web Site

Wouldn't it be nice if you could smell the smoke of a security hole before it becomes a fire? That's the objective of the CyberIntelligence firm iDefense (www.idefense.com), which employs an entire group of intelligence analysts charged with identifying and fighting hacker attacks. For a yearly access fee, you can access the latest information on any computer virus, DoS attacks, or cyber-terrorists, as well as a full assessment of your e-business's current security infrastructure.

Customers and potential customers are comparing your business to the competition and telling stories about you according to their experiences. In the offline world it's hard to track what individuals say about a company, but on the Web you can monitor comments and participate in these interactions.

Prior to the Internet, consumers had a hard time finding others who purchased products that they were considering. Not so on the Net.

Monitoring Consumer Comments

The Net enables people to spread the word about what concerns them. Every time someone interacts with your company, he or she is forming an opinion of you, your company, its products, and its people. For good or bad, newsgroups, discussion lists, newsletters, chat rooms—even personal Web sites—have given consumers and competitors the chance to talk about your company and the goods and services you offer.

The oldest form of consumer interaction is Usenet, which has several thousand newsgroups where people post opinions on practically everything. Over the years, consumers have exchanged experiences and opinions about merchants—both online and off—in such groups as `misc.consumers` and `alt.consumers.experiences`.

But these conversations are not invisible to the e-marketer. With sites such as Deja.com (`www.deja.com`), e-marketers can locate and read comments made about their company. Deja.com has organized the Usenet discussions and categorized them for easy searching on a particular subject or issue. In addition, services that combine Web postings with email discussion lists, such as Topica (`www.topica.com`) and eGroups (`www.egroups.com`), make it easier to monitor such discussions.

Discussions in these communities could touch on a particular product or company like yours and occasionally, there is so much discussion—both positive and negative—that it becomes easy for prospective customers to develop a profile of your company that you would not like. Monitoring these discussions and responding to negative comments will help protect your company and brand reputation in the marketplace.

Monitoring customer comments about a company on the Web can be a full-time job in itself, or marketers can monitor these discussions with a variety of services such as eWatch (www.ewatch.com), MarkWatch (www.markwatch.com), and WebClipping (www.webclipping.com). If you are a public company, it would be wise to monitor the stock message boards like the ones at Yahoo!. What investors are saying about your stock can impact your company's reputation with the investment community. Monitoring these various investor message boards can give you good ideas, suggestions, and notice of legitimate concerns from investors and a chance to respond to them.

Finally, over the last couple of years, a whole new set of sites has sprung up to fulfill a customer-service need that had long been felt by consumers. Sites like ePinions.com (www.epinions.com), ConsumerReview.com (www.consumerreview.com), and Shopserve.com (www.shopserve.com) all enable consumers to post raves and rants about their experiences at stores, both on and offline. These sites should be monitored as well because these are places where consumers can get frank opinions about products, services, and vendors from consumers that are either disappointed or delighted. When you see a negative comment posted, respond to it and show that your company is customer-focused and open to change.

At least with these types of Web sites, the comments about your company and any damage to your brand can be remedied with monitoring. But there is a more insidious threat to your brand that has arisen over the last year or so. One that is practically invisible and one you should be aware of—the screen scrapers.

The Threat to Brand of Screen Scrapers

You've spent time, money, and energy building and promoting your brand. And now, there are companies on the Net that can take your Web site and your brand apart, piece by piece, and scatter it across the Net.

One such company is Yodlee (www.yodlee.com). Yodlee is one of several new companies creating a new way to view content on the Web. Rather than treat the Web as a collection of sites and pages,

Stay Current on Customer Complaints

At Feedbackdirect.com (www.feedbackdirect.com), consumers can initiate the customer service process with thousands of companies across more than 14 vertical categories. Using their service, consumers can fill out forms and fire off complaints and suggestions to e-businesses like yours.

Yodlee and others, such as CallTheShots (www.calltheshots.com), Moreover.com (www.moreover.com), Octopus.com (www.octopus.com), and OnePage.com (www.onepage.com) literally scrape the content from Web pages, reorganize the content according to the wishes of the consumer, and serve it up in smaller components. These components can be as small as a headline, a table, or a single word, and then the pieces are shuffled into new forms. The goal is to reduce information overload by making it easier for users to snatch the needles they want out of the haystack that is the Internet.

The problem is, when this data is scraped and reorganized your company and brand can be lost in the process.

No Web site is immune. These companies can work their magic without the cooperation, permission, or even knowledge of the sites whose content is being scraped. What's the point of spending hundreds of thousands of dollars building a noticeable brand to drive customers to your site when your content can be sliced and diced and reorganized at will by a consumer?

And the news gets worse. Not only is the scraper technology a bane to one's brand, but it is both necessary and inevitable. The rise of mobile wireless devices will encourage more companies to pull content from Web sites and assemble it in ways that are appropriate for small screens. Web sites, as we know them, will not survive on these small screen devices. Also, many feel that the on-the-go user will not tolerate that stalwart advertising vehicle known as the banner ad—not that the tiny screen can accommodate it.

CASE STUDY

WASHINGTONPOST.NEWSWEEK INTERACTIVE

New technologies like Web scrapers are breaking up Web sites into bite-sized pieces and e-businesses can do little to stop it. So if you can't fight the trend, join it. At least that's what *The Washington Post* did.

The Washingtonpost.Newsweek Interactive (WPNI), the new media arm of *The Washington Post* company, is adapting its content to wireless devices and other non-browser access methods for the Net. *WAP (Wireless Application Protocol)* users can read ad-free, full text articles from *The Washington Post* at twp.com on their cell phones and PDAs. By positioning WPNI now and offering its own version of scraping its Web site, WPNI hopes to get the jump on headline aggregator

Not that this scraping process is new. That's exactly what search engines like AltaVista do when they scour the Web and return search results on a custom formatted page. Comparison shopping engines do the same. They visit online merchant sites, view their product offering, and return with the lowest price for a product available, serving it all up on a customized page for the shopper.

What makes this new generation of scrapers unique is their vast reach and the sophisticated search technology that far surpasses the crawler software that just grabs pages used by search engines. Yodlee, for example, can pull individual snippets of content and personal information from some 1,300 different data sources on the Web.

Yodlee's cofounder, Venkat Rangan, believes that the aggregation model of the screen scrapers will be a boon to consumers who are now busy searching for data across the Internet. "Each Web site on the Internet is like an island," he says. "People are trying to hop from island to island trying to gather their content." Now intelligent software and services, such as Yodlee's, will gather content from various sites and bring it to a user's PC, cell phone, PDA, or any Net-enabled device.

A similar technology comes from companies such as OpenTV (www.opentv.com), Oracle's Portal-to-Go (www.oracle.com), and Pumatech's Browse-it (www.pumatech.com) that chew up Web sites built for PC browsers and spit out versions reformatted for display on Net-appliances such as phones, set-top boxes—even voice-enabled Net gateways.

Screen Scrape Your Intranet

Plumtree Software (www.plumtree.com) provides software to create corporate portals for company intranets. Its Corporate Portal software brings together in one simple, personalized Web page all the information and productivity tools relevant to a corporate user. In one place, employees, partners, and customers can review product and market news, analyze key performance metrics, launch productivity tools, and complete e-commerce transactions.

Moreover.com and personalization service Octopus.com.

Nothing has been decided yet, but it could include carrying small ads, or the company could charge a subscription fee to the service. Or WPNI could give the content away free as a loss leader that can draw readers to revenue producing places on its Web site.

As new software technology and Net-enabled devices come online, WPNI will face all kinds of new challenges to its e-business. Although WPNI's forward thinking will not guarantee its dominance in the news content field, it's sure to be in the lead of other content providers who are waiting to see what shakes out in the nonbrowser space before acting.

As consumers choose these approaches over the traditional ways to view the Net, e-businesses will certainly have to start to think hard about how they do business. Or, in the words of Jakob Nielsen of the Nielsen Norman Group, "It's a great example why, when one is thinking about the future of the Internet, one should not get too involved in the way it is now."

The battle lines are being drawn. The old guard has hundreds of years of copyright law on their side—the new guard has the new technology on theirs.

Copyright issues in the New Economy will be one of many battles fought over the law that is and the technology that it is becoming. Technologies like Napster and Gnutella are just tips of the iceberg. Napster is an open target for the law because their technology is served from a central sever which can be closed down. On the other hand, technologies like Gnutella, which are distributed across millions of individual PCs, are impossible to control.

History has shown that laws have to catch up to technology, so some kind of agreement has to be reached between the creators of content and those that use it. Without the compensation for one's content, there is no motivation to create it.

We'll just have to wait and see what the answer to this dilemma will be. In the meantime, keep in mind that it is open season for the new technology and "not to get too involved in the way [the Net] is now."

PART II

Rules for Success in the New Economy

Rule #1—Selling Anywhere

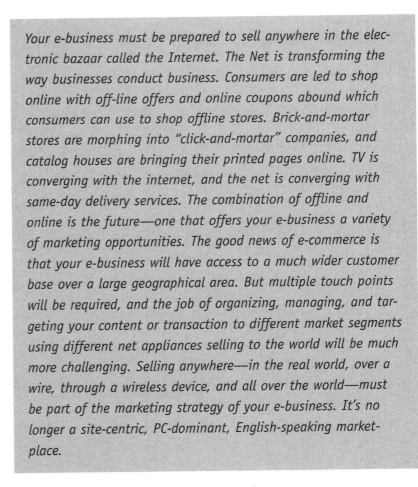

Your e-business must be prepared to sell anywhere in the electronic bazaar called the Internet. The Net is transforming the way businesses conduct business. Consumers are led to shop online with off-line offers and online coupons abound which consumers can use to shop offline stores. Brick-and-mortar stores are morphing into "click-and-mortar" companies, and catalog houses are bringing their printed pages online. TV is converging with the internet, and the net is converging with same-day delivery services. The combination of offline and online is the future—one that offers your e-business a variety of marketing opportunities. The good news of e-commerce is that your e-business will have access to a much wider customer base over a large geographical area. But multiple touch points will be required, and the job of organizing, managing, and targeting your content or transaction to different market segments using different net appliances selling to the world will be much more challenging. Selling anywhere—in the real world, over a wire, through a wireless device, and all over the world—must be part of the marketing strategy of your e-business. It's no longer a site-centric, PC-dominant, English-speaking marketplace.

onsumers are already receiving offers offline to shop online, and online coupons used to shop offline stores are already in existence. Brick-and-mortar stores are transforming themselves into click-and-mortar companies and printed catalog houses are morphing into *click-and-flip* merchants. TV is converging with the Internet, and the net is converging with same-day delivery services. Even banks are getting into the act, turning ATMs into Internet kiosks.

A 1999 study by Forrester Research suggests that, when done right, established brick-and-mortar companies have the same chance, if not a better chance, to dominate their product category on the net. In its first ever PowerRankings study, which ranks e-commerce sites in the most popular categories, Forrester Research found that many real-world companies are leading their category on the Web. Charles Schwab led the brokerage division, Lands' End was top in apparel, and Hallmark was first with online flowers. Forrester Research director David Weisman said, "What this suggests is that the strong brands, established order fulfillment systems, and good customer service these companies have offline is starting to make a difference in the online world."

Clicks and Bricks

It looks like the brick-and-mortar companies and their online strategies are poised to win the next round of the e-commerce battle. Their marketing strategies will offer the purely dot-com companies a run for their money. It would be wise now to take a leaf out of their notebooks and realize that the combination of offline and online is the future, one that offers your e-business a variety of marketing opportunities. After all, an offline presence for your e-business adds more than the opportunity for a sale. It builds brand recognition and the medium for customer acquisition and retention. It also gives online and offline companies the chance to form affiliations that would benefit both.

For example, take America Online (www.aol.com) and the Blockbuster video stores. AOL uses Blockbuster to help it acquire new customers. Blockbuster hands out those free AOL membership CDs that we've all come to know. In return, AOL promotes Blockbuster on its service. Another customer acquisition partnership is the affiliation between the TV network CBS and Medscape—they create co-op ads that benefit both.

Click-and-Flip

As brick-and-mortar stores come online and become click-and-mortar companies, printed catalog companies, such as Lands End and L.L. Bean are also doing the same. These online catalog companies are called click-and-flip companies.

TV-Web Convergence

HyperTV Networks, at www.hypertv.com, offers a unique way of combining the excitement of television with the interactivity of the Internet. When a user downloads its free software, he can automatically receive exclusive Web content on his computer that complements a program that he's watching on TV.

Cutting Down Return Rates

Return rates for clothing are one of the highest in e-commerce. EZsize (www.ezsize.com) seeks to trim those returns by fitting buyers the first time around. EZsize sets up a pavilion at a brick-and-mortar store, and consumers can measure their bodies in 3D. They then plug their measurements in the pavilion and order clothes that fit.

Another example of blending the online and offline world is BarPoint.com (www.barpoint.com). BarPoint brought an innovative twist to the clicks and bricks marketing model. The company has combined traditional process of everyday shopping with the power of the wireless Net.

For the die-hard comparison shopper, BarPoint.com is manna from heaven. As you stroll down a brick-and-mortar merchant's aisle, BarPoint.com makes it easy to learn everything about any product you choose. Just enter any barcode number of any product directly onto the BarPoint.com site. After you do, you can find all types of information on the item, check prices, read reviews, and, if you want, purchase it from one of more than 350 affiliate merchants.

But visiting the Web site is only one of the many ways that BarPoint.com delivers information. BarPoint.com can also turn your portable wireless device—cellular phone, PDA, or pager—into a wireless comparison-shopping tool, putting the power of product-specific information in the palm of your hand while comparing prices from other merchants. BarPoint.com lets users compare and save right in the store by providing an optional scanning gun for discreetly swiping the UPC tag. Affiliations like this can be used not only for customer acquisition, but for customer retention as well. Drugstore.com (www.drugstore.com) and the click-and-mortar drug store RiteAid have integrated their services so that customers can place their prescription online and pick it up at the local RiteAid drug store. Both benefit by giving their customers a reason to continue doing business with them.

Finally, the combinations of offline and online marketing venues are nearly endless. New companies routinely appear that bring a new twist to combined online and offline marketing strategies. Selling anywhere, online or off, wired or wireless, and all over the world, must be part of the marketing strategy of your e-business. Looking at how other e-businesses are selling anywhere can give you ideas when it's time to form your marketing strategies.

The Strip Mall Goes Virtual

At first glance, the Internet seems to signal the end for anything local. But local has its advantages. As the months go by, in fact, it

Spin Off Your Online Operations

If you're a brick-and-mortar store with a click-and-mortar strategy, consider spinning off e-business to compete with the pure e-commerce plays. Both American Airlines and Barnes & Noble used this strategy to recruit and retain good people (using stock options) while also providing access to low-cost capital.

seems that local entities might just have the advantage over the be-alls and end-alls of the large e-businesses on the net. Whether the brick-and-mortar store is a local store or part of a chain, they both have a common competitor: the pure dot-com player. Your company can learn the advantages that the brick-and-mortar companies have and can apply them to your e-business.

One of the most important marketing advantages of selling both online and off is for the customer. Pity the consumer who has to return a product for whatever reason. In its very nature, returning a product purchased online over the phone or through the mail is a cumbersome and inconvenient process for the consumer, no matter how well designed the system. If your company has a local offline presence, customers can return the product easily and quickly. Obviously, the large chains selling nationally online have the advantage over the small local stores. But if your local e-business sells where it is located, you still can have this marketing advantage, one that the pure dot-com plays can't duplicate.

Easy handling of returns is only one advantage of a click-and-mortar business. When a customer is in your real world store for a return or a customer service problem, there's an opportunity to make another sale. One tactic is to give them a discount coupon that's good for a return visit to your store or to use on your Web site. A customer service problem then becomes an opportunity for customer retention.

The net gives consumers "virtual mobility," but what consumers need now is trust, loyalty, and service with their purchase. Linking consumers with a local business can meet this challenge. But local delivery is only one marketing advantage of a click-and-mortar strategy. Enter still another: the desktop-to-doorstep revolution.

Desktop-to-Doorstep Revolution

A young MBA student once submitted his concept for an overnight delivery service as his MBA thesis. His professor gave him a poor grade for the business concept because he couldn't see why anyone *had* to have anything overnight. The U.S. Postal Service was delivering mail twice a day and once on Saturday, servicing our needs very nicely.

e-Certificates Hit the Real World

Recipients of Web certificates have always been able to spend them at online stores. But now they can spend them in the real world as well. Ecount (www.ecount.com) has a Web certificate shopping card that's good at any brick-and-mortar merchant. If the recipient of an online Web certificate wants to make an offline purchase, Ecount issues a prepaid plastic card (that acts like a debit card) to use.

Of course, that MBA thesis went on to become Federal Express and proved that people *did* want things overnight. Today, we not only want what we buy overnight, but we want it right now.

Here's where local brick-and-mortar companies shine again. Local e-businesses can offer something that few dot-coms can: not only easy product returns and real-world customer service, but same day delivery as well.

Several new e-businesses are capitalizing on this same-day delivery strategy. Kozmo.com (`www.kozmo.com`) delivers to certain locales videos, games, DVDs, music, magazines, books, food, and more—all in less than an hour. Kozmo currently delivers to 10 major cites, including Atlanta, New York, Los Angeles, Seattle, and Washington, D.C.

UnderGroundOnline (`www.ugo.com`), a media distribution company, consists of more than 300 owned and affiliated Web sites showcasing exclusive content featuring games, film and TV, music, technology, animation, and freestyle entertainment categories, and has another interesting approach to this type of marketing. It has decked out two mobile Web assault-type vehicles that hit events such as skateboard competitions, concerts, and comic book conventions to reach its target market of 18- to 34-year-olds. The company's "Road Rave" vehicles and staff members invite visitors to play video games onsite, participate in contests, and take home promotional merchandise. Similar to click-and-mortar stores, UGO's marketing strategy is to be "on the ground" to bring its e-business to where its target market lives.

Online at the Corner Shop

A new company in England, called Dropzone1 (`www.dropzone1.co.uk`), is making online shopping a little easier. Although more people are shopping online, few of them are home during the day to take delivery of the goods they have ordered. Modeled after companies in Japan, Dropzone1 is signing up petrol stations and corner shops across the country that will accept delivery on behalf of online shoppers, who then pick up their packages on the way home from work.

CASE STUDY

REI

REI, a 62-year-old outdoor gear and clothing retailer, has made a big success out of the bricks and clicks marketing strategies. The Seattle company has seen its online sales grow a whopping 237% since last year, making its Web site, `www.rei.com`, the chain's biggest store.

Yet, REI claims that its Web site sales are not cannibalizing its traditional store sales. In fact, the opposite has occurred. Online customers who also shopped REI's stores spent 22% more in the brick-and-mortar stores than the previous year. Both in-store and online sales grew together without any sign of cannibalization.

REI's success can be traced back to its customers, a fanatical following of hikers, campers, skiers, cyclists, and other outdoor enthusiasts. REI has been capable of channeling its success through the retail stores, its

A variation on marketing to where the customer lives is practiced by OpenTable.com (www.opentable.com). OpenTable is developing a massive nationwide network that will eventually handle tickets to restaurant tables in every major city. Consumers who want to book a reservation at a participating restaurant simply go to OpenTable's Web site, choose the restaurant that they want, and book their reservation for the evening. The reservation shows up instantly on the screen of a small box at the restaurant. This service is free to the consumer—it's instant, and the customer's reservation is confirmed. The restaurant pays $100 a month for the service. OpenTable plans to add other services for the consumer, such as ordering flowers on the table and registering events for birthdays and anniversaries.

Wedding Traditional Media with Interactive Services

Closing fast behind click-and-mortar companies are click-and-flip companies, which market over the Internet and through printed catalogs. Catalogers were quick to build online stores in response to the their dot-com challengers. In turn, the pure dot-com plays have turned to printing and sending catalogs to customers and prospects to increase their reach and build their brands.

Familiarity with a brand, such as catalog merchants L.L. Bean (www.llbean.com) and Sharper Image (www.sharperimage.com), makes consumers more comfortable with their online purchases. On the flip side, online merchants can extend their brand

Web site, and its printed catalog. The company has successfully wedded both traditional media and nontraditional interactive services and has cross-marketed its offers to its wide range of customers. REI's marketing strategy is to give its customers every opportunity to purchase products from stores, the catalog, or the Web site.

In addition, REI's in-store cash registers are net-enabled, allowing their cashiers to order for customers who couldn't find an item in the store. In-store kiosks, and "shop the Web site" messages are imprinted on every sales receipt, newsletters, emails, and other forms of communications with customers.

REI is a prime example of a successful clicks and bricks marketing strategy, and it gives us a glimpse of the future in which all marketing engines are effectively in play.

awareness and reach into new consumer segments by publishing a printed catalog. Greatfood.com (www.greatfood.com)—now part of 1-800 Flowers—was one of the first pure dot-coms to launch a *netalog*. Its printed netalog was used to drive new traffic to its Web site.

Using print by pure dot-coms to sell merchandise is not the only example of wedding traditional media with interactive services. Content can be sold as well. Take Yahoo!, for example. That dot-com has a very successful magazine that it markets called *Yahoo Internet Life*. Not only is it a magazine in its own right, but it also acts as a branding and traffic-generating vehicle for Yahoo!'s Web site. It has a paid circulation of more than 750,000—higher than some decades-old popular magazines, such as *Esquire*.

On a more mundane note, companies such as Mimeo (www.mimeo.com) supply a software package that lets a consumer or business print and send documents over the net. These documents then are printed, bound, and delivered the next day via Federal Express.

As you can see, using a click-and-mortar strategy is not just a way to handle returns. By studying companies like those mentioned here, your e-business may be capable of applying these marketing techniques to help sell wherever your customer may be. Someday soon, selling entirely through a pure dot-com will seem as ludicrous as having a catalog company without a toll-free number.

m-Commerce: Wireless Commerce Is Coming

Ready or not the wireless masses are coming. Armed with every kind of net-ready device, millions of consumers will soon be demanding wireless access to your e-business. Shut them out, and they'll turn to your nearest wireless competitor as fast as you can say "Out of business."

Consumers are already using their mobile phones for a variety of mobile e-commerce services. This even has a name: *c-commerce*, for cell commerce. Consumers are using their phones for banking, obtaining stock quotes, ordering movie and train tickets, and buying from vending machines. Although consumers in the United

States use only some of these services, the rest of the world—especially Europe and Asia—see their phones as the preferred medium of getting information, making transactions, and checking on the status of their affairs.

However, the craze for net appliances does not stop at the cell phone (see Table 6.1). Virgin Entertainment (www.virginmega.com) distributes 10,000 Virgin-branded Web players to qualified consumers who can use them to buy CDs and videos from Virgin's online store. America Online and Gateway Computers are working on a net appliance that will provide Instant AOL access as well.

What's c-Commerce?

c-Commerce is a subset of mobile commerce, or m-commerce. When transactions are made using a cellular phone, as opposed to any other net-enabled wireless device, this is called c-commerce.

Table 6.1

World Wide Information Appliance Shipment Forecast			
	1999	2004	Annual Growth
Net TVs	6.1	17.8	6.2%
Net Screenphones	1.1	3.6	26.2%
Net Gaming Devices	2.0	22.6	28.1%
Email Terminals	0.1	4.6	70.6%
Web Terminals	0.006	6.5	124.2%
Net-Smart Handhelds	1.7	33.2	77.4%
Other	0.01	0.69	94.7%
Total Appliances	11.0	89.0	33.5%

Source: IDC

But c-commerce is only the tip of the iceberg. Hot on its heals is m-commerce, or mobile commerce. m-commerce consists of selling anything over a mobile wireless device or net appliance. International Data Corporation (IDC) (www.idc.com), a leading provider of information technology industry analysis, predicts that net appliances will surpass U.S. shipments of personal computers by 2002, and forecasts the net appliance market to grow to 89 million units, or $17.8 billion, in 2004 (up from 11 million units, or $2.4 billion in 1999). IDC's definition of net appliances includes Internet gaming consoles, net TVs, handheld devices, and Web and email terminals and screenphones.

Wireless Comparison Shopping

Deja.com (www.deja.com) offers its Precision Buying Service as a wireless application. Its comparison shopping service give consumers the ability to research products on the Internet and compare prices from individual merchants.

Speech-Driven Telephones for e-Business

NetByTel.com (www.netbytel.com) brings e-commerce home to the common telephone. The company offers an automated, speech-enabled interface to e-commerce Web sites so that a customer can call from anywhere and conduct business over a wired or wireless phone.

But of the 500 million m-commerce users in the year 2005, only 22% will be in North America. Western Europe and Asia will make up almost two-thirds of the usage. That means that your e-business must not only provide a seamless way for your customers to access your offers over a range of mobile net appliances, but it also must be ready to sell to a global market. As consumers and business customers make the shift from wired to wireless net access, your e-business marketing strategy will need to make some profound shifts as well.

The good news of m-commerce is that your e-business will have access to a much wider customer base over a large geographical area. But the job of organizing, managing, and targeting your content or transaction to different market segments using different net appliances will be much more challenging. Wireless Application Protocol (WAP) is attempting to standardize access to the net through any and all wireless devices. Your e-business cannot ignore WAP if you want to reach your target customer base. Your customers around the world will expect to have a seamless interface to your content and to perform transactions from whichever wireless appliance they use.

Today GeePS.com (www.geeps.com) provides a wireless shopping portal. By year-end, 1 million WAP phones will be in use, and GeePS.com plans to capitalize on it. While driving, strolling, or shopping, merchants can pinpoint your location and present offers to you as you pass by their establishments. You can walk past the Gap, for instance, and your cell phone will ring—and a discount offer from the Gap will appear on your cell phone or Palm Pilot. This pinpoint targeting is the result of the FCC 911 mandate (in place by 2001) that all wireless devices must be capable of pinpointing your location within 100 yards.

Your typical consumer in the not-so-distant future will use the net like this.

Let's call our typical m-commerce consumer Bob. Bob's job keeps him constantly on the move. He has a computer at home, but his preferred way of accessing the net is his wireless net appliance, a combination cell phone and personal digital assistant (PDA). He takes it everywhere—it contains his calendar, appointments, his Rolodex, and the shortcuts to all his favorite Web services.

On the long subway commute home from work in the evening, Bob takes this opportunity to catch up on a few things that he still needs to do. Accessing the city box office, he checks to see if he was able to buy those tickets to *Phantom of the Opera*. The show was sold out, and he was on the wait list. He then checks to see if the stock trade he ordered went through that morning and if the proceeds were credited to his account. He sees that he did get the two tickets to *Phantom*, so he reserves a table for him and wife that evening at their favorite restaurant for after the show.

At home, he turns on his interactive television and accesses the local Gourmet Meals on Wheels and orders a steak-and-lobster dinner for him and the wife. As an afterthought, he quickly jumps to a floral shop and orders a dozen roses to arrive with dinner. He then accesses his brokerage account to research that stock tip he got from a colleague that afternoon. He calls up a video of the CEO of the company reporting that the company will hit its revenue target for this quarter. Bob decides to buy the stock. He enters his brokerage account PIN number, and his trade is confirmed.

Your company must be prepared to service the customer anywhere and on any net access device that the customer chooses to use at the moment. This means that your marketing strategy must include a stable of m-commerce marketing essentials.

m-Commerce Marketing Essentials

Within just a year or two, your customers will prefer to interact with a company via both wireless and wired net appliances. Your challenge will be the one of content and transaction management through all these points of contact. Here are some m-commerce essentials to keep in mind:

> **Plan for multiple touch points**—As the world moves toward wireless, your marketing strategy must be designed for multiple touch points, that is, the many ways to reach consumers through multiple net-enabled devices that are here now and are coming in the near future. For example, consumers are not using just Netscape or IE to access the Web anymore. More are accessing the net through their Palm Pilots, Web TV, cell phones—even their Sega Dreamcasts and Sony

Plan for Multiple Touch Points—Wireless Net Devices

When planning your offer to be displayed on a wireless net device, streamline is the key here, not graphics or logos. Make access to menus quick, use short text phrases, and present just a few simple menu choices.

Plan for Multiple Touch Points—Web Site

Customization is important when planning your Web site. Use the virtually unlimited space of your site to personalize the shoppers' experience, offering content and offers based on what you know about each customer's visit and what that person wants to accomplish.

Playstations. Jupiter Communications predicts that in 2003, net-enabled video game consoles will surpass 16 million units in the United States alone.

Presenting your company content and offers through a Web site, WAP-enabled wireless net devices, cell phones, game consoles, and interactive TV is enough of a complex task. But tomorrow there may be three times that many net appliances to market your message through. You'll have to code and repurpose your information differently for each platform.

Plan for interactive marketing—Think about our friend Bob. While he's on your Web site reserving a table at your restaurant or your Gourmet Meals on Wheels service, what additional products or service can you sell him? Flowers for his wife at his restaurant table, or maybe a nice bottle of wine to go with the delivered meal? If he won't take the up-sell offer then and there, inform him that he has a discount coupon waiting for him at your Web site. These are simple up-selling techniques.

But suppose that you wanted to present a more sophisticated offer, perhaps some other investment alternative to the stock that he bought? For that, you need to know more about Bob than just this one transaction. You need to have formed a relationship with him—a relationship formed over so many transactions that your company has built a profile of his preferences. This is the payoff of a good customer relationship marketing program.

Plan for different languages and cultures—If you're going to market to a global audience, you'll need to do it in their language and be sensitive to cultural differences. Your content and product offerings must take into account local customs and must be perceptive of the difference between theirs and yours. An Italian consumer will want to perform tasks differently than a Japanese shopper.

Plan for different laws and tariffs—What's considered a final price in one country is not the same in another. If you're selling globally, your company needs to know the various duties, taxes, and shipping fees for different countries.

It's going to be a multitouch-point, multilingual, multicultural world. Prepare for it.

Selling to the World—Going Global

Did you know that when in Japan, you should always present a gift with two hands? This is also true with presenting business cards. And did you know that you should avoid giving gifts in sets of four? The word *four* in Japanese is *shi*, which is also associated with the word for death. White symbolizes death, too, so packages should never be wrapped in white paper.

I bring these up as examples of how easy it is to make mistakes when dealing with another culture. If you're going to sell into the global marketplace and you don't understanding the culture of the customer you're selling to, you're setting your company up for costly mistakes. Building an international marketing strategy is more than just translating your site into another language. Of course, your company faces not only the challenges of language, but also the regulatory challenges of import and export rules, taxation, social and political issues, and fulfillment and customer services problems. Any one of these items, if mishandled, can quickly torpedo your global marketing efforts.

How important is a global initiative for your e-business? Let's put it this way: In the future, if you're not selling everywhere, you're selling nowhere. And by *everywhere*, I mean technologically (on wired and portable wireless devices) and geographically (selling anywhere in the world).

The global market will soon represent a large portion of e-commerce. Preston Dodd, an analyst at Jupiter Communications, says, "Basically, two-thirds of the world online audience within a few years will be non-English-speaking." IDC, another Internet research firm, predicts that two-thirds of all e-commerce spending will take place outside the United States by the year 2003. In that year, the firm reports, consumer spending at U.S. Web sites will reach $119 billion, but overseas sites will garner $209 billion in business. This business will come not only from e-commerce Web sites, but also from cell phones, PDAs, and other wireless net-enabled devices.

Plan for Multiple Touch Points— Interactive TV

Use the capabilities of the television medium to use animation, video, and audio to grab and keep shoppers' interest. Use the technology to create presentations that enhance and influence a customer to consider your product or service offers.

Free Translation Service

Need a quick and simple translation of your offer? How does free sound? At the FreeTranslation.com site (www.freetranslation.com), you can do it for free, *libre*, *libero*, *frei*, and *livre*!

But selling internationally is not easy. Challenges abound. When designing your international marketing strategy, there are a number of elements to keep in mind.

Designing for a Global Market

With more than 30% of online shoppers located outside the United States (and growing), it's imperative that your e-business develop marketing strategies for the countries that you target. Your e-business cannot hope to reach buyers from around the world through a simple English-speaking Web site. Your marketing strategy will have to deal with many issues not normally a concern with selling from a U.S. Web site. MRI International (www.mediaresources.com) tells a visitor right on its home page that shoppers from around the world are welcome.

First let's address the language and cultural challenges. Mere word-for-word translation of your product or service offer is not enough. Cultural nuances also must be considered. Certain products may be offensive in certain cultures. A good example is selling leather products made of pigskin to a Muslim audience. Pigskin comes from pork, and pork is considered sacred in the Muslin religion. Another cultural misunderstanding to avoid is the incorrect tone of product instructions. In Japan, for example, you wouldn't say, "Don't press the right button." You should say, "It would be much better if you pushed the left button."

Every element of your visual offer, including language and navigation, whether seen on a Web site or a net appliance, must be designed with this kind of cultural sensitivity.

In addition to the language and cultural challenges, there are the local customs and legal issues for individual countries. Customs, tax, or tariffs charges must be easily figured into the final sale to an international customer. Finding the right software that can calculate international shipping charges, value-added taxes, duty, and other international charges is of prime importance if you're going to sell in the global market.

Before the first order is taken, however, your company must think about fulfillment. Will you ship from one country to another, or will you set up a local warehouse and shipping center in the countries in which you do business? And what about customer service and merchandise returns?

Building a global e-fulfillment system is one of the biggest challenges that your e-business will face. One of the best solutions to these problems is to outsource your fulfillment and customer service operations to companies that actually reside in your customer's country. One company that has been very successful at selling to a global market is Dell Computers. The Dell site is aimed at more than 85 different countries and territories, and uses a decentralized approach with its international sites. Dell created a common technology platform for each of its global sites, including templates for ordering and product information, which provided a consistent user experience across all the sites.

Dell then provided several hundred language specialists to train and advise the local managers of each site. And customer service? The company solved that problem by employing a local customer service team so that anytime a customer picks up a phone, they're dealing with someone local. To top off this global marketing strategy, Dell built manufacturing plants and distribution centers in each of the regions that it serves.

And don't think that selling services is any easier or has fewer problems when selling products internationally. Take Charles Schwab as an example. Selling financial services in Europe should be a breeze, right? That's what Schwab thought, too. Europeans know all about buying stocks, bonds, and mutual funds. So, when the online broker Schwab (`www.schwab.com`) opened a site for clients in Britain in 1998, many of the Brits bulked at online trading. They were accustomed to trading paper stock certificates, not electronic trades. Because Schwab refused to issue paper certificates to its online customers, the site generated only 15,000 new accounts in 12 months.

Even if your e-business does not have the resources of Dell to plan and execute a global business, some companies can help. US-Style.com is one such company. US-Style.com (`www.us-style.com`) will handle the front end of your e-business if you are marketing to customers in Japan. The company serves e-tailers (B2C), manufacturers, and wholesale distributors (B2B) who want to sell products to the growing global online markets outside North America.

Will That Be Cash, Check, or Charge?

Most of the world does not use credit cards. So, when you market to your global customers, make sure to let them know that you can and will take other forms of payment, including checks, debit cards, or electronic forms of cash.

Parlez-Vous Email?

Selling anywhere also means selling any way. Using email is a way to offer products or services to your global customers. VeloMail (www.velomail.com) is a free email service that gives you the ability to write and receive emails in 40 languages. Velomail makes typing in foreign languages easy by providing a virtual keyboard on your screen, showing what each key will produce when used in the language you are typing in.

What's important about US-Style.com is that it provides not only translation, but also cultural relevance. Specialists actually rewrite your product description to make it more compelling to a Japanese shopper. The company also handles inbound customer service calls and translates your outbound customer service replies.

A company on the net that can help your e-business on the fulfillment side is From2.com (www.from2.com), an international logistics company that provides an all-inclusive solution for e-commerce merchants to deliver goods to international customers. From2.com offers a complete suite of traditional logistics functions through its domestic and international facilities, including warehousing, fulfillment, and international door-to-door delivery services. Without ever leaving your Web site, your customers can calculate freight, insurance, duties, taxes, customs clearance fees, and other import charges associated with shipping a product across international borders.

As for the offer itself, your e-business can use any one of several translation companies on the net to translate your offer from English to other languages. One such service is Wholetree.com (www.wholetree.com). This company offers technology for your e-business that handles multiple currency purchases, provides multilingual technical support, and recognizes input and provides output in multiple languages.

It's no longer a site-centric, PC-dominant, English-speaking marketplace. Your e-business must be prepared to sell anywhere in the electronic bazaar of the Internet.

BARPOINT.COM

BarPoint.com (www.barpoint.com) brought an innovative twist to the clicks and bricks marketing model. The company has combined the traditional process of everyday shopping with the power of the wireless net.

For more than 20 years, the barcode has been used by manufacturers and retailers alike to track inventory. But waiting silently between those cryptic black lines was information that the consumer could use; information that BarPoint.com has made accessible to the general public.

For the die-hard comparison shopper, BarPoint.com is manna from heaven. As you stroll down a brick-and-mortar merchant's aisle, BarPoint.com makes it easy to learn everything about any product you choose. Just enter any barcode number of any product directly onto the BarPoint.com site. After you do, you can find all types of information on the item, check prices, read reviews, and, if you want, purchase it from one of more than 350 affiliate merchants. Unlike traditional search engines that return all kinds of irrelevant data, using the product bar code and BarPoint.com's service returns complete and accurate information on any product.

But visiting the Web site is only one of the many ways that BarPoint.com delivers information. BarPoint.com can also turn your portable wireless device—cellular phone, PDA, or pager—into a wireless comparison-shopping tool, putting the power of product-specific information in the palm of your hand while comparing prices from other merchants. BarPoint.com lets users compare and save right in the store by providing an optional scanning gun for discreetly swiping the UPC tag.

With information in hand, you don't have to pound the pavement looking for a better deal, and you don't have to stand in a cashier's line. Just pull out your Palm Pilot, punch in the product bar code information, and you'll be told the cheapest place in the area to buy it.

BarPoint.com seamlessly weds the real world with the cyber world.

Rule #2—Selling Anything

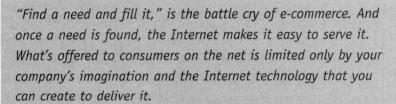

"Find a need and fill it," is the battle cry of e-commerce. And once a need is found, the Internet makes it easy to serve it. What's offered to consumers on the net is limited only by your company's imagination and the Internet technology that you can create to deliver it.

This ability to create something new, something that has no real-world counterpart, is driven by the unique technology of the Internet. You might think that finding a unique selling category is close to impossible. This is not so. New ideas for products and services are invented each day—some that can be provided only using the Net.

But the Internet's unique capability has its critics. Not only has it opened doors to commerce opportunities, but it also has started a battle over who really owns the content of the Internet. Screen scrapers, bots, and content-on-the-edge technologies have raised copyright concerns. But although the copyright holders have won the court battles, they might have lost the war. As more e-businesses remodel themselves toward information companies, the debate over who owns this content will come to center stage. At issue here is the debate between the protection of intellectual property and free speech. And the solution will not be quick in coming. This debate will affect what your e-business can or cannot sell now and in the future.

As the months go by, it seems that companies are selling almost anything to any audience on the Internet. Just about every traditional and conceivable product or service has been explored and offered to online consumers. In addition, an alphabet soup of selling channels has emerged, including business-to-consumer (B2C), business-to-business (B2B), business-to-government (B2G), business-to-employee (B2E), and consumer-to-consumer (C2C) companies, each with a particular approach to selling products, services, or information online.

The ingenuity of today's e-businesses is limited only by its capability to slice and dice the marketplace into an almost infinite variety of *niche markets*. This capability is driven by the unique technology of the Internet that in many cases have no real-world counterpart. But this unique capability of net technology does not escape its critics. While having opportunities to e-commerce, at the same time it has launched a highly charged debate over who really owns the content on the Internet.

As more e-businesses remodel themselves toward information companies, the debate over who owns this content will come to center stage. And this debate will affect what your e-business can or cannot sell—sooner rather than later.

Motivating the Consumer

Every e-business wants to have the "next big thing" or the "next killer app" for the Internet. Whatever that may be, to succeed it must seize and hold the consumer's attention. So how do you seize this attention? By finding out what motivates the consumer.

Human beings are neither rational nor irrational. They're arrational. What they feel is in their best interest is what motivates them. As an e-business, you need to know what your buyers think is in their best interest, what motivates them. Of course, different things motivate different people, even at different times. So, when trying to have the next big thing for the net, keep the following human motivations in mind:

> **Information**—One of the great human motivations is the need for information—and that's where the Internet shines. The Internet is like the Library of Congress multiplied

What Is Niche Marketing?

Selling fitness equipment to health buffs, shock absorbers to auto manufacturers, or stock quotes to investors is a niche market—one in which you meet the needs of a particular buying audience.

The Next Killer App?

EXP.com is one of a new type of e-businesses: expert services. It wants to be the next killer app of the net, with person-to-person Q&A. It specializes in connecting people who have questions to people who can answer them.

What's a Bot?

A bot, short for *robot*, is a software tool for searching the Internet to find and organize data. You give a bot directions, and it brings back answers. There are shopping bots, news bots, stock bots, research bots, search engine bots, and many more that can scour the Net and retrieve data for their user.

millions of times. But it's also a vast information storehouse that is hard to navigate. This navigation problem has proven to be a rich vein of e-commerce opportunity. First exploited by search engines such as Yahoo!, Excite, Alta Vista, and Hotbot, this area has lured others, such as Google (www.google.com) with more sophisticated search technologies.

If you think that the major search engines are the only place to find information, think again. CNET's Search.com (www.search.com) is a perfect example of a comprehensive search service and an infomediary. True to the definition of an infomediary—most of the search engines that they offer really don't belong to them. Search.com links users to specialized engines on Web sites all around the net, searching more than 700 different engines with one search.

Economic—A second very strong motivation is economic in nature. And what motivates a shopper to buy? A quality product, a nice selection, a secure and convenient way to purchase—even a great deal! All these and more would entice a shopper to open his wallet and buy from your online store. But looking at the multitude of different kinds of products and services that you can buy today on the net, you might think that finding a unique selling category is close to impossible—not so. New ideas for products and services are

CASE STUDY

ABOUT.COM

When About.com (formerly the Mining Company) began four years ago, critics said that its business model would never work. Based on volunteer guides being paid a small stipend as independent contractors, About.com's strategy was to create a network of expert professional guides in more than 700 subject categories.

Critics couldn't see how a group of underpaid volunteers would create what was to become one of the hottest properties on the Internet.

The critics were proven wrong. About.com became a roaring success.

About.com's success stems directly from two factors. First, its guides live and work in more than 20 countries. Guides are specially selected to lead based upon a demonstrated expertise in a particular topic, and each must have the desire and ability to help others who share an interest in that topic.

Second, About.com provides its guides with infrastructure support. All the "back office" technology such as chat rooms, discussion invented each day, some that can be provided only by using the net.

For example, career sites are not limited to just consumer-oriented jobs. Personics (www.personic.com) is building a B2B trading hub that links human resource departments, recruiting companies, and electronic job boards. Personics does not seek resumes from individual job-seekers. Rather, it aggregates data from individual job sites as well as from recruiting and staffing companies to create a central marketplace. Companies submit job requisitions and, in turn, receive data on candidates that fit their qualifications.

Entertainment—We all love to be entertained. We'll even pay for it if we feel that the value is there. So, entertainment is another good motivation. Entertainment sites of all stripes have blossomed on the net, including sites for movies, games, music, and TV. Most are content sites, but more are turning into portals where individual consumers can entertain and interact with each other.

Napster (www.napster.com) is a good example. Napster has created a new way to find and exchange music entertainment on the net. Using the company's Web portal, consumers who collect MP3 files can exchanged them with each other. Users download the Napster software and then are able to search the MP3 files of other users and download the ones they like.

Private Label for More Margin

Are your product margins under pressure? Then turn to an old retailing standby: private label manufacturing. Private labeling products that you sell with your own brand can give you higher profit margins and better control of inventory.

boards, newsletter maintenance, member services, and ad-generating revenue are handled by a cadre of top-notch IT professionals, software engineers, marketing mangers, and advertising representatives that support the guides at every turn.

What makes About.com so unique is that each guide site is devoted to a single topic, allowing the guide to focus on his or her expertise. Each of these highly targeted, topic-specific sites provides a comprehensive experience, including the Internet's best link directories and original content and perspective. The topic-specific nature of the sites also brings together a network of active members who can assemble around their interests and share their own personal experiences, opinions, and passions.

About.com not only creates an in-depth content site, but it also sets up an active community of users around each of the 700 subject areas.

Social—Finally, the urge to interact with other people is a strong motivational force. The opportunity to hobnob with those of similar interests can be turned into a profitable business. Large community sites such as Yahoo!/GeoCities (geocities.yahoo.com), Xoom (www.xoom.com), and Delphi (www.delphi.com) have developed successful community-generating sites. Delphi, in particular, has built a successful site with its discussion board building model. Delphi has hundreds of thousands of discussion boards run by individuals on every conceivable subject. The company also provides live chat for each of the boards on its site. Companies such as Yahoo!/GeoCities also have attracted millions of users who have built home pages using their services on the net.

All the online companies mentioned have succeeded in one way or another by identifying a human motivation and seeking to meet it. But this success hides a growing problem and a rising debate over who owns the content of the Internet. The question raised is this: Can a company sell anything using the technology of the net? And just because it could, should it?

New Opportunities Bring New Challenges

We've only just scratched the surface of what can be done on the Internet. New hardware and software applications have opened up some intriguing and controversial uses of the capabilities. *Screen scrapers*, bots, and content-on-the-edge technologies have raised copyright concerns.

None of these uses of net technology is without controversy. Even the simple service of providing free home pages for users has had its share of controversy, one that revolved around three simple words "terms of service."

A few years ago, Yahoo! bought GeoCities, the granddaddy of all community sites. Shortly after the sale, a dispute erupted on the net that led to a boycott of Yahoo! itself. Yahoo! made changes to

What's a Screen Scraper?

Screen scrapers are software applications that enable users to pull information from one Web site and deposit that information onto another Web site or into a database, even if the two sites are not connected.

the GeoCities' terms of service (TOS). Here's the paragraph in the Yahoo!/GeoCities TOS that sparked the controversy:

> By submitting Content to any Yahoo! property, you automatically grant, or warrant that the owner of such Content has expressly granted, Yahoo the royalty-free, perpetual, irrevocable, non-exclusive and fully sub-licensable right and license to use, reproduce, modify, adapt, publish, translate, create derivative works from, distribute, perform and display such Content (in whole or part) worldwide and/or to incorporate it in other works in any form, media, or technology now known or later developed.

In other words, all material—that is, a user's personal Web page—that a user posted on Yahoo!/GeoCities became the intellectual property of Yahoo!/GeoCities, and they had full copyright and permission to do whatever they wanted with it. With that, GeoCities users fired a shot across the bow of Yahoo!, demanding that the company delete such a reference in the TOS, and an Internet-wide boycott was declared until Yahoo! did so. Comments like these were posted all over the net in newsgroups, through email, and on discussion boards.

In a few short weeks, the matter was solved. Yahoo! gave in and revised its Yahoo!/GeoCities TOS. The revision directly incorporated the demands of GeoCities users and received favorable comments from Internet rights experts. Win one for the net consumer.

Another service to the consumer was not so lucky. Napster created a new software application and technology that lets users easily find and download MP3 music files from more than a million libraries on the net. Those libraries existed on individual users' PCs that were connected to the net. Anytime a Napster user came online, the software application would read the MP3 files on the user's computer and upload the filename and location of the files on the user's PC to the central library on Napster's site. This eliminated the need for FTP, broken links, and downloading from slow Web sites or Web searches.

In effect, Napster became the music version of *TV Guide*. It didn't create the music or really supply it. The music came from individual users' PCs, and all Napster did was create a directory on its site of the music files on all the PCs connected to it. Napster's service and software became one of the fastest-rowing services on the net, growing to million of users in a few short months. But with this speedy success came an even speedier controversy.

Because the music files didn't belong to Napster, the company had no control of the files that were being uploaded into its directory. Some of these files were copies of music CDs that were sold in stores and were protected by copyright law. When original artists and music companies found out what was going on at the Napster service, the Recording Industry Association of America (RIAA) (www.riaa.com) brought a suit against Napster to cease and desist. The RIAA sought damages of up to $100,000 per pirated song, although Napster said that its software exchanges no files and that it was not legally responsible for any pirating done.

The suit against Napster is still pending but a similar suit was against Mp3.com by RIAA and Mp3.com lost its suit. Win one for the content suppliers.

Are Your Prices Competitive?

Does your e-business sell products on the Internet? You can keep track of the price at which your competitors are selling the same products by using shopping bots. You can find a list of them at www.botspot.com/search/s-shop.htm.

Another copyright controversy is still brewing. This one revolves around the bots. Although most of the bots that consumers use are fairly noncontroversial, there's a love/hate relationship between the comparison-shopping bots and the merchants that they shop. On the one hand, shopping bots drive traffic to e-commerce sites that they would not normally acquire. Consumers looking for products or price comparisons on different products would visit a comparison-shopping site such as Dealtime (www.dealtime.com) or Bottom Dollar (www.bottomdollar.com).

By using such a service, consumers are introduced to shopping sites that they did not know about before and might actually visit and buy from those online merchants. This is a plus for the online merchant. On the other hand, merchants are not pleased with the fact that they are competing for business with these bots based on price alone. Next-generation shopping bots such as Frictionless Commerce (www.frictionless.com) are trying to remedy this problem by offering a more sophisticated shopping bot. This bot not only will present the price of a product, but it also will include other offer information, such as shipping and handling fees charged for the product, merchant satisfaction guarantees, and return polices—that is, it will provide the full selling position of each merchant.

One company in particular is refusing the access of bots to its site. eBay (www.ebay.com) wants to keep bots from displaying its listings without its permission. Auction aggregators such as BiddersEdge (www.biddersedge.com) let shoppers compare prices for specific items at more than 80 auction sites. What's good for the shopper, however, is not deemed appropriate by eBay. eBay has sued BiddersEdge for displaying listings culled from its site. In response, BiddersEdge has filed a countersuit calling eBay a monopoly, and the Justice Department is investigating the case. eBay also asked comparison-shopping agent mySimon to remove eBay's listings from its search criteria. Unlike BiddersEdge, mySimon complied.

eBay claims that BiddersEdge is free-riding on its content (sounds like *TV Guide*, right?) and that eBay has a fundamental right to control access. Not so, says BiddersEdge, claiming that the net is an open environment and that the listings belong to the sellers, not eBay.

Whatever the outcome of the legal wrangling is, the questions remains: Whose Internet is it, anyway? As companies create e-businesses that act increasingly like infomediaries and less like purveyors of matter, the controversies will get worse before the situation gets better.

Enter the screen scrapers. When you visit Amazon, you're greeted by name and offered books and CDs that the company thinks you'd enjoy based on your past purchases. Portal sites such as Yahoo! let you create a personalized page with filtered headlines, local weather, and a personal stock portfolio. But screen-scraping tools take the concept of personalization one step further, one that has copyright issues written all over it.

The technology behind screen scrapers is quite simple. The net is basically one big database, and it's not hard to pull pieces of information from one URL and display them on another. That's what bots do, to some extent. Companies such as CallTheShots.com (www.calltheshots.com), QuickBrowse.com (www.quickbrowse.com), and Yodlee (www.yodlee.com) make it easy for consumers to combine different content from multiple Web sites on a single page of their making.

Serving an Auction Niche

AuctionWatch (www.auctionwatch.com) has cut out a niche in the online auction space. It specializes in boutique auctions that search more than 300 boutique auction sites for products such as antiques and art, collectibles, and entertainment items.

A Web Account Aggregator

Vertical One (www.verticalone.com) consolidates, organizes, and presents Internet users' personal account information with one master password, providing consumers with a single, easy-to-access interface for personal account information such as bank and brokerage statements, credit card balances, voice mails, emails, household bills, and travel award programs.

What's an ISP?

ISP stands for Internet service provider and provides Internet access to its subscribers. Like a phone company, your ISP connects you to the Internet.

None of these new e-businesses has explored the legal questions that their screen-scraping technology raises. The problem with all these sites—and where copyright issues will be raised—is in the way in which they let consumers grab content at a very basic level and then present it in ways that the creator of the content did not have in mind.

These types of issues and more will almost certainly be raised when companies begin to realize the true potential of selling anything through the technology of the net.

Whose Net Is It, Anyway?

Whether your e-business sells products, services, or information, the infomediary component of your company will—and must— grow if you're to stay competitive in the future. Information is the stock in trade of the new digital economy, whether you produce it, provide it, or package it. But how do you protect those who create the information without controlling the technology that sells it?

Stewart Brand, founder of the Whole Earth Catalog back in the '60s, once said, "Information just wants to be free." If so, making a buck in the information economy will be harder than ever. Some kind of compromise must be made between those who create information in the digital marketplace and those who use it. A host of new court cases is hoping to decide that issue. First brought to court by software companies wanting to protect their intellectual property, non–software-producing companies are using the Digital Millennium Copyright Act (DMCA) of 1998 against several new Internet companies.

One of these was Napster. Another was DeCSS. DeCSS is a software application that cracks the Content Scrambling System (CSS) by reading media files directly from a DVD disc without a decryption key. Supporters of DeCSS said that they were just building a Linux DVD player and had to crack the DVD encryption to make one. Napster now claims that it is just an *Internet service provider (ISP)* and thus is protected under the DMCA and can't be held liable for what its users do as long as they act when they get notice of a copyright infringement. Napster did just that when it banned certain members from its service for pirating copyrighted music.

But despite the fact that copyright holders have won the court battles, they might have lost the war. Millions of consumers have downloaded the DeCSS code-breaking software; in spite of the copyright holder's efforts, Napster has been as popular as ever. It's just a matter of time before applications such as these show up for movies and any other tightly controlled industries. The disintermediation of the Old Economy is moving into full swing.

Even the toy industry is vulnerable. Mattel, one of the biggest and best-known toy manufacturers in the world, got into technology by buying Microsystems Software Inc., makers of the Cyber Patrol censorware program (www.cyberpatrol.com). When hackers in Canada and Sweden published a method for seeing what sites Cyber Patrol blocks, cracking its encryption in the process, Mattel sued under the DCMA and won a restraining order. It also got the hacker code back and then tried to close a host of mirror sites that emerged to support the hackers. The result? Mirror sites that supplied the code increased dramatically, and the Electronic Privacy Information Center and the American Civil Liberties Union (ACLU, the stanch defender of free speech) joined forces to defend the mirror sites.

At issue here is the debate between the protection of intellectual property and free speech. And the solution will not be quick in coming. Do search engines, bots, and screen scrapers have the right to cruise around the net plucking content from the vast database that we call the Internet and then repackage it with no regard for its source? Does the copyright holder of the information have a right to determine how its intellectual property is to be used?

Old Economy businesses see the Internet as another money-making platform and want ownership over what content it produces. Consumers, including new infomediaries such as Napster and BiddersEdge, see the net as a giant information bazaar where ownership claims of content should be kept to a minimum. The problem is that digital information is seen most often as copied information. But digital information is the stock in trade of the

Manipulation of Content Without Detection

You might not always be able to see how consumers perceive the content on your Web site. Companies such as Third Voice (www.thirdvoice.com) let anyone who downloads its browser plug in to "post" comments on any Web site. These comments can be viewed by anyone with the company's browser plug-in. The only way that your company can see these comments is to use the Third Voice plug-in.

New Economy. By its nature, you can't access or use digital information without making copies.

So what does this all mean to your e-business? If you decide to position your company in the new digital marketplace as an infomediary, or if you plan to create an infomediary component of your e-business, then business on the net will not mean business as usual. Do you see your company positioned as a content guardian or content harvester? Prepare to be both.

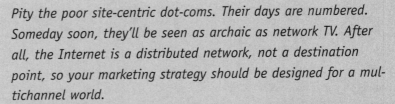

Pity the poor site-centric dot-coms. Their days are numbered. Someday soon, they'll be seen as archaic as network TV. After all, the Internet is a distributed network, not a destination point, so your marketing strategy should be designed for a multichannel world.

A multichannel marketing strategy is needed if your company is to survive and prosper in the new digital economy. Selling anywhere is not enough. Your e-business will need to market to your buyers not only wherever they are, but whenever they spend their time on the Net. As the focus of the Internet changes from a site-centric model to a distributed selling model, the marketing battles are moving from your company's Web site to your customer's PC desktop, TVs, cell phones, personal digital assistants (PDAs), Net appliances—wired or wireless—and even to other Web sites.

Your e-business must be ready to sell whenever your buyer is ready to buy and should have a marketing plan to do it. Your marketing strategy should include the creation of new distribution channels by affiliating with other content, community, and commerce companies on the Net. Affiliate marketing is a great way to market to potential buyers wherever they spend their time, whether that time is spent on their favorite Web sites or reading their email.

One of the unique aspects of the Internet is that it allows companies to conduct business 24 hours a day, 7 days a week, every day of the year. It's the convenience of buying on the Net that comes up time and again as the top reason for shopping on the Internet. Up until now, just about all of this business has been conducted from a company's own Web site. This *site-centric* business model—selling only from one's Web site—leads to a site-centric marketing strategy. Build it. Promote it. Drive buyers to it, and then sell to them.

But there are problems with this type of approach.

First, if you're starting a new e-business or want to add a different market niche to your e-business, few usable dot-coms are left for the picking. An April 1999 survey of 25,500 standard English-language dictionary words found that 93% of them had been registered as dot-coms. You could register words that are not necessarily English words, but you run the risk of coming up with a word for your company that means "idiot" in Japanese. Just remember the mistake Chevrolet made when it marketed the Chevy Nova in Mexico. *No va* in Spanish means no go.

Second, your visibility on the Net is limited by having a single Web site. The marketing costs of driving qualified buyers to a Web site are a huge cash drain on dot-coms, bringing many of them to the brink of bankruptcy (see Table 8.1).

Table 8.1

Cost of Customer Acquisition	
Business Type	**Cost of Acquisition**
Internet-only retailers	$82
All online retailers	$32
Brick-and-mortar stores	$31
Printed catalogs	$11

Source: April 2000 Boston Consulting Group/shop.org

Third, believing that the mass of consumers who will soon use the Net for commerce will access it only when in front of their Macs or PCs is a marketing calamity waiting to happen. Your customers expect 24/7 availability, and not only at their computers. They'll want to shop your company anytime, at their convenience and on any Net-enabled device—wired or wireless—that they have at the time.

Yes, this is a challenge. But it does have its benefits. One of the benefits of positioning your company to sell anytime through many channels is that the acquisition cost per customer drops. According to the Boston Consulting Group, in 1998, the cost for each customer acquired through purely online businesses was $42 per customer. In 1999, that number rose to $82. But companies that sold through a variety of channels saw their customer acquisition costs drop from $22 per customer in 1998 to $12 in 1999.

As you can see, it's important to build a marketing strategy that includes the opportunity for consumers or businesses to buy from you whenever and wherever they have the time. Your e-business must be ready to take an order anytime—on the buyer's schedule—whenever the buyer is on the Net. The days of bookmarking commerce sites and shopping them one by one are on their way out.

Dot-Coms—Who Needs Them!

Got a dot-com? Too bad. Someday soon, it'll be bronzed and seen as a classic.

More than 10 million dot-coms are registered today, and thousands of new ones are being added everyday. This poses an immense problem for buyers searching for products and services to buy—it's like finding a needle in a cyber-haystack. Second, even with the help of more sophisticated search engines and shopping bots, finding a site is getting more difficult.

Let's face it, browsing shopping sites on the Net is inefficient and time-consuming Worst of all, it requires one of the most user-unfriendly devices created by man: the personal computer. And if you believe that the great unwashed masses that are arriving soon on the Net will use an intimidating technology such as the personal computer, you are wrong.

With today's technology, it's not necessary for potential customers to either use a PC or visit a merchant's commerce site. So, new

What Is Site-Centric?

A site-centric business model consists of selling primarily from one's own Web site accessible only from a computer.

Finding Sites Is Getting Harder to Do

A recent study showed that even the best search engines search only 40% of the Net, while the comparison-shopping bots search only a relatively small handful of shopping sites.

ways must be found to market your product or service. Remember that the Internet is a distributed medium, and more companies are understanding this and including it in their marketing plans. So should you.

The battle for your buyer's attention will not only take place on your company's commerce site, but throughout the network. Your company must market to wherever the consumers spend their time. That will include the TV shows that they watch and the content and community sites that they visit when working at their computers, using their cell phones, PDAs, or other Net-enabled appliances.

Site-Centric Versus Distributed Selling

Imagine that you're sitting in front of your TV, with remote control in hand. You're watching the Super Bowl, and a small ad appears in the lower part of your TV screen for Pizza Hut. It offers you a Super Bowl Special of two pizzas for the price of one if you order within the next 10 minutes. You click on the Order Me button, and a small pop-up window appears asking for your phone number. You type it in, and the pizzas are charged to your phone bill.

Picture another scenario. You're in your favorite food store. You walk down the personal care aisle and head for a tube of Crest toothpaste. You take out you PDA and scan in the code number on the toothpaste box. You are immediately connected to the Crest virtual private network. You begin to negotiate with Crest for the price of the toothpaste, promising to commit to buying a certain number of tubes over the next few months at a certain agreed-upon price.

In either case, did you visit a Web site? The answer is no.

Sure, these scenarios won't happen right away. But the future has a nasty way of becoming the present on the Internet. And if you're one of those cyber-squatters holding those cool domain names, take my advice: Sell now, while you can. Those names won't be worth a penny in the near future. The Net is a distributed network, not a destination point. Visiting Web sites will become passé.

e-Commerce to Go

The mySimon To-Go service (www.mysimon.com/ consumer_resources/ mySimon_To_Go/index.anml) allows consumers to comparison-shop the Net while cruising their favorite brick-and-mortar stores. They can find out whether that hyped bargain at Best Buy is as good as it seems by running a quick comparison on their mySimon To-Go-enabled Palm Pilot.

Speedier Purchases on the Net

PlanetRx.com (www.planetrx.com) has made ordering off the Net a lot easier. Using ScanCart, their new handheld scanning device, you can load your PlanetRx shopping cart with all your favorite products from home. Just point it at an empty shampoo bottle or toothpaste tube, and it reads the bar code. Then upload the data into the PlanetRx shopping cart on the Web site.

Here is proof. See those icons on your start bar or on your computer screen's desktop? When you click on a certain type of icon, a small window could pop up through which you can conduct an activity. If you've downloaded an *applet* from Real Audio (www.realaudio.com) for example, the Real Player icon would appear on your start bar or desktop. In Real Audio's case, you could listen to streaming audio from radio stations and other broadcast sites on the Net—no need to open a Web browser, no need to type in a URL, no need to visit a Web site.

The result? Your computer's desktop is becoming one of the next marketing battlegrounds. And it gets better.

Not only is the computer desktop going to be an area contention, but now the common keyboard will as well. Hot keys on keyboards have been around for while. When an Internet hot key is pressed, the user is sent to a specific Web site on the Net. Compaq Computers (www.compaq.com) was one of the first companies to place hot keys to the Internet on their computer keyboards. Compaq did it with a one-key Internet search using Alta Vista (www.altavista.com) as its default search site. Hewlett-Packard (www.hp.com) soon followed.

But a new company called RocketBoard (www.rocketboard.com) has gone a step further. It's giving its keyboard away for free. Each keyboard has 18 keys that link to more than 300 online merchants. Its market is the mass of new consumers who are arriving on the Net daily and who don't have a clue on how to use the Internet. So how does RocketBoard make money if it gives its product away for

CASE STUDY

ICHOOSE

iChoose (www.ichoose.com) was founded in April 1999. The company's goal was to create an online savings alert that would bring consumers and e-tailers together in ways not possible in the physical world.

iChoose created the iChoose Alert, a small, downloadable applet or software program that's installed on a consumer's computer. After a consumer downloads the iChoose software applet and installs it, a small icon appears on the taskbar of that user's computer. The consumer then shops e-commerce sites for products such as books, toys, music, videos, hardware and software, consumer electronics, and pet supplies as he or she normally would. When a consumer finds a product to buy, that user places it in the merchant's shopping cart.

That's when iChoose Alert goes to work.

When the iChoose Alert icon spins on the taskbar, this signals the consumer that it's free? The company gets a piece of each sale made by the keyboard owner when that user buys from the sponsoring online merchants.

Your e-business marketing plan should include not only the marketing of your URL around the Net, but also the distribution of a desktop applet on as many computer desktops as you can. Whether you sell to consumers or businesses, distributing a desktop applet to your potential buyers is an important marketing tool. In addition, your e-business should be alert to new innovative marketing companies such as RocketBoard that can present your company to new users on the Net. Ideas like these are an important component of a multichannel marketing strategy that can market to your buyers wherever they spend their time.

Affiliate Marketing

How would you like other Web sites to market and sell your company's products and services? And how would you like to pay the Web site only when its users buy your product or service or perform a task? Sound like a marketer's dream? Well you can take advantage of it if you use another form of distributed selling called affiliate marketing.

Affiliate marketing has been around for quite a while, but it has been getting quite a bit of attention over the last couple years. Back in 1996, Amazon.com launched the first popular affiliate program (also known as Associate Programs) on the Internet. Jeff Bezos, the CEO and founder of Amazon.com, was attending a cocktail party when a woman he was chatting with expressed

An Applet

A program designed to be executed from within another application. Unlike an application, applets cannot be executed directly from the operating system. A well-designed applet can be launched from many different applications.

looking for a better deal on the product in the shopping cart. If the icon flashes, iChoose found a better deal, and it presents it to the consumer. The consumer is then provided a choice: either decline the offer and continue the transaction, or accept the offer. When a customer accepts the offer, iChoose automatically transfers the contents of the shopping cart to the new merchant's order page. And the iChoose Alert does all this with one effortless click of a mouse.

Consumers can configure the iChoose Alert so that offers are displayed only when saving thresholds are met. These savings can be price differences that are realized from lower delivery costs, or through instant coupons or from special offers available only from iChoose partner merchants.

The iChoose Alert applet allows consumers to do "horizontal surfing," becoming aware of better offers from other Web sites without actually visiting them or the iChoose Web site.

Two-Tiered Affiliate Marketing

Affiliate marketing can be even more effective when the two-tiered model is applied to a program. This model allows affiliates to sign up other affiliates below themselves. When the second tier affiliates earn a commission, the affiliate above it also receives a piece of that commission.

Build Versus Buy?

You can use one of the existing affiliate solution providers such as BeFree or Linkshare to track your affiliate program—or build your own. If you decide to build your own, check out either the Affiliate Program (www.theaffiliateprogram.com) or Pro-Track (www.affiliatesoftware.Net/main2.html) for affiliate program management software.

interest in selling books about divorce on her Web site. Bezos thought about it for a while and then came up with the idea of having Web sites sell Amazon's books for commission. This gave the Web site a way to make a little money at the same time providing both additional visibility and revenue for Amazon.

It seemed like a win-win situation, so Amazon introduced the Amazon Associates Program. It was an immediate success and now claims to have more than 300,000 Web sites linking to Amazon's Web site and selling its books. The idea was simple: A Web site would place a small banner on its site telling its visitors that they can buy books on a particular subject right from the site. The visitor clicked on the Amazon banner and was whisked off to Amazon's Web site where the site user bought the book that gave the Web site a small commission on the sale.

Since then, affiliate marketing has caught on like wildfire. It's estimated that more than one million Web sites participate in some kind of affiliate program with dot-com companies. This novel marketing idea proved to be an economical and effective way to reach potential online customers. In April 1999, a Forrester Research survey ranked affiliate programs number one in effectiveness, ahead of email, public relations, television, and all other marketing methods. It also stated that affiliate programs accounted for 13 percent of 1999 online retail sales. Jupiter Communications reports that affiliate programs account for 11% of the $5.8 billion of consumer transactions online and projects that figure to grow to 24%, or $37.5 billion in total sales, by 2002.

At first sight, affiliate marketing seems like an easy and inexpensive way to market your e-business. But don't let the simplicity of the concept fool you. Launching and running an affiliate program is far from easy. First of all, the percentage of affiliates that sign up for your program and then become active is quite low. Forrester Research says that the average affiliate program has about 10,000 affiliates. But only 10–20% of the affiliate sites actually participate in the program—that is, place your affiliate icon or banner on their sites. And of those 10–20% of active affiliates, only 20% of those are superaffiliates, those that produce the majority of the revenue for your program.

To run a successful affiliate program, your company must continually recruit new affiliates and reach out to existing ones to motivate them to become active in the program. Running a successful affiliate program is not easy, but when done right, affiliate marketing is a great way to market to potential buyers wherever they spend their time. Whether that time is spent on favorite Web sites or reading email, there is an affiliate marketing strategy for both.

Site Affiliate Marketing

Since its introduction in 1996 by Amazon.com, affiliate marketing has grown and flourished, spawning a variety of new and innovative models. It works well as a marketing tool for individuals and for both small and large e-businesses.

Affiliate programs come in four types, and your company can offer any or all of them to potential affiliate partners. Combined, they represent the different ways that Web sites can generate revenue from the program and merchants can acquire prospects and customers. They include banner links, storefronts, pop-ups, and email.

Banner Links

Web sites that join your banner links of programs agree to place a small banner or icon on their Web pages. The banner has the name of your company promoting what the merchant is selling. eToys is a good example. A Web site might place a banner for eToys on its Web pages, promoting the fact that great toys can be bought from eToys. Some promotional copy on the banner would get the Web site visitor to click on it—perhaps, a 10% discount if you buy now. When the user clicks on the banner, it brings up eToys site, where that user might buy a toy. If the shopper buys a toy, the affiliate site gets a commission.

However, banners are not limited to products. Some financial institutions promote their different credit cards using affiliate marketing. NextCard (`www.nextcard.com`) is a good example. Affiliate Web sites place a banner persuading visitors to apply for a NextCard Visa card at a very low percentage rate. When the user clicks on the banner, the NextCard site comes up, where the user can fill out an application. If the user is approved for a Visa card, the affiliate site gets a commission.

Use Affiliate Program Directories to Recruit New Affiliates

To gain exposure for your affiliate program, you should be sure to submit your program to the affiliate program directories, such as Associate-It (www.associate-it.com), AssociatePrograms.com (www.associateprograms.com), and Refer-it (www.refer-it.com).

Other revenue model using banners don't depend upon commissions. Instead, you can offer Web sites a "click-through" affiliate program. In this method, Web sites earn revenue every time one of their visitors clicks through to your Web site or performs a task, such as filling out a survey form or enters a contest. No sales are made, but your company can build up an email list of prospects that you can market to later. Examples of pay-per-lead networks include WebSponsors (www.websponsors.com) and DirectLeads (www.directleads.com).

Storefronts

Although the banner links programs have been successful for online merchants over the years, they haven't been that great for affiliate Web site partners. The banner links approach has its drawbacks for affiliates. Primarily, when a Web site's visitor clicks on an affiliate program banner, the visitor leaves the affiliate site to complete the transaction. The affiliate Web site loses the traffic that it has worked hard to acquire with the small chance that the visitor would actually complete a transaction at your online store.

This is why pay-per-click programs are more liked by affiliate Web sites. If the Web site loses its traffic, at least it has the guarantee of being paid for it.

But a new affiliate marketing model has entered the picture and has revitalized the sales commission model. With the storefront model, visitors don't leave your affiliate partner's Web site. In the

CASE STUDY

VSTORE

Vstore (www.vstore.com) is one of the new breed of affiliate programs that not only enable any Web site to open a store of its own, but also keep the traffic generated to that site.

One of the main complaints with affiliate programs is that visitors are sent away from an affiliate site to the merchant's site when the visitor is ready to buy. That doesn't happen with Vstore. Vstore creates a complete online store with the look and feel of the affiliate's partner site that make shoppers think they are buying from the affiliate's own store while staying within the navigation of the site. Vstore serves the affiliate store from its servers, branding the affiliate store with the company's own logo, color scheme, and site navigation. Visitors stay and buy while remaining within the affiliate's site.

Another complaint was the limited amount of product offerings that any one merchant could offer in the affiliate program. If an

storefront model, you actually create a complete online store that looks like it resides on your affiliate partner's site. Nexchange (www.nexchange.com) and Vstore (www.Vstore.com) are good examples of this affiliate marketing approach. At both Vstore and Nexchange, an affiliate partner can open a store that is embedded in the its site that can sell products in a variety of categories.

Vstore offers its affiliate partners a way to seamlessly integrate a complete online store on their sites. They can build a store right from Vstore's Web site in a variety of product categories.

Pop-Ups

Affiliate models that use storefronts keep the affiliate partner's traffic on its Web site; its visitors never leave the site. With pop-ups, visitors never leave the affiliate's *page*. An example of this type of technology is ePod (www.epod.com) and IQ (www.iq.com). Both of these companies use a Java or Java-based technology that offers products and services to Web site visitors through a small pop-up widow. When visitors come to a Web site, they may see a small banner or icon advertising a product or service of an online merchant.

At first glance, the banner looks like a traditional affiliate banner link. But instead of being whisked off to another Web site—or even another page on the existing Web site—when clicked on by the visitor, a small pop-up window appears with the offer inside. The original page still appears in the background, so when the visitor is finished reading the offer—or even completing a transaction—that

Check Out the Experts

Declan Dunn, the renowned affiliate guru, sells a great training system for affiliates called "Winning the Affiliate Game." Another book/program that can really assist your affiliates is *Make Your Site Sell*, by Ken Evoy. *Nothing But 'Net*, by Michael Campbell, is also a very useful title that will help your affiliates optimize their sites and convert shoppers into buyers.

affiliate wanted to sell more than just books, or toys, or CDs, he had to join three, four, or more merchant affiliate programs. Vstore gives the affiliate the capability to open one store offering products in multiple categories. Vstore offers more than one million products to sell, including full customer support, order fulfillment, high-speed hosting, and transaction processing.

And with Vstore, any content or community Web site can join its affiliate program and

build a complete online store to its liking in just 10 minutes. Vstore supplies the entire front-end and back-end infrastructure. Vstore eliminates the traditional barriers to e-commerce faced by individuals, online communities, and Web sites. Affiliate partner sites just offer the products to their visitors, and Vstore does the rest.

visitor is still on the same Web page when the pop-up window closes. However, pop-ups do have their disadvantages. Because the pop-up window is small, a limited amount of space is available to present your offer and complete a transaction or a task or to collect information.

Email

Web sites aren't the only places to conduct an affiliate marketing program. Over the last year or so, a new ripple to affiliate marketing has appeared: email affiliate programs. Barnes&Noble (www.bn.com) offered the first email affiliate program through an affiliate solutions company called BeFree (www.befree.com).

With Barnes&Noble as its first client, BeFree launched B-Intouch, an email marketing service designed to expand affiliate e-commerce capabilities to anyone with an email address. B-Intouch gives merchants an opportunity to commerce-enable Internet users who don't have their own Web sites. This means that anyone with an email address can participate in an affiliate program. With a service like B-Intouch, you can make anyone with an email address an e-marketer for your e-business.

You do so by enabling them to earn money by selling products or services through a text link placed in the *signature option* of their email messages. When a person signs up to become a Barnes&Noble affiliate, this person places a small snippet of code in the signature of his or her email. This small piece of code calls a program from BeFree that automatically inserts a promotion for Barnes&Noble at the bottom of an email message.

Here's how the B-Intouch program could work for you. A person visits your company's Web site, which is part of the B-Intouch network. On your site, the person clicks on a link and registers to become an electronic marketer for your e-business. Each time this person sends an email, your message is then embedded into the bottom of the email, providing a link to your Web site. If the recipient of the email clicks through to your Web site and buys a product or service, the sender of the email gets a commission.

It's quick, simple, and easy. Your company gets the sale, and the email sender gets a commission.

What Is an Email Signature?

The signature option allows for a brief message to be embedded at the end of every email that a person sends.

But why stop at text links in the signature field? With the growth of HTML-enabled email, complete images can be tagged at the end of mail messages, imploring the recipient to click on the image offer for discounts or special deals on a product or service. It can also be used to direct the recipient to surveys and free offers, where their email address can be captured and then marketed to at some later date.

Affiliate marketing is one way to be there whenever a potential buyer is in the mood to shop. When you have settled on the type of affiliate model, your company will have to decide on a compensation plan for your affiliates.

Compensation Models

Your affiliate program can pay out commissions on the basis of clicks, leads, or sales. Which payment plan is appropriate for you depends upon the marketing strategies of your e-business. Are you looking to make an immediate sale from a click-through to your site? Or perhaps you're interested in building database of prospects that you hope to convert to customers later. When you've determined the objective of your affiliate marketing plan, then you can design a compensation plan for your affiliates.

Basically, there are three types of plans:

- **Pay per sale**—The affiliate is paid either a flat fee or a percentage of each sale referred from the affiliate site to the merchant.

- **Pay per lead**—The affiliate is paid a commission for each lead (membership registration or click to the merchant Web site) referred from the affiliate site.

- **Pay per click**—The affiliate is paid on a cost-per-click (CPC) basis for each time somebody clicks on a link to your site.

Another aspect of compensation to keep in mind is the payment threshold—that is, how much your affiliates will have to earn before you issue a check. You might consider holding back payment until an affiliate earns at least $25, $50, or $100. Then there's payment frequency to consider. Do you pay your affiliates weekly,

Be Clear About Your Compensation Plan

Affiliates need to know in clear and concise language what your compensation plan is. When do they get paid? Weekly? Monthly? Quarterly? How long do they have to be in your program before they get their first check? Do they need to reach a minimum commission before a check is sent to them? Affiliates need to know your payment rules.

Nothing Succeeds Like Success

One the first things to do when creating a successful affiliate program is to find out what works for others. Affiliateselling. com (www.affiliateselling. com) has a list of the top 50 affiliate programs on the Net.

monthly, every other month, or once a quarter? These decisions must be designed into your affiliate marketing program.

Don't Make These Affiliate Marketing Mistakes

On the surface, affiliate marketing looks simple. A Web site joins your program, a visitor to the affiliate's site clicks on your offer, you make a sale, and the Web site makes a commission. Under the surface, however, it's not so simple. There's a lot involved in creating and running an affiliate marketing program—and if not done right, it could undermine all the objectives of your plan.

So don't make these affiliate marketing mistakes:

- **Mistake #1: No contract**—You must have an affiliate partner contract drawn up and ready to read on your Web site. No affiliate worth his salt will sign up for your program without knowing the rules, limitations, and compensation structure. And by the way, don't write your contract in legalese. Use everyday language, and make it easy to understand. Also spell out in detail the terms of your agreement: when they get paid, how they get paid, and how they can be dropped from your program.

- **Mistake #2: No FAQs**—Well-written contracts are good, but for a quick read on your program, your company should provide a set of frequently asked questions (FAQs) on your site. List everything that your affiliate partner needs to know in an easy-to-understand question-and-answer format. As your program grows, you'll receive questions from your affiliates. So, whenever you answer a new question, add that to the FAQ.

- **Mistake #3: No affiliate manager or affiliate support**—Don't think that once a program is launched and Web sites are signed up, there's no further need of your program commitment. It's not so. Affiliate marketing programs are *not* self-administered. It's necessary to have a full-time affiliate manager—and even a staff—dedicated to the day-to-day operations of your company's affiliate marketing program. This person should be easily reached by your affiliate partners to answer their questions and solve their program problems. Without this kind of support, your program is doomed from the start.

Affiliate Solution Providers

Affiliate solution providers provide a combination of the network, software, and services needed to create and track an affiliate program. Here are three of the biggest on the Net: Be Free (www.befree.com), Commission Junction (www.cj.com), and LinkShare (www.linkshare.com).

- **Mistake #4: No privacy statement**—State categorically that you will not share your database of affiliates with any other company for any reason. Affiliates don't want their names and email addresses showing up on *spam* lists. Let your affiliates know that their privacy is secure.

- **Mistake #5: No marketing help for your affiliates**—Thinking that a sale will just happen on an affiliate partners site is a big mistake. Affiliate partners must be trained and educated on how to sell your product or service and the objectives of your program. They need to know the best ways to promote your program and how they can increase their potential revenue. You should also change your banners, links, and offers regularly—offering fresh content to your affiliate's sites.

- **Mistake #6: No reports**—It's critical that you provide your affiliates online, statistical reporting. They need to know impressions per day, click-throughs, and sales and performance figures on a 24/7 basis. They will expect this feature, so either design a reporting mechanism yourself or use one of the third-party affiliate solution providers such as BeFree, Linkshare, or Commission Junction.

Be alert to these common affiliate program mistakes, and you'll be well on your way to creating a successful affiliate marketing program.

Spam

Posting an unsolicited commercial message to a newsgroup or sending unsolicited email.

Post a Privacy Policy on Your Site

Make sure that you have a posted privacy policy on your Web site. You can create a privacy policy by using the TRUSTe wizard at www.etrust.com/wizard.

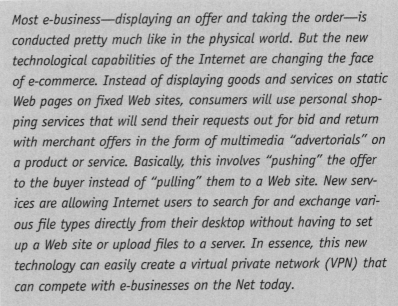

Most e-business—displaying an offer and taking the order—is conducted pretty much like in the physical world. But the new technological capabilities of the Internet are changing the face of e-commerce. Instead of displaying goods and services on static Web pages on fixed Web sites, consumers will use personal shopping services that will send their requests out for bid and return with merchant offers in the form of multimedia "advertorials" on a product or service. Basically, this involves "pushing" the offer to the buyer instead of "pulling" them to a Web site. New services are allowing Internet users to search for and exchange various file types directly from their desktop without having to set up a Web site or upload files to a server. In essence, this new technology can easily create a virtual private network (VPN) that can compete with e-businesses on the Net today.

Finally, digital cash—or e-cash—will eventually become the dominant way of paying for products and services on the Internet. Net consumers not only have the option of what and where to buy, but also how. Although the credit card or bank account is where payment will come from, how the payment is made on the Net will take a variety of forms. New e-cash services are both a boon and a bane to your e-business—a boon because you can easily set up consumer-to-consumer transactions at your e-business, but also a bane because these methods introduce a new level of competition.

When you think about selling on the Net today, buying from a Web site that imitates the experience of a real-world store is the first that comes to mind. Doing business on the Net was a fairly simple procedure: Set up an electronic storefront with a series of Web pages displaying your product or service offering, and then tie them together with a simple-to-use navigation structure. Finally, provide a shopping cart of some type for the shopper to use, and offer to take a credit card or mail-in check for payment.

Most businesses on the Web today are mirror images of their real-world counterparts. Very few are using the capabilities of the selling technology of the Net and are merely applying old rules to the New Digital Economy.

The selling rules are changing, and they're changing fast. New ways of accepting digital payment for products, services, and information have appeared. Buyers will be using new methods to find and view your company's offers. Web pages will give way to new forms of media that will present your company's offers in unique and dynamic ways. And selling on the Net will decentralize in ways not even dreamed of just a short while ago.

Your emerging marketing plans must incorporate selling into multiple channels and in multiple ways.

The Bots Are Coming!

The fastest-growing area of personal software agents is the e-commerce bot. These bots consist of both shopping bots and selling bots. Now, bots in general have been around the Internet for more than four years—that's practically prehistoric in Internet time—and have been getting more sophisticated as the years go by. But they are undergoing some fundamental changes in their application for e-businesses, changes that your marketing strategy must take into account.

In the not-so-distant future, shoppers and merchants will never need to see each other because e-commerce bots will soon make "face-to-face" transactions unnecessary.

A Bot for All Seasons

A Jupiter Communications conference on shopping bots in May 2000 reported that in the future, shopping bots will deliver all the objective information that the consumer needs for a purchasing decision— price, shipping time, service quality, merchant ratings, and so on—and that customers will fill out their credit card and delivery information in the bot itself. They may never have to visit the site from which the product is purchased.

What Is Rich Media?

Rich media is an Internet advertising term for a Web page ad that uses advanced technology such as streaming video, downloaded applets (programs) that interact instantly with the user, and ads that change when the user's mouse passes over them.

So much for all that work and expense put into a Web site, huh? The future of marketing on the Net will shift from a site-centric, page-centric mentality to *rich media* presentation. I'll talk about that later in this chapter in the section entitled "Rich Media— Streaming Ahead." First, let's take a closer look at the e-commerce bots: shopping bots and selling bots.

Selling with Bots

Like any evolving organism, shopping bots have grown in sophistication from generation to generation. First-generation bots were crude in comparison to today's bots. Bots such as Junglee and Jango—both of which have been purchased by other companies and have disappeared into the bowels of their offerings—were more or less databases of merchant Web pages that they searched for the best price. These first-generation shopping bots needed the cooperation of the merchants that they shopped to work. The participating merchants either placed some code on their product pages or allowed the shopping bot to import data into its database. This, of course, limited the number of merchants that a shopping bot could shop.

Second-generation shopping bots, such as mySimon, could build a database of merchants to shop without the merchants' involvement. mySimon engineers write a small script for each merchant site and use it to search the entire product offering without the merchant knowing. In cases like mySimon, the consumer must visit mySimon's site to do comparison shopping.

Not so for third-generation shopping bots. Bots such as Dealtime (www.dealtime.com) can be accessed directly from the consumer's desktop, which lets them start price comparisons instantly while they are browsing any leading online store without leaving the merchant's Web site. Dealtime calls this technique "horizontal surfing"—it allows consumers to seamlessly leap from one Web page to another with related content.

Fourth-generation bots such as SmartShop (www.smartshop.com) and Frictionless Commerce (www.frictionless.com) look for total value, including promotions and shipping costs. These bots work on the assumption that shoppers are not necessarily shopping on price alone. And that's correct. What's good value to one shopper is not so to another. Many considerations enter the buying decision of a shopper. Price, delivery time, shipping and handling costs, guarantees, rebates, and other factors all determine in a shopper's mind what's the best value.

This need for the best value for each individual points finally to the ultimate shopping bot—and the bot that your e-business will have to contend with in the near future. The best way to work with these new bots is to first cooperate with them—they're going to find your site and comparison shop it eventually. Then you'll need to give to the agent and the shopper a presentation of your offer that provides the shopper with the full selling position of your company and the product. Another use of the shopping bots is to keep tabs on what your competition is offering.

Picture this: It's early Monday morning. Before Stephanie leaves for work, she programs her personal shopping bot to look for an anniversary gift for her parents by filling out a form similar to Table 9.1.

Shopping Bots May Lead to Higher Prices

As more e-businesses use shopping bots to monitor the prices of their competitors, this may lead to higher prices instead of lower ones. With bots, online merchants can quickly and easily track what price their competitors are selling at. Competition does not necessarily lead to lower prices. Take the airline industry, for example. After it was deregulated, this kind of instant price monitoring and fast follow-up led to ever-increasing fares for business customers.

Table 9.1

Agent's Shopping Task	
Product Description	Anniversary gift for my parents
Consumer Description	Married couple: male 55, female, age 53, good health, love to travel and dine out, contemporary homeowner
Price Range	U.S. $90-175
Options	60-second rich media presentation
Consider	Crystal, pewter, art, collectibles
Consider Not	Furniture, clothes
Terms & Conditions	Money back guarantee, toll-free phone number, return policy, delivery time, shipping and handling information, and online security information

Rich Media Email

Now you can send your product or service rich media offers via email. RadicalMail (www.radicalmail.com) delivers streaming content directly into emails without requiring a plug-in. There are no executable files and no lengthy downloads, and the email recipient requires no software.

She hits Send, and her agent takes off for the Net while Stephanie takes off for work.

On the Net, her personal shopping bot is diligently filling Stephanie's request. In its travels, her bot meets a selling bot from ContemporaryGifts.com. The selling bot informs Stephanie's bot that it can fulfill her request for an anniversary gift for her parents—a hand-blown crystal vase from Venice—and downloads a short video of the product offer into her interactive TV. When Stephanie returns home, she views the video offer and decides to buy it. She informs her shopping bot to negotiate a price and goes to the kitchen to make dinner.

The shopping bot and the selling bot negotiate the price, terms, and conditions, and finalize the purchase using Stephanie's shipping information and credit card number. Deal done—and without the shopper or merchant in direct contact with each other and without the need of the merchant's Web site.

Are selling bots just creatures of the future? Will it be years before your e-business marketing strategy has to cope with them? Sorry, they're already here. Selling bots are still primitive, but the use of these types of bots must become an important part of the way to sell to your potential buyers in the future.

Here are two examples of selling bots that you should incorporate into your marketing plans today. Shoppers that visit myGeek (www.mygeek.com) fill out a request for a product or service, and myGeek broadcasts their request anonymously to its pool of online merchants. When the merchant responds to myGeek, it sends the shopper an email with the merchant's offer. Respond.com (www.respond.com) is another type of selling bot similar to myGeek. Shoppers submit a request for a product in their own words. Respond.com forwards the request to the appropriate merchant, and the shopper receives a personalized response from the merchant via email.

The easiest way to get incorporated into these selling bots is to join them. You can become a myGeek merchant (www.mygeek.com/seller_overview.jsp) and a Respond.com merchant (www.respond.com/apps/seller).

These selling bots may be primitive compared to the shopping bots, but they do give you a preview of a way of selling that will dominate e-commerce in the future. It would be wise to join these new upstarts and start using their services to learn the ways of selling to buyers without the use of a Web site. Right Now Net communication is email over the wired Internet. Tomorrow it will be a multimedia presentation or automated phone call through a wireless device.

Presentations, *Not* Web Pages

Your e-business needs to start planning to offer your product and services through more than a static Web page. Pushing the offer to the buyers instead of pulling them to a Web site will become the dominant way of selling on the Net.

On-Demand Video Presentations

See It Work at www.seeitwork.com/ offers on-demand video presentations profiling more than 10,000 top selling SKUs. e-Businesses can syndicate the product presentations to be used on their own Web sites.

shopper a response. Best of all, Respond.com is absolutely anonymous and totally free.

Merchants benefit by receiving highly targeted leads from shoppers who are ready to buy. Every day, thousands of customers visit Respond.com looking for products and services. Respond.com has partnered with America Online and American Express. These relationships have extended Respond.com's reach to more than 40 million potential

shoppers, probably the largest reach of any online shopping service.

The kicker is that using Respond.com, a selling agent, you don't need to have a Web site because the service is done entirely through email. In addition, Respond.com is more effective than traditional advertising because it exposes targeted, ready-to-buy customers to a merchant's offer. Services such as Respond.com should be part of the marketing strategy of every e-business.

Push Technology

In the normal course of events, a consumer goes to a Web site to look for goods and services to buy. The consumer asks for the content of the site to be displayed in his Web browser on his computer. In a word, the consumer *pulls* the content to him on demand. With *push technology*, the content or offer is *pushed* to the consumer's PC without asking for it at regular intervals. Stock tickers are good examples of push technology.

What Is a T1 and a DSL?

A *T1* is a high-speed digital network connection at speeds up to 1.544Mbps. *DSL* is the phone company's answer to cable modems. Unlike a cable modem, where many subscribers are on the same line, a DSL circuit connects two specific locations and is much faster than a regular phone connection.

Push marketing is not new. It, too, has been on the Net for several years. Pointcast, now called EntryPoint (www.entrypoint.com), was one of the first players on the Net to introduce a push technology. Pointcast pushed content to Net users in the form of news, weather, sports scores, and stock quotes. It became so popular, in fact, that it became a bane to network administrators. All this pushing of data ate up a large amount of bandwidth at companies, and many made their employees remove it from their desktops.

But push technology combined with rich media will grow because this is how product offers will be presented to consumers in the future. It's only a matter of time—perhaps as short as a few years—before the bandwidth will open up for just about everyone using the Net. Most businesses have a fast connection—either at least a *T1* or a wireless dish—and cable and *DSL* are making inroads to our homes as each day goes by. Increased bandwidth will allow users to experience all types of rich media offers in streaming audio, video, and multimedia product and service presentations.

Currently only about 5 percent of the Internet population has the bandwidth necessary to view rich media offers at this time. But your e-business will need to prepare for it now. And then think in terms of transmission sites—not Web sites to present offers to buyers.

Companies like Emblaze Creator 2.5 (builder.cnet.com/Graphics/Media/ss02.html), Flash 2 (builder.cnet.com/Graphics/Media/ss03.html), Microsoft NetShow 2.1 (builder.cnet.com/Graphics/Media/ss04.html), RealPublisher 5.0 (builder.cnet.com/Graphics/Media/ss05.html), and VivoActive Producer 2.0 (builder.cnet.com/Graphics/Media/ss06.html) supply streaming media technology to create rich media presentations.

Rich Media—Streaming Ahead

When rich media first started, it was used to perk up advertising banners on the Net. With rich media, static banners started to move and were made interactive. Soon, users could play simple games, view animated product offers, and even conduct transactions through banners on a Web site. Attempts were made to offer a richer multimedia experience, but they mostly failed due to the limited bandwidth available to the average Net user and slow downloads of the media files.

In response, companies turned to technology called "streaming media." Using streaming audio or video, users do not have to download the entire media file onto their computer. They have to download only the first several minutes of the file, and then the rest is streamed to them as needed. Although streaming has increased the download speed in most cases, without a cable modem or DSL connection, the experience is less than satisfactory.

Streaming audio and video are still in their infancy. Video streams cannot provide complex images fast enough. Images are smeared, audio is out of sync from video, and there are gaps and stalls in the stream. But this isn't stopping consumer-oriented companies such as AOL from forging ahead. AOL's merger with content giant Time Warner signals its intent to make multimedia play a large role on AOL in the future.

And AOL is not alone. Companies such as New York-based Internet news channel iNexTV (www.inextv.com) and Los Angeles-based movie channel CinemaNow (www.cinemanow.com) demonstrate full-blown streaming video with elements of interactivity.

Your e-business could and should make streaming media a part of its marketing plans today. Don't wait until the technology has been perfected. Keep up with the current rich media technology—as much as you can—to be prepared for when a standard emerges. Start experimenting with the different types of streaming media software turning your Web page presentations into 10, 30, and 60 second multimedia streaming presentations of your offers.

Make your IT and software engineers familiar with rich media technology. Buy the software and invest in the media servers to familiarize them with the technology. If you can't make such infrastructure investments at this time, use a media firm like Enliven (www.enliven.com) that provide rich media advertising solutions to the Internet advertising community.

Experiment with and learn how to use streaming media, and your e-business will be prepared for when bandwidth is not a concern for the majority of Net users and when shopping bots are ready to retrieve your offers.

Fashion TV Hits the Net

FashionTV.com (www.fashiontv.com) provides Internet viewers runway shows, photo shoots, fashion news, seasonal collections, and events in the fashion industry from around the world. FashionTV.com plans to feature and sell designer clothes and market its own line of casual clothing, swimwear, clubwear, and accessories.

Forum to Set Broadband Content Delivery Standards

The Broadband Content Delivery Forum will write guidelines and forge standards for the delivery of Internet content over broadband access links. The Forum will unite all the players in the broadband space—equipment manufacturers, content providers, and content creation and distribution companies—in focusing on streamlining and personalizing content delivery.

Content-on-the-Edges: The Decentralization of the Net

It's the online search engines' turn to be threatened by disintermediation. Companies such as FileFury (www.filefury.com) and iMesh.com (www.imesh.com), and programs such as Gnutella, are taking a leaf out of Napster's book and are turning the Internet inside out. These Web sites allow users to search for and exchange various file types directly from the desktop without needing to set up a Web site or upload files to a server. In essence, this new technology can easily create a *virtual private network (VPN)*.

Gnutella, for example, is a new kind of network architecture that enables real-time searches of vast libraries of content. That's in stark contrast to current search engines such as Excite and AltaVista that use Web crawlers that search one site at a time. It takes weeks or months for a search engine to crawl the Web and add new Web sites. Gnutella's peer-to-peer network works like the old game of telephone. A user's computer is connected directly to 20 others, and those in turn are connected to 20 more for a total of 400. Add only two more layers, and the original computer can talk to 160,000 computers on the network. It also means virtually no dead links.

Where Napster has a centralized Web site that can be blocked, the Gnutella program has none. Gnutella is distributed across hundreds of thousands of individual computers. Clay Shirky, a new media professor at Hunter College in New York, calls this "content at the edges."

CASE STUDY

GNUTELLA

A team of programmers from inside America Online released Gnutella on a Web page March 14, 2000. The program is a simple way of trading files without requiring participants to connect with any central server or Web site. Soon hundreds of programmers on the Net downloaded the program before AOL removed the site that Gnutella was on. Shortly thereafter, Nathan Moinvaziri, one of the programmers who downloaded the software, set up a new Web site, and the GnutellaNet was born. Now, dozens of developers are continuing the Gnutella project in a Linux-like collaborative effort like at gnutella.wego.com.

All kinds of information is available on the GnutellaNet, and when you get a search hit, it's virtually guaranteed to be there—no stale links and no irrelevant hits. The other half of Gnutella is giving back. Almost everyone on GnutellaNet shares their stuff. Every client on the GnutellaNet is also a server, so you not

According to Shirky, this violates the Net's current "content at the center" data model, relegating it to nothing but brokering connections. Content at the edges reinvents the PC as a hybrid client/server and places it squarely in the center of a new architecture of the Net.

Content at the edges accomplishes a number of unique things:

- It dispenses with uploading and leaves the files on PCs. This eliminates the cumbersome use of an FTP process.

- PCs running on the new network do not need a fixed Internet address of which there is a finite number.

- It ignores the reigning Net paradigm of client and server. If you can receive files from one PC, that PC can receive files from you.

All this proves that PCs can act as servers and that they are powerful enough to fill this new role. For e-commerce, this means competition, and more of it from a most unlikely source.

Content at the edges makes a PC act like a Web server that can be searched by anyone on the virtual private network created by content at the edges technology. That means all the money, time, and energy that large e-commerce sites have spent, building a brand and hoping to lock out the Johnny-come-lately players, may be all for naught. With this new technology, e-commerce virtual private networks—or shopping malls—can be easily set up by anyone with a product or service to sell. PCs act as Web servers, and requests

Creating the World's Largest Computer

Centrata (www.centrata.com) is creating the world's largest virtual hard drive and most powerful virtual computer using PCs connected to the Net. Centrata has a unique business model that will enable the hundreds of millions of computer owners with Internet access to sell their unused computer resources over the Web.

only can find stuff, but you also can make things available to others.

Because of the autonomous nature of Gnutella, no one knows for sure how many people on the Net use the program and are hooked into the GnutellaNet. Estimates range in the millions and are growing steadily. Perfect anonymity is its key strength and its key threat because there is little way to oversee the activities of the GnutellaNet users.

Still, software such as Gnutella posses a real challenge to e-business in the future.

GnutellaNet is a virtual private network, and an infinite number of them can be created with Gnutella-like software. Whole groups of shopping sites can be tied together into a VPN that neither search engines nor shopping bots can find. Joining or even starting a "stealth" shopping community could be an interesting and effective way to sell a company's goods and services.

Searching the Net Without a Central Server

FileFury (www.filefury.com) allows users to share files of any type and search other user's computers all over the Internet. Users can surf through any computer that has FileFury installed and copy whatever they want.

WAP—Wireless Application Protocol

Wireless application protocol (WAP) is an application environment and set of communication protocols for wireless devices. It's designed to enable manufacturers and vendors to have access to the Internet and advanced telephony services that are technology-independent.

for goods and services can be pointed quickly accurately to users' machines.

Now anyone with a PC has the ability to compete with even the largest of the e-commerce sites on the Net. Think of these VPNs as private shopping districts without the problem of setting up complicated Web servers and the expense of Web hosting.

In addition, *WAP*, the 500-pound gorilla of wireless commerce, is focusing on access and control of centralized commercial services. But with content-at-the-edges technology, a shopper can bypass the central service and go directly to a PC that has the product or service that the shopper desires.

And here's another challenge to your e-business: Gnutella-like technology is anonymous. Current e-commerce sites keep logs on their visitors so that they can target ads and offers to their visitors. This ends when Gnutella-like technology is used. When a user sends a query to a Gnutella VPN, not much in the query links it to the user. In short, there may be no safer way to use the Net without being watched—or known by the competition.

So, how far in the future is this new e-commerce model? How about now?

A company called Lightshare (www.lightshare.com), is preparing a service that will allow individual computer users to sell digital goods directly from their computers rather than going through centralized servers from companies like eBay or Amazon.com.

And how real is Lightshare? Very real. It is staffed largely with former Netscape, America Online, and Time Warner engineers and is funded by executives from Microsoft, Netscape Communications, and Google. The company will be Web-based and anyone who wants to sell or buy something will go through the Lightshare site to make the transaction. But the products themselves—initially digital files like songs or software—will actually be traded between individuals' computers, the same way that songs are swapped through Napster.

Content-at-the-edges technology is important to keep tabs on and, perhaps, use in your marketing strategy. Some of the best sites on the Net to keep up with content-on-the-edges technology like

Gnutella and Napster are at `gnutella.wego.com`, `www.surfacelayer.nu/gnuworld/basic.shtml`, and `www.napstermp3.com`. They offer the latest news, chat, and discussion boards for those wanting up-to-date information.

New Payment Solutions

Actual money—the paper and coins that we've come to love—is fast becoming information.

When you pay your credit card bill, the mortgage, or the utility bill, the transaction is an information exchange. When you've written that paper check, data is transmitted between your bank, your creditors, or your vendors. Money has become simply a sequence of bits and bytes of electronic information and, for e-commerce, payment for goods and services through electronic means is a natural extension of the same process.

Although many of the current online payment schemes that most companies use are still rather conventional, changes are in the air. Your e-business must be prepared to accept payment for goods and services in new ways, and these payment changes should be considered in your marketing strategy.

Digital cash—also called e-cash—will eventually become the dominant way of paying for products and services on the Net. Net consumers not only have the option of what and where to buy, but also how. Although payment will come from the consumer's credit card or bank account, how payment is made on the Net can take a variety of forms: as a prepaid payment option, as a person-to-person (P2P) service, or in the form of an Internet escrow service.

Examples of these types of payment methods include eCount (`www.ecount.com`) and RocketCash (`www.rocketcash.com`). eCount lets Net consumers conduct secure online transactions at any online store through the use of prepaid personal accounts. Consumers can add as little as $5 to their "ecount" to open an account. When they register and are accepted, they choose a unique user ID and password and are issued a 16-digit MasterCard account number and an expiration date, which together can be used to access the balance of their ecount at online merchants that accept MasterCard. eCount was developed for those consumers

Visa Plans Mobile Device Bill Payment

Visa has partnered with the wireless services firm of Aether Systems to bring card payment services to wireless devices. One of the first services that that they will co-develop is an e-wallet for handheld devices.

P2P: Peer-to-Peer or Person-to-Person

P2P is used to mean two things: Peer-to-Peer computing and Person-to-Person transactions. Peer-to-Peer computing allows computers to locate and share information directly with each other without going through large intermediary servers. Person-to-Person transactions (also known as C2C—consumer-to-consumer) occur between two consumers on sites like eBay and Amazon Auctions.

unable or unwilling to use their credit cards to pay for goods and services online. With eCount, consumers never have to give out their credit card online again.

RocketCash allows kids to purchase goods online without their parents' credit cards. Parents—or anyone, for that matter—who want to extend a prepaid purchasing limit to another party can set up an account at RocketCash. A credit card number is entered into the RocketCash system, a spending limit is assigned, and a password is given to the user of the RocketCash. The user can then shop at the different authorized merchants that are on the RocketCash site.

One problem that companies such as eBay (www.ebay.com) have had to deal with is the opportunity for fraud by users of their service. Scam artists on eBay promising one thing and delivering another have cheated many eBay buyers. Up to now, the best way consumers could protect themselves was through the use of an Internet escrow service such as TradeSafe (www.tradesafe.com) and iEscrow (www.iescrow.com). Now, companies such as PayPal (www.paypal.com), eCommony's Pay2Card (www.pay2card.com), and ProPay.com (www.propay.com) have entered the P2P space, offering secure payment services between consumers. With these P2P payment services, any consumer can become a seller and can set up business on the Net.

These new P2P eCash services create an interesting twist to e-commerce. They're both a boon and a bane to your e-business. They're a boon because your e-business can easily participate in the consumer-to-consumer market space. However, they're also a bane because these new sales methods have the potential to introduce a new level of competition.

When you combine these P2P payment systems with the capability to set up virtual private networks through the use of programs such as Gnutella, you have the potential for a new type of competitor entering your marketplace: the average Net consumer. Many consumers already have set up successful small, one-person businesses using eBay. Imagine others like them doing the same on their very own PCs connected to a Gnutella network. These types of "stealth" competitors would be impossible to find using traditional search engines and shopping bots, and would promote themselves in the hundreds of thousands of discussion boards and chat rooms around the Net.

You could have competition without ever knowing about it. It would be wise to study these new e-commerce and Net technology initiatives and to prepare for them when designing your e-business marketing strategy.

CHAPTER 10

Rule #5—Selling at Any Price

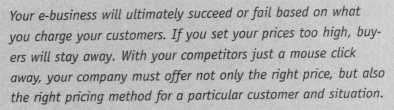

Your e-business will ultimately succeed or fail based on what you charge your customers. If you set your prices too high, buyers will stay away. With your competitors just a mouse click away, your company must offer not only the right price, but also the right pricing method for a particular customer and situation.

The one major fact of e-commerce today is that the customer is in control. The one price fits all model is obsolete. Pricing will get personal, with customized price offers to each and every buyer. Auctions, reverse auctions, Dutch auctions, comparison shopping, group buying, exchanges, bartering, and a host of other buying schemes will each offer their own individual trade-offs for the ability of buyers to choose their own price.

These pricing models will work their way into every form of e-commerce. It is important to understand and incorporate these new dynamic pricing models and their trade-offs into your e-business marketing strategies if you want to stay atop the e-commerce wave and not be swamped by it.

What new combinations of flexible pricing are on the horizon, no one knows. But to be sure, they will change how, when, where, and at what price buyers will purchase goods and services over the Internet in the future. And those e-businesses that succeed in the dynamic pricing game will come out winners, gaining the loyalty of their customers in the process.

I magine the day when consumers can surf over to their favorite online e-tailer and demand the price they want and how they want it. Well, that day is fast approaching, and your e-business must be prepared for it.

The state of e-commerce today is that the consumer is in control. He or she can surf from site to site and business offer to business offer, comparing prices, using automated shopping bots that can ferret out the lowest prices for any product or service that they seek, playing one merchant against the other, and forcing profit margins down to near zero. Given this reality, the current "one price fits all" model is obsolete.

Pricing will get personal. And by *personal*, I don't mean just preferred pricing for repeat customers, but the delivery of customized price offers to each and every buyer.

Personalized Pricing

Compared to other pricing models in the commerce world, fixed pricing is relatively new. From the earliest days of human commerce thousands of years ago, all types of flexible pricing methods have existed. Bartering at the community bazaars, auctions, and co-op buying, in which farmers banded together to get volume discounts on feed and equipment. In comparison, fixed pricing has been around for only about 100 years.

But with the help of the Internet, dynamic pricing schemes are making a comeback, turning the current fixed-pricing model on its head with more power being transferred to the buyer—whether that buyer is a consumer or a company purchasing agent. The Internet easily allows hundreds of thousands—even millions—of buyers to band together and buy. And although many of the dynamic pricing methods that the Internet supports are not new, the Net makes using these models more efficient—and a challenge to your e-business fixed-pricing model.

But there is a silver lining to the dynamic pricing challenge. By being capable of offering customized sales offers to each individual buyer, your business may regain the price model equilibrium and restore margins while, at the same time, building customer loyalty. In its very nature, the dynamic-pricing model responds to the

A Collusion of Buyers

Companies such as Mercata (www.mercata.com) may be a sign of consumer power to come. Mercata lets consumers band together to get the lowest price on a product by using group purchasing power. This could revolutionize the power structure between buyers and seller. One day, Congress might have to pass anticonsumer trust legislation to protect sellers from the unfair collusion of buyers.

buyer's demand for a preferred price in return for making certain trade-offs in time, selection, limited warrantees, and other value-added elements.

Very soon, we will see many dynamic-pricing models for e-business that couldn't even exist in the real world. Jay S. Walker, founder of Priceline (www.priceline.com), talks of how the future of dynamic pricing will mirror the equities market, where the traditional equities bid/ask model has been complemented by more complex and flexible pricing models such as puts and calls, derivatives, and strips.

What's Walker's vision of an e-commerce future?

Consider a manufacturer that might accept or offer a different price if it has the option to deliver the product to the customer within a one-month window. With such an option, the manufacturer can manage his inventory and distribution channel much more efficiently and cost-effectively. Similarly, the manufacturer or retailer may accept or offer a different price if it can sell—or choose not to sell—a product based on its future availability. Or, different prices can be offered to consumers who agree to take a specific product or a similar product from the manufacturer's product line.

Borrowing another pricing method from the financial industry, future pricing for consumer goods could include consumer-friendly forms of derivatives. For example, in future holiday seasons, a consumer might pay a small amount to a toy manufacturer or retailer, which gives that consumer the option to buy a specific toy at a prespecified price. In cases where the toy turns out to be very popular, these prepaid options can give the manufacturer a better idea on how many toys to build, thus reducing the shortfall and giving the manufacturer a good idea of demand.

In Walker's vision of the e-commerce future, dynamic pricing, combined with an almost infinite choice and expert automated sales help from bots, will give the Internet the power to deliver all the elements that consumers are looking for—"Wal-Mart pricing with Nordstrom service and 7-Eleven convenience."

Walker believes that these pricing models will work their way into every form of e-commerce. But that's the future—let's look at the dynamic pricing methods available now for your e-business.

Dynamic Pricing

In the real world, it's very difficult for retail stores to change prices after the price tag is applied. To do so would be a very labor-intensive process. But on the Net, prices can be changed in a second.

It's obvious that your e-business will ultimately succeed or fail based on what you charge your customers. If you set your prices too high, buyers will stay away. If you set them too low, profitability is impossible. With your competitors just a mouse click away, your company must offer not only the right price, but also the right pricing method for a particular customer and situation.

And what about the consumers? How will their growing control of the transaction impact the sales method of your e-business? Will consumers be buying strictly on price alone, and will the low-price leader win every sale?

Not likely. Consumers buy for different reasons, and price is not the only determining factor, although it is an important one. So, you must be prepared to offer a number of dynamic pricing strategies that fill a consumer's price demand. These demands will be filled in exchange for certain value-added elements that a sale might contain, such as these:

- Product selection

- Convenience factors

- Customer service and purchase guarantee information

- Rebates

- Personalized services

Auctions, reverse auctions, Dutch auctions, comparison shopping, group buying, exchanges, bartering, and a host of other buying schemes will each offer their own individual trade-offs for the ability of buyers to choose their own prices. It is important to understand and incorporate these new dynamic-pricing models and their

A B2B Auction Exchange

At TradeOut.com, companies with excess inventory can list them at auction for other companies to buy. There is no cost to register and no fee for buyers, and sellers pay a commission only when products are sold. Geared primarily to businesses, the average transaction at TradeOut.com is $20,000.

trade-offs into your e-business marketing strategies if you want to stay atop the e-commerce wave and not be swamped by it.

Haggle Pricing

Haggling, although not new in the real world, has come to the Net. This type of pricing model is a one-to-one exchange. You either personally haggle—or negotiate—a price with a seller, or you can use an intelligent software agent. You're beginning to see sites use this pricing model because the technology of the Net makes it possible. Two examples of haggling services are eWanted.com (www.ewanted.com), which lets buyers post what they want sellers to bid on, and NexTag.com (www.nextag.com), which offers online negotiations for computer products, software, and consumer electronics.

Another form of one-to-one haggling is the "name your price," or demand pricing, model, such as with Priceline. Priceline started out letting consumers name their own prices for airline tickets. Since then, the company has added hotel rooms, car rentals, home mortgages, and even groceries to the lists of things that you can demand a price for online. The trade-off for consumers is that they cannot choose a particulate brand—or, in the case of airline tickets—a date or time that they can buy the product or service. The consumer trades off price for convenience or brand.

PRICELINE

Priceline claims that it's not so much a place to shop, but a way to shop.

Priceline pioneered the "name your price" selling method in April 1998 when it launched its service enabling consumers to name their own price for leisure airline tickets. It followed up with "name your own price" for hotel rooms, new cars, home financing, long-distance services, rental cars, and groceries. The Priceline service enables consumers to use the Internet to save money on a wide range of products and services while enabling sellers to generate incremental revenue from unused inventory.

As a Web site, Priceline is attractive and relatively easy to use. It first collects consumers for the products and services it carries. Consumers guarantee their demand with their credit cards. Then Priceline communicates the offers directly to its participating sellers. Consumers agree to hold their offers open for a specified period of time to enable Priceline to fulfill their offers from inventory provided by their participating sellers. But once offers are fulfilled, they cannot be canceled.

Since then, other sites have caught on to this pricing model. Microsoft Corp.'s Expedia travel service (www.expedia.com) will also let consumers set their own prices for hotel rooms, and eCollegeBid.org (www.ecollegebid.org) will even let students set their own tuition and see if a college is willing to match it.

The consumers may not get exactly what they want, but they will get it at the price they want.

Online Auctions

One of the most successful and most imitated dynamic pricing methods on the Net today are online auctions. Online auctions are becoming increasingly popular (see Table 10.1). Forrester Research reported that goods sold through online auctions are expected to grow from $1 billion in 1998 to $6.4 billion in 2003. Jupiter Communications predicts that online auctions will grow to $27 billion during the same period.

There are basically three main segments in which auctions are used: consumer to consumer (C2C), business to consumer (B2C), and business to business (B2B). Each method serves a different market space.

Haggle-Equip Your e-Business

HaggleWare (www.haggleware.com) uses electronic salespeople to provide product information and pricing decisions that match buyers and sellers in online negotiations. You could haggle-equip your company Web site with the company's unique online negotiation technology.

Place an Auction on Your Site

Want to add an auction to your site? Two companies to consider are Fair Market (www.fairmarket.com) and Open Site (www.opensite.com).

To get a better price than they normally would for the products and services that Priceline offers, consumers must make a trade-off. They must be flexible with respect to brands, sellers, and product features. They may not get a flight at the most convenient time, or a rental car brand that they want. But they could get the price they demand. As for the sellers, Priceline enables them to generate incremental revenue without disrupting their existing distribution channels or retail pricing structures.

How successful has Priceline been?

A study conducted by Opinion Research Corporation International of Princeton, New Jersey, found that seven Internet-related companies are now recognized by more than 50 million U.S. adults, or more than 1 in 4. Priceline was one of the seven, right up there with Yahoo!, Amazon, AOL, and Netscape. Priceline is a proven leader in ushering in an era when fixed pricing is no longer the norm and when real-time pricing on-demand will dominate e-commerce.

Table 10.1

Purchasers at Online Auction Sites	
1999	1.9 million
2000	2.9 million
2001	4.4 million
2002	6.5 million

Source: Forrester Research

eBay Makes Life Easier for Sellers

eBay's payment subsidiary, BillPoint (www.billpoint.com), can now sign up sellers as small-volume Visa-accepting merchants. Sellers who sign up for BillPoint can accept Visa debit or credit cards for their sales. This is as close to a person-to-person payment solution that any site so far has reached. Visa benefits by encouraging more people to use their Visa cards online for purchasing products at eBay.

C2C auctions are an open market where anyone can sell anything to anyone at anytime. It's like a virtual flea market. eBay (www.ebay.com) is one of the most successful companies in this online auction space. B2C auctions sell either new or refurbished products from e-tailers or manufactures. Merchants either have a limited supply of a certain product that they put up for auction, or they may put up a small amount at a time, replenishing the products from inventory when the original supply is auctioned off. B2B auctions are in their infancy compared to the B2C auctions, but these are growing fast as more businesses see this sales method as a way to sell both excess and new inventory.

As in the real world, online auctions come in different flavors:

- **Standard auction**—The standard auction has grown exponentially on the Net over the last few years. It was the first alternative to fixed pricing, and the number of sites offering this pricing model has grown dramatically. The standard auction is a seller-dominated market that pits buyers against each other to determine the highest price of an item. The highest bidder gets to buy the item. Online auctions are generally timed, so bids must come in before a predetermined point. A variation of this auction is the *reserve* auction. In this case, a minimum price is set for an item; if that price is not reached, the item is withdrawn from sale.

- **Dutch auction**—Unlike a standard auction, in which bidders see prices steadily climb, the Dutch auction works backward. Dutch auctions are typically used when a seller has many identical items. In this case, many buyers can win a bid and buy as many of the items for sale as they want. Multiple people can win, and winners can buy more than one item. All winners pay the lowest successful winning bid.

- **Reverse auction**—Reverse auctions turn the standard and Dutch auctions on their head. When buyers dominate an auction, the reverse auction is used. In this case, buyers name the desired quantity and price of an item or service, and sellers bid down to get the sale. Here the seller is competing against other businesses instead of the buyer competing against other buyers.

Aggregate Buying

Remember those loud ads on TV many years ago—usually from some home stereo discount store? They claimed they could beat any price because they bought on *volume*! In fact, that's close to the truth. Wal-Mart was built on that business strategy, and it's reflected in the many discount mail order catalogers in business today.

This concept of volume driving down prices has hit the Net. It's called *demand aggregation*, or aggregate buying. Aggregate buying is different than other dynamic pricing models. In aggregate buying, buyers band together to negotiate a better price through volume discounts. The basic theory is that the more items sold, the cheaper the cost of any individual item. It's sort of like an electronic co-op.

Examples of the aggregate buying model include MobShop (www.mobshop.com) and Mercata (www.mercata.com).

Where aggregate buying really shines is for products and services in which an affinity group exists—for example, people in a book club who need to buy the same book, or people who have signed up for a class and all need the same software.

Exchanges—Flex Pricing

Auctions, haggling, and aggregate buying are good examples of dynamic pricing methods. But the closest to an equities market model of dynamic pricing is the Exchange.

Exchanges, which use flex pricing, are basically two-way, simultaneous auctions in which both buyer and seller price quotes float in response to supply and demand. This is very similar to a stock

Warning: Buyers and Sellers of Hazardous and Unlawful Product Auctions

The Consumer Product Safety Commission (CPSC) (www.cpsc.gov) has partnered with two of the biggest online auction sites—Amazon and eBay—to protect people from buying dangerous second-hand products via online auctions. The two sites will share links with CPSC that lists hazardous items that they deem dangerous or that have been recalled by manufacturers. Agreements between organizations such as the CPSC and online consumer-to-consumer auction sites will protect Net consumers in the future.

market. Although this method seems to be labor-intensive, making the merchant respond to every bid with an ask, in reality, the technology of the Net can automate the process.

Here's how it would work: A merchant would set some starting price point for a product or service. He then would choose a set of rules that the flex price computer program would follow. He would choose how much or what percentage a product would rise whenever it's bought. Conversely, he would choose how much or what percentage a product would fall—and over what period of time—if the product does not sell. Eventually, it would reach a point—high or low—at which the product would clear the market. All this would be done automatically by the computer.

Although this dynamic sales method will result in a more efficient sales method for companies than current dynamic pricing methods, it's also the most complicated and uncertain because the prices are always in flux. Some exchanges using flex pricing are developing now in the fragmented and large B2B sectors, and it's only a matter of time that it migrates down to the consumer level because the technology of the Net can make it happen.

Concurrent Dynamic Pricing

For the most part, current dynamic pricing methods have been a duplication of the sales methods in the physical retail world. At its heart, Web-based e-commerce today is little more than a reflection of the way business has always been conducted in the brick-and-mortar world. After all, fixed-price buying at a fixed location, online auctions, and group buying merely mimic the retail world, as we've always known it. And exchanges, in and of themselves, are a reiteration of the equities world.

Concurrent dynamic pricing is a next-generation application of flexible pricing and has no analogy in the brick-and-mortar world. Concurrent dynamic pricing combines several of the current flexible pricing methods into one, allowing merchants to sell more products faster and at higher prices than other pricing systems. With concurrent dynamic pricing, an e-business doesn't have to decide whether to sell its goods via a fixed-price model such as Amazon.com's, an auction model such as eBay's, or a "name your own price" model such as Priceline's. Instead, an e-business can sell goods and services through all these methods concurrently, with the price of the goods or services fluctuating minute by minute, based on actual customer demand and price sensitivity.

Concurrent dynamic pricing turns the business paradigm on its head. Instead of companies competing against companies for a consumer's business, consumers compete against other consumers for a company's business. Here's an example of how concurrent dynamic pricing would work. A company that we'll call Office Supplies-R-Us sells a wide variety of office supplies, including stationery, pens, pencils, and small office machines, through catalogs distributed throughout the country. The company has established an e-commerce Web site in recent months as well.

Among the products that Office Supplies-R-Us resells is the Acme Faxomatic, Model 101, which has sold below the company's expectations. Acme has just begun selling the enhanced Faxomatic Model 102, and Office Supplies-R-Us must quickly sell its excess stock of Model 101 units to make room for the new product.

Traditionally, getting rid of the excess inventory would involve sharply discounting the product, marketing it through the company's Web site or through printed catalogs. These methods would result in reduced margins that barely covered the cost of maintaining inventory. In other cases, the entire lot might be sold to a liquidator for pennies on the cost dollar. In an effort to reduce the inventory cost quickly and maximize the return on the outmoded product, however, Office Supplies-R-Us has elected to sell the excess items via the concurrent dynamic pricing method on its Web site.

After setting a few simple business rules, Office Supplies-R-Us is ready to sell its fax machines. The fax machines will be offered to buyers via the flex pricing, "name your price," and auction pricing methods simultaneously.

Flex pricing allows a buyer to purchase the fax machine at a price that fluctuates based on supply and demand over a certain period of time. If demand for the fax machine goes up, the concurrent dynamic pricing method automatically raises prices. If demand is slack, the price is automatically lowered, based on the business rules configured by Office Supplies-R-Us.

Concurrent Dynamic Pricing a Reality

A new company called Concurrent Commerce Technologies (CCT) has patented a concurrent dynamic pricing system that lets merchants and manufacturers sell their goods in three or more dynamic pricing methods concurrently. Using CCT's technology, a merchant can dynamically price-enable any product offered on the Web site.

Simultaneously, faxes are also being sold through the "name your price" method. Offers are accepted or rejected based on a formula that incorporates the value that Office Supplies-R-Us has assigned to the entire lot of the Faxomatic Model 101 fax machines.

Meanwhile, the Faxomatic 101 sale also has stirred the interest of customers who prefer to buy via auctions. Auctions start at $1, and Office Supplies-R-Us has set a reserve bid price for the fax machines. Because the available stock of fax machines could be depleted by customers who are buying them via the flex pricing and "name your price" methods, the supply of fax machines via the auction method is constantly being reduced. Eager bargain hunters will have to wait until the time period that the product is offered has ended to find out whether their bids are accepted. Much like other auctions, bidders can increase their offers right until the end of the auction, increasing their chances of winning.

If the Faxomatic 101 turns out to be a very popular product, few, if any, will be left at the end of the time period for the auction. If so, buyers are compelled to buy at the current higher flex price, thus giving Office Supplies-R-Us a better price for the product than if they sold it to liquidators. On the other hand, if the Faxomatic 101 produced little demand from buyers, Supplies-R-Us could still clear the lot in the auction process.

This application is only one example of concurrent dynamic pricing. There are others. For instance, a company wanting to test-market a unique product could use concurrent dynamic pricing to help determine an acceptable price point. B2B Web exchanges such as VerticalNet (www.verticalnet.com), which already bring buyers and sellers of goods and components together, can use concurrent dynamic pricing as a means of helping sellers make the most profit possible and help buyers get the best deal possible.

As Web-enabled wireless devices proliferate, buyers will have the ability to access product or service offers while away from their computers. For example, a warehouse manager could determine right from the warehouse floor whether he has excess inventory and could offer his products through a concurrent dynamic pricing process right from his cell phone.

What new combinations of flexible pricing are on the horizon, no one knows. But to be sure, they will change how, when, where, and at what price buyers will purchase goods and services over the Net in the future. And those e-businesses that succeed in the dynamic pricing game will come out winners, gaining the loyalty of their customers in the process. And that's priceless.

PART III

Promotion Strategies for the New Economy

CHAPTER 11

Driving Traffic to Your e-Business

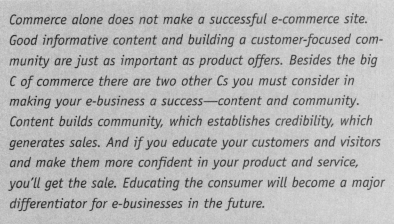

Commerce alone does not make a successful e-commerce site. Good informative content and building a customer-focused community are just as important as product offers. Besides the big C of commerce there are two other Cs you must consider in making your e-business a success—content and community. Content builds community, which establishes credibility, which generates sales. And if you educate your customers and visitors and make them more confident in your product and service, you'll get the sale. Educating the consumer will become a major differentiator for e-businesses in the future.

People go online not just to be informed but also to interact with other people. Filling this need at your Web store will help you turn shoppers into customers and customers into repeat buyers. If done right, an interactive community on your site will increase the number of page-views per visit, giving you opportunities to offer merchandise to your shoppers. In addition, online communities are not limited to site-centric e-businesses. In fact, community might turn out to be the force that drives the wireless Net.

Finally, the best kind of marketing is the kind you don't have to do yourself. And that's the beauty and power of viral marketing. When you use viral marketing as a tool, you're using the Net creatively, the way it was meant to be used.

With customer acquisition costs running at unsustainable levels, tomorrow's e-businesses must find more cost-effective ways to attract customers to their sites.

This is achieved by giving Net users what they want.

There are two schools of thought on the Net. One school believes people use the Net for information. The other firmly believes that people want to do things on the Net—not just read about them. The answer to these two different opinions—like most anything else in life—lies in the middle.

Just slapping together pages and pages of product connected to an online shopping cart might or might not get you sales, but customers don't live on offers alone. Besides the big *C* of commerce there are two other *C*s you must consider in making your e-business a success—content and community. Relevant content can help support your online offer, while at the same time, helping your visitors and customers interact with one another can increase repeat visits to your site. Content builds community, which establishes credibility, which generates sales.

Table 11.1   Acquisition Costs Are Climbing (1999)

	Q1	Q2	Q3	Q4
theStreet	$113	$224	$168	$619
e*trade	$258	$286	$250	$362
EarthLink	$121	$126	$173	N/A
MindSpring	$21	$202	$324	N/A

Source: Jupiter Communications

Finally, besides adding relevant content and community elements to your Web site, word-of-mouth programs can substantially increase the number of customers driven to your e-business with little or no acquisition cost.

Content—Smart Shoppers Buy More

The fundamental purpose of the Net is to provide information. Too many e-businesses have ignored this fact. A user of the Net is there to find an answer to a question—not perform a transaction.

Targeting with Sub-Sites

If your e-business targets different types of customers with different products, create *sub-sites* for people in each targeted audience to find what they're looking for. About.com is a good example of using sub-sites. Each of their guide sites has the name of the site before About's domain name, such as onlineshopping.about.com, pets.about.com, health.about.com, or fashion.about.com.

According to a study by ActivMedia (www.activmedia.com), e-commerce still accounts for less than 2% of total retail sales in the U.S. Of those sales, the majority was for books, music, and videos. Notice these are all commodity products found everywhere with little or no depth of information needed by buyers to decide on a purchase. If your e-business sells anything else, providing informational content on these products should be a primary strategy for attracting and retaining customers.

If you educate your customers and visitors and make them more confident or add to their interest, you'll not only get the sale—and more of them—but sales of better, often higher-priced products as well.

Micron PC has a partnership with Ziff-Davis Education. When Micron PC offered courses on how to shop on the Web, it saw a rise in buying activity and the average sales prices to customers rose with their confidence as they purchased more sophisticated computer hardware.

Martha Stewart is another example of good customer education. Martha ties her merchandise promotions to the focus of her editorial pieces in her magazine and on her Web site. Want to make Christmas cookies? She'll show you how—and sell you cookie cutters in the process.

So, do you begin pouring resources from your e-business into designing slick courseware for your site? Not really. You're in the business of selling, not training. So, creating relationships with Net-based training companies would be a good strategy. Firms such as notHarvard.com (www.notharvard.com) build compelling *eduCommerce* courseware for online stores. And it works.

Their eduCommerce courseware improves the stickiness, or customer retention, and customer interaction of their clients' sites. And this must be the goal of any e-business if it's to succeed. Educating the consumer will become a major differentiator for e-businesses in the future. Educating the consumer kills two birds with one stone. An educated consumer will not only buy—and buy more—but the rate of product returns is much lower, which reduces the cost of customer support and service.

The informational content you provide to customers does not need to be formal courseware. There are other types of information, such as news, product features, and reviews that can help inform your customers and help them make a purchasing decision. However, before you lay down your money for informational content, consider these issues first.

Content need not be strictly educational. Another content strategy is to offer informational content. iSyndicate (`iSyndicate.com`) aggregates free content from more than 500 different providers in categories such as Top News and Weather, Sports News, Business and Finance, Entertainment and Lifestyles, Technology, and Health News—even Fun and Games. News providers include CNet, *Rolling Stone* magazine, CBS Market Watch, and Sporting News. And most of the content is free to use on your Web site.

A similar site to iSyndicate is Screaming Media (`screamingmedia.com`). With Screaming Media, you can display news stories based on any keyword that you choose. The story headlines and full stories are integrated into your site pages.

Will the Content Support Your Site?

The latest news from Reuters or national sports scores might bring some visitors to your site, but you should try to make the content relevant to what you are selling. Useful content is a tool for suggesting an action. Next, see if the content you're buying is restricted in some way. Can you edit or personalize the content specifically for your offers? If the content provider is selling the very same information to other sites, then your e-business will have no differentiation.

At the end of the spectrum, there are those online companies whose services commerce-enable content. If your e-business's stock and trade is content, then online companies like ePod (`www.epod.com`) and Pop2it (`www.pop2it.com`) help content publishers link their articles to related products and services.

For example, suppose you have an outdoor hiking site. Your Web site is filled with content informing visitors about how, where, and why to hike the great outdoors. A small micro site using either a fixed or pop-up window can be placed in the articles that offers to

What Is eduCommerce?

eduCommerce is the process of offering free consumer education as a powerful customer acquisition tool that enhances an e-business's customer value proposition resulting in increased stickiness and greater sales.

Flyswat Brings Net Searches to Any Web Page

Flyswat (`www.flyswat.com`) lets Web surfers click what they call *flycons* attached to any word on a Web page or a computer screen and get a choice of links related to that information. These links let them go directly to the Web page they need. Flycons can be used within a Web sites' email, word processing, or any Windows application.

sell a product related to the article being read. This is what Pop2it and ePod do. By merging the shopping experience directly into the editorial content, users never leave the content to make a purchase and your Web site receives a percentage of the sale.

Does the Content Reside on Their Server or Yours?

It's important to know whether the content on your site is owned by you or just leased from the content provider. Does the content reside on your server or does it reside on theirs? If it resides on theirs, they usually brand the content with your name and site navigation structure dressing up pages on their server to look like yours.

The problem with leasing content is that when you decide to end the contract with the content provider, all your content disappears and you're back at square one. If you own the content and not just lease it, you keep the content on your site after the relationship is terminated.

Another thing to consider if the content resides on the provider's server is that search engines will not direct surfers to your site because the content resides on the provider's server. If the content is not on your site, your site won't show up in the search engines. Because most people use search engines to find content, they won't find it on your site even though you're paying fees for the content.

CASE STUDY

FLYSWAT

Flyswat is a free service that delivers answers on-the-fly, no matter where you are on the Web or desktop. Flyswat transforms key words in any application—Web based or PC based—into live links to information and resources on the Net. Flyswat delivers information on finance, sports, travel, shopping, entertainment, and more—when a reader needs it. Simply click a yellow-underlined Flyswat link in Internet Explorer or Alt-click any word in any Windows application to pop up Flyswat's concise menu of additional information choices.

Flyswat offers your e-business a quick and easy way to add content to your site without sending your visitors off to somewhere else on the Net. Flyswat's technology lets people searching for information find it without

Getting the Right Content

It's wise to know the ultimate provider of the content that you're buying. Some content providers have bought their content from someone else. You need to know which providers have.

Why?

First, does the content provider have the legal right to sell the information to you? Be sure the content provider is not breaking any copyright laws. Second, your site visitors will think that the content is coming from you so it's important that your content be accurate and of high quality. After all, it'll be a reflection of you.

Finally, before you sign on the dotted line for content, make sure you know what your exit strategy is. Are you committing your company's resources to buying content for the next year or two or more whether you use it or not? If you decide to stop using the content, can you easily extricate yourself from the contract? Remember, things change fast on the Net. Today's hot content could be tomorrow's old news.

Community—User Generated Content

Buying content from service providers is one way to place relevant content on your site. Another is to have the very people who use your site generate content. The strategy here is to encourage contributions from visitors to your e-business.

visiting a separate Web page like Yahoo! or the other search engines.

Flyswat was launched in 1998 by a group of Massachusetts Institute of Technology engineers. In addition to underlining words in a Web document that users can click for more information, Flyswat's user interface includes a toolbar that sits underneath the browser. The application is available for use only with Microsoft's Internet Explorer browser 4.0 and higher.

Flywswat's revenue stream comes from transaction fees. For example, if an instant search on a book title leads to a sale of that title through an online bookseller, Flyswat collects a fee. Flyswat must have done something right because they caught the eye of NBC Internet (NBCi) and was purchased by them in May of 2000 for $70 million.

Encourage Contributions

Offer a process for visitors to submit articles, allowing their experiences to be included on your site or in your newsletter. Not only do you get free help in building your site content but you also gain long-term, repeat visits from people whose content is included on your site.

People go online not just to be informed but also to interact with other people. Filling this need at your Web store will help you turn shoppers into customers and customers into repeat buyers. Content can attract shoppers to your site. But to generate a continuous flow of repeat visitors, you need to provide access to an interactive community. If done right, an interactive community on your site will increase the number of page-views per visit, giving you more opportunities to offer merchandise to your shoppers.

Community features can be used to encourage customers to return to your site. Establishing a *learning community* can help shoppers develop expertise through the interaction with other shoppers who visit your site. Asking questions, discussing problems, raising issues, and the general camaraderie that develops in an interactive learning community breeds a kind of loyalty that is beneficial to the success of your Web store.

And loyalty breeds repeat visits.

Another benefit of an interactive community is that it can add content to your site. Discussion boards and forums, chat rooms, and discussion lists can provide content by their very nature of generating information. You can take a short quote from one of your forums or discussion lists and post it each day on your site as fresh content to generate interest in your product or offer. This type of content can act as a traffic magnet bringing a steady stream of visitors to your site.

A good example of this is my online shopping site (`onlineshopping.about.com`). Visitors to my site can join in discussions, vote in polls, and participate in live chat sessions on the topic of online shopping. I also make reference to these interactive community forums on my home page.

Communities can build your business. The more times a shopper visits your site the more familiar they are with it. The more familiar they are the more comfortable they become making a purchase from you instead of some unknown merchant a mouse click away. Look at it this way. Communities are sticky. Visitors tend to spend longer periods of time at your site than before. The stickier the communities, the more loyal the visitors. Loyalty builds trust and trust is the currency of business.

You should include as many interactive community tools as possible on your Web site. The major tools of the interactive community are discussion boards or forums, chat rooms, and discussion lists.

Discussion Boards or Forums

Everyone has an opinion and most people want to know that their opinions are taken seriously. Some enjoy helping other people and others have a desire to learn more about a subject, issue, or product. It's this willingness of your visitors to help others that builds a learning community at your e-business. As word gets out that serious discussions are going on at your Web site and if you can promote those discussions on your site, shoppers will come back on a regular basis to see what's discussed next.

Discussion boards need to be programmed. But if you don't mind using a message board service, you can add a discussion board to your site for free! A free discussion board service and one that offers many options is Delphi Forums (www.delphi.com). Their administration tools are very sophisticated and they also provide a free live chat room for your site's use.

Chat Rooms

The stickiest interactive community tool of all is the live chat room.

Having a live chat room on your Web site can keep visitors on your site for hours at a time. That's a lot of face time for one Web page. During this time, you could place offers on the chat discussion page pitching your products or service. You could even join in the chat about your product or product category identifying yourself as the merchant and offering to answer any questions about your company, its products, and types of products it sells.

There is, however, a downside to chat rooms. Unlike discussion boards where you can read all the messages posted there and remove any that are deemed unfit for your board, chat rooms are open free-for-alls. To supervise them would take a staff of people monitoring them 24 hours a day. To solve this problem, you could open the chat room at certain times of the day when monitoring is available.

Build Your Community with No Programming

Your Own Community offers software to buy that lets you build guestbooks, discussion forums, polls, and many more great interactive features including start pages for visitors that direct them right to your site. Find Build Your Own Community at www.buildacommunity.com.

Here's another use for chat. How about real-time customer service? Lands End (www.landsend.com) provides live customer service through a chat interface. If you need help with a product, you click the Live Help button and it opens a chat window and initiates a chat session with a live customer service representative.

Discussion Lists

Although discussion boards and chat rooms require that shoppers visit your site, there are other ways to build a community with shoppers that do not require a site visit, yet build loyalty and keep your e-business in their mind.

One of the best and least expensive ways to build community is through the use of an email discussion list.

A discussion list is a discussion board via email. Subscribers to your discussion list receive emails on a regular basis containing comments that are *echoed* to every other subscriber on the list. Every subscriber on the list receives every post to the list. All posts to the list are done via an email message sent to the list. In a typical discussion list, the software enables a member to send his or her message to the list address, and then broadcasts or echoes that message out to all the list members—all within a few minutes.

A well-executed discussion list can gain wide visibility and a very good reputation for your business and for the products or services you sell. Members of a popular discussion list can number in the thousands and offer a great opportunity to sell your product or service.

CASE STUDY

DELPHI FORUMS

Delphi Forums started out as Delphi—an Internet services company that once was the linchpin of News Corp.'s online efforts. Since then, Delphi has revamped itself and was reborn as Delphi Forums—an online business that provides community tools and services that are integrated into high-traffic Web sites.

Adding Delphi's service to your Web site creates a valuable resource on a vast array of subjects for anyone seeking information, advice, or friendship. Delphi currently provides discussion boards and chat rooms for client sites such as About, Xoom.com, and News Corp.'s Fox Sports and Fox News online units.

Millions of individuals have chosen to take advantage of free forums on Delphi. Delphi Forums currently has more than two million registered users, in 80,000 active Forums, posting 50,000 messages each day.

And how can you use such a list?

You might use a discussion list as a communications platform for customers who use your manufactured product. If you sell other company's products, you can use the discussion list to inform your subscribers about the product's category. For example, suppose you sell collectible first-edition books. You could form a discussion list for collectors to exchange ideas about collector books. You could participate and answer their questions about first edition books showing off your knowledge of the market and building trust in the eyes of your subscribers for your business.

To get the software to run a list, you can use one of several free services on the Net. One is MSN's ListBot (www.listbot.com) and another is eGroups (www.eGroups.com).

With eGroups you can set up your own private discussion list for your shoppers. Your shoppers can send and receive emails, schedule meetings, share files and photos, or have private group chats.

There are three types of discussion lists:

- Unmoderated discussion lists

- Discussion list digests

- Moderated discussion lists

An unmoderated discussion list sends all messages received out to all members of the list. If the number of members on the list is small and the list is not very active, then this is not be a problem.

Those who register with Delphi.com enjoy personalized features like their own My Forums page, which keeps track of the communities they participate in. Users who participate in message board discussions also get email notification when somebody replies to their messages and when there are new messages in the Forums they're interested in. Delphi.com also offers Profiles, where members can post an image and personal information to share with others.

Delphi Forums earns revenue by selling advertising on its site. It offers a unique advertising model in which users entering Delphi Forums are presented with a choice of advertisers. After the session ends, the visitor can choose to use more interactive methods, such as pop-up windows, to continue looking at products from selected merchants.

Who Builds an Online Community?

Keep in mind that an e-business doesn't build an online community—the users do. To have a successful community at your e-business, the community features must reflect the users' point of view. The users define the subject matter—you respond to it.

What's a Killer App?

A *killer app*, short for killer application, is a software program that makes performing a function or task exceptionally easy. Killer apps are the kind of programs that make you wonder how you ever got along without them. But it could also mean the application of a concept like interactive community or specialized content.

But if the list is large and very active, it could generate hundreds of messages a day and swamp the users of the list.

One solution is to create a list digest. The digest collects all the messages sent to the list first, then bundles them, and emails them—in one email—to the list members. The digest can be either daily or weekly.

Another way to cut down on the number of emails to the list is to have a moderated discussion list. You'll find that the free services only provide what's called unmoderated discussion lists. That means that all posts that are sent to the list appear without any review. If you want to control what is said on the list or the number of posts sent to the list, you need to bring the software in-house.

Web Marketing Today (`www.wilsonweb.com/reviews/ free-lists.htm`) has a good review of free mailing list programs. They review eGroups.com, OneList.com, Topica.com, and ListBot.com. The review explains the main features and points out differences and advantages of each.

Communities and the Wireless Web

Are online communities only relevant to site-centric e-businesses? Far from it. It fact, community might turn out to be the *killer app* that drives the wireless Net.

At least, Joe Cothrel, vice president of research at Participate.com (`www.participate.com`), thinks so. He states that most of the attention of the wireless application developers today is focused on content—what to deliver, how to deliver it, and how to make money doing it. But he's not at all certain that content is the killer app that will drive widespread adoption of the wireless Net. And there's a good historical basis for doubting. Just look at how the Net developed. Initially content was king, but it was later followed by all kinds of interactive community elements like discussion boards, live chat, instant messaging, and email discussion lists.

Cothrel thinks the wireless Net will follow a similar evolution.

Like the broadband connections to the Net that are always on, wireless online community members will be always accessible, because communities will always be using their cell phones, PDAs, and pagers. This will take the instant messaging service of today to the nth degree. In fact, a company in Japan is already doing it.

A wireless operator in Japan offers a mobile dating service called Cupid. When two Cupid customers are in the same geographic area, their cell phones sound an alert. They can then arrange an instant date. Add to this the capability to screen a profile ahead of time and you have the instant equivalent of the Web dating services.

Even users themselves will devise new ways for community interaction. Cothrel notes that a short messaging service, which allows users to send and receive text messages from a wireless phone, was added to the global system for mobile communication protocol almost as an afterthought.

Without major marketing efforts from either network operators or phone manufacturers, Single Messaging System (SMS) usage—similar to AOL Instant Messaging on a PC— reached more than one billion messages per month last year in the European market.

Is your e-business ready to capitalize on this new form of community interaction?

Adding content and community elements to your e-business is not the only way to drive customers to your site. One of the best cost-effective methods of driving traffic to your e-business is viral marketing.

Viral Marketing

The best kind of marketing is the kind you don't have to do yourself. And that's the beauty and power of viral marketing. Viral marketing is just like it sounds. It's word-of-mouth advertising, spawning, self-propagating, and organic.

Communication through word-of-mouth was the world's first form of marketing. Viral marketing is just the Internet equivalent of I'll tell two people, and they'll tell two people, and so on. But the Internet has taken this organic form of marketing to new heights by making communications better and communities of people tighter—thus making word-of-mouth even more effective. When you use viral marketing as a tool, you're using the Net creatively, the way it was meant to used.

Venture capital firm Draper Fisher Jurvetson supposedly coined the term viral marketing in 1998. With viral marketing, word-of-mouth advertising turns into word-of-Net advertising. According to a December 1999 Jupiter Communications survey, 80% of all online companies benefit from some form of viral marketing. Of the people who receive the viral messages, 91% pass them on to at least one other person and nearly half are likely to pass that message on to two or three others.

Viral marketing on the Net has a long history. The first use was by Netscape. The small "Designed for Netscape" icon was first used as a status symbol by Webmasters to show that their site was the latest in Web page design. It didn't take Mr. Gates very long to see the power of viral marketing and soon "Designed for MS Internet Explorer" icons quickly spawned next to Netscape's.

A couple of years later, the creative marketers at Amazon took viral marketing beyond this simple link. When Amazon created the first affiliate program on the Net, they spawned a whole new generation of viral partners eager to promote Amazon's book site to their Web site visitors. Today, they have hundreds of thousands of affiliates promoting Amazon and gaining a small commission on each sale directed to them.

But you don't need to have a costly or complex affiliate program to benefit from viral marketing in your business. There are other ways to motivate your customers and visitors to do the marketing for you.

Viral Tactics

The granddaddy of the new viral marketing has to be Hotmail which was soon copied by Yahoo! and anyone else who had a free email service. It was simple. Attach your URL to every email that your users send out. Before they knew it, Hotmail had more email users than the largest ISP. You can do the same. Make sure that every email sent out from your company has your URL on it. Or create a funny newsletter or an email virus alert that people would pass on to friends.

Get Your Visitors to Market You

Here's a good idea to spread the word about your Web store. Ask visitors who like what you offer to email your URL to a friend along with their comments. Place a form on your Web site that can be filled out by visitors and emailed to any address they enter. If you want a free service that does this and is easy to place on your site, check out Recommend It! (www.recommend-it.com).

Another way to get your message passed along is to reward your steady visitors for bringing new visitors to your site. Create a special referrer program that your steady visitors can sign up for. Have them invite their friends to visit and if they do, have them mention the referrer's email address and the referrer earns something free from your site.

Finally, don't just send out a notice about new content on your site—send out summaries by email and ask people to forward it on (with copyright and URL attached, of course). A variation on this is to let other sites reprint your content on their site, with appropriate credits and links to yours.

But viral marketing can be a doubled edged sword. The downside to viral marketing is that you're letting others do your marketing for you. Although this will save you money, your message and your brand are in the hands of some one else. There's a fine line here of spreading the word and diluting your brand. But, if you master this technique, your message and your site can spread as quickly as the common cold.

Don't expect a viral marketing program to pay off immediately. Like a real virus, computer viruses don't become epidemics until they reach critical mass. Your virus must propagate through the host population until it reaches a certain threshold of visibility and scale.

Think of it this way. Suppose a real-world virus doubles every year. In the first few years it's scarcely detectable. But within a few years after that it suddenly becomes an epidemic. You should understand that you're playing the same game. Viral marketing takes time. So be patient, be fruitful—and go out and multiply!

CHAPTER 12

Permission Marketing

Email marketing is one of the key marketing strategies that e-businesses are using on the Internet today. But not all emails to consumers are created equal. Without gaining the permission of the people you email to, your email marketing campaign could easily be perceived as unsolicited spam—and spam is the bane of any good email marketing program.

Although sales are made from spamming email addresses, your e-business reputation can be harmed in the process. Permission marketing means getting the consumer's permission to email an offer before it shows up in the email box—and just as easily, offering the recipient the ability to be easily removed for your mailing list. It also means protecting consumer privacy—don't give consumers' email addresses to other marketing companies.

With this in mind, you should consider outsourcing your email marketing and list management to a third-party source that specializes in managing email marketing programs. Don't do email marketing in a vacuum. Treat your mailings as part of an integral marketing program. Make sure that everyone in your organization is kept up-to-date with the information that you send. Finally, selling products isn't the only use of direct email marketing—you can use it to sell services, too.

W hat could be better than a marketing piece that's easy to use, that costs no money to produce, that costs next to nothing to send, and that reaches millions of prospects in a matter of minutes? That's email marketing, one the most cost-effective ways for an e-business to market goods and services to potential consumers. There simply isn't an easier, cheaper, or more direct way to reach your customer.

Although it sounds easy, email marketing does take a lot of work to do it right. You must start from a clean email list of people who have confirmed their willingness to receive your email offer, and then you must target and personalize that offer for the best response.

Just how important is email marketing to an e-business? Because of its cost-effectiveness, it's becoming more important as time goes by (see Table 12.1). According to Forrester Research, 77% of e-marketers send email to customers; by 2004, Forrester predicts that U.S. e-marketers will send almost 210 billion emails a year to people who want them. And that's the most important part of email marketing—sending only to those who have asked to receive your offers.

The opposite of responsible, or *opt-in*, email marketing is *spam*. Spam is the bane of any good email marketing program. Although sales can be made from spamming email addresses, your e-business's reputation can be harmed in the process.

Table 12.1

Type of Sites That Send Marketing Email	
Type of Business	Percentage That Use Email
Consumable products	50%
Personal interests	45%
Computers and electronics	43%
Fashion and style	43%
Collectibles and hobbies	41%
Toys, games, and entertainment	38%
Investments	38%

What's Opt-In Email?

Opt-in email is the direct opposite of spam. People who opt in to an email list have said in advance that they are willing to receive unsolicited email from companies on the Net that meet the list criteria. For example, someone who wants to be kept informed of newly released software might opt in to an email list that announces new software products.

What's Spam?

Spam is unsolicited email, the junk mail of the twenty-first century. It clogs email servers around the world and sucks up needed bandwidth on the Net, and it's the quickest way to create a bad reputation for you, your company, and your product.

Table 12.1   (continued)

| Type of Sites That Send Marketing Email | |
Type of Business	Percentage That Use Email
Office supplies	37%
Travel and entertainment	32%

Source: ActiveMedia Research

So, before you plan your grandiose email marketing scheme, be aware that opt-in email marketing is really permission marketing. It's a good idea to find out how to get that permission and how to get the best results.

Best Practices of Permission Marketing

Companies that want to grow and sustain a profitable Internet business will have permission-based email as a key ingredient of their marketing mix.

A recent study by FloNetwork, Inc., (http://www.FloNetwork.com) reported a sampling of 1,011 Internet users who were asked how they learned about the goods and services offered by Internet merchants. Nearly 60% said that they usually find out about new products, services, or promotions offered by their favorite online merchants via permission-based email. FloNetwork reports that this is twice as high as banner ads and 11 times higher than magazines and TV advertisements combined. In addition, according to the study, 73% of online buyers listed email as the medium of choice for notifications. In addition, those consumers who purchase from the same online merchant on more than one occasion said that they were even more likely to prefer permission-based email than one-time buyers.

So, just what is meant by permission marketing? Permission marketing means getting the consumer's permission to send emails about an offer *before* your message shows up in the email box.

It works like this: When a consumer visits a permission marketing-enabled e-business and registers or buys something from it, the consumer is asked, "Would you like to receive information from us periodically about new sales, or receive our newsletter?" The consumer then responds with either a "yes" or a "no" by clicking in a box. If the answer is "yes," the consumer has given permission. If it's "no," the customer hasn't.

This process seems very simple, but that's not all.

First, if the consumer wants to opt out of your email marketing pieces, he or she should be able to do so easily by visiting your e-business. Either set up an automated process that automatically removes an email address from your database when a recipient emails it, or create a separate opt-out URL on your site that recipients can visit to remove their email addresses from your list.

Second, the consumer gave *you* permission to send emails, not anyone else. Don't give or sell customers' email address—that is, their permission to be emailed—to any other company or person.

So, how can you get the permission of consumers? You can offer them a chance to win a prize in exchange for their email address. Or, you can offer them points that they can exchange for products after they've accumulated enough of them.

Paying people for permission is what made Cybergold (`www.cybergold.com`) a success. It pays cold, hard cash to consumers for visiting its member Web sites. Recently, it ran ads on bus boards showing a young man or woman saying, "I got paid for doing it." The ads were pulled after receiving less than favorable press coverage that they were sexist. Still, the message was right on target. In permission marketing, you *get* by *giving*. And while spammers are currently getting good response rates on their email blasts, that's changing fast. Consumers are wising up and are demanding that the spammers be curbed.

If you're thinking about spamming, think about this first: Antispammers rarely complain just to their Internet service provider (ISP). They complain to *your* ISP, your ISP's backbone provider, and just about everyone else in between you and the electronic path to the recipient. These providers will often terminate your Net connection, if just to stop the complaints.

If losing your Internet connection is not scary enough, then listen to this: The Mail Abuse Prevention System (`www.mailabuse.org`), which runs the Realtime Blackhole List (RBL), has compiled a list of *IP addresses* of known spammers and offers this list to subscribers. And who are these subscribers? Email administrators.

Don't Pre-Check Permission

When collecting information from the consumer as a way to build your customer database, make sure that you ask permission to send emails. Even if a customer has bought from you previously, has answered a survey for a free gift, or has given you information for whatever reason, you still should provide a check box on the form asking if that person would like to receive further emails from you. Do *not* automatically pre-check the box; have the customer check it manually.

What's an IP Address?

An *IP address* is a unique 32-bit Internet address consisting of four numbers, separated by dots (such as 209.12.152.00). Every server connected directly to the Internet has an IP number.

Using the RBL list, these administrators reject any email that originates from those IP addresses. That's right, *any email*—not just *bulk* email.

You're probably thinking that the RBL list includes only pornography sites and get-rich-quick spammers. It doesn't. It also includes what the antispam community calls "mainsleaze," a combination of mainstream and sleaze. These are legitimate companies that use questionable email practices. That is, they don't use opt-in email lists—or, in other words, permission marketing.

Obviously, getting permission is extremely important for your email marketing strategy and the reputation of your e-business.

Permission Marketing Elements

Although permission email marketing is one of the most cost-effective tools that marketers have ever known, mass emailing campaigns can damage your company's brand credibility and provoke consumer hostility, if they're used improperly.

So how do you do it right? Based on an email marketing practices survey of 400 email users and 200 marketers, IMT Strategies (http://www.imtstrategies.com) recommends the following eight best practices for leveraging the potential of permission email while avoiding the pitfalls of spam:

- **Gain active consent**—Make it clear that consumers are agreeing to a permission email relationship. What you want to avoid is consumers feeling that they were tricked into a relationship. Remember, over the long run, opt-in strategies lead to higher response rates and lower overall list management costs, even though having the consumer consciously and deliberately agree to receive email offers from you builds an email list slower.

- **Deepen personalization**—Personalize your email messages—make sure that your offer matches the recipient's interests. Not only include the name of your recipient in the message, but also target that person by going deeper into his or her consumer profile to create relevant content, products, and offers. This will help you maintain permission list loyalty and increase your response rates. In other words, don't send steak offers to vegetarians.

- **Recognize levels of permission**—Although you should permit consumers to opt out of the marketing relationship with each email message sent, forcing your consumers into a strictly "on" or "off" marketing relationship is unnecessarily limiting. Customize your e-marketing offerings. Allow consumers to choose among a menu of different email offerings, such as a newsletter, discount offers, and product-specific updates. Give consumers the ability to convey specific information about their interests and the frequency that they would like to receive your offers.

- **Deploy reminder services**—More than half of the leading marketers that IMT Strategies surveyed have already experimented with reminder services and scheduled alert programs, including event reminders (for birthdays, for example), replenishment (for refills and upgrades, for example), and service ticklers (for scheduled maintenance, for example). Research showed that 33% of email users have registered for reminder services.

- **Expand use of advocacy**—Join the 50% of leading marketers who are experimenting with viral marketing. Leverage the trust that prospects have for recommendations from friends about new Web sites. Keep in mind that more than 75% of consumers report that they have received online referrals from trusted acquaintances. More importantly, 20% of email users surveyed cited word-of-mouth as their primary means of discovering new Web sites, after search engines and random surfing, and well ahead of marketing strategies requiring actual expenditures of cash for Web banners or TV and print ads.

- **Adopt cross-brand/cross-vendor programs**—Pursue co-marketing promotional strategies across brands and with partner companies as part of your email marketing practice. Developing these programs enables you to realize higher levels of trust within your core consumer communities, reach new consumer communities, and create marketing leverage.

Cross-brand and cross-vendor programs also enable you to expand the breadth and value of permission email campaigns by cross-fertilizing permission communities with a broader range of offers, content, and solutions.

- **Measure performance and return on investment**—Any campaign is only as good as its return on investment. Identify the overall response rate for a given campaign, and track responses to the level of individual consumer profiles so that you can target future campaigns to segments that have exhibited certain buying or response behavior in the past.

- **Improve frequency management**—Different consumers expect to receive emails at different times. Align the frequency of email contact with your consumer's expectations and needs. Their frequency expectations vary significantly by circumstance, ranging from daily or weekly offers to only once a month—and only when the offers are relevant to their needs and interests.

Sustained high volumes of untargeted email communications will cause consumers to withdraw their consent to the marketing relationship.

Managing and Prospecting with Email Lists

Strictly speaking, any marketing message sent by email is email marketing. Managing your email marketing efforts takes some thought and planning.

Any email program, such as Microsoft Outlook, Eudora, or Netscape Messenger, can be used to send out email marketing messages. But if your list is large or you want to target specific offers to specific groups of recipients, these programs will limit your email marketing campaigns. Building a sophisticated email marketing system in-house requires a database server and an email server, both different from your Web server from which you serve your Web site.

Another alternative is to outsource the management of your email marketing efforts. Companies such as Message Media (www.messagemedia.com) will build and manage your opt-in email lists and send customized messages when needed; they can send email messages in either text or HTML formats. Or, if you want to operate your own email marketing system, you can install UnityMail. UnityMail is Message Media's email marketing software that links directly to your database. With UnityMail, you can send individualized, focused email campaigns, with trackable URLs, to your customers and prospects.

Of course, to run any email marketing campaign, you'll need an email list. You can either build your own through visitors to your e-business or rent opt-in email lists to use—or you can do both. Even if you do have a house list that you use for emails, you can use the services of the opt-in list companies on the Internet to prospect for new customers. If you want to email responsibly, first turn to these sites to purchase targeted opt-in lists.

When renting an outside, third party opt-in email list, I strongly suggest that the company you're renting the list from use a double opt-in process to create their lists. A double opt-in process means that consumers who sign up to be list members are emailed a confirmation by the creator of the list. Recipients of the confirmation emails must confirm that they want to be part of the database *before* they are added.

Many list rental companies do not do this because it's time consuming but it is the only way you can be sure that recipients of your rented email list really want to have emails sent to them.

The first company to collect, categorize, and offer for sale non-spam opt-in email lists was NetCreations (www.netcreations.com) formerly known as PostMasterDirect. If you're looking for numbers, this is the place. NetCreations works with more than 250 partner Web sites that ask visitors if they'd like to receive mailings on certain topics. NetCreations uses a "double opt-in" process and you can choose from more than 10 million opt-in email addresses in more than 3,000 categories.

Stay Up-to-Date with Email Marketing

The Direct E-Mail List Source (www.copywriter.com/lists/index.htm) is a directory of voluntary email marketing lists. This is a resource for opt-in lists, newsletters, email discussion lists, advertiser-supported email services, and email list brokers where you can advertise without spamming.

Heads Up

Want to keep up on the newest happenings in the New Economy? Then check out the New Economy Index at www.neweconomyindex.org. This site provides a set of economic indicators specifically geared to the New Economy gathered from both private and public sources.

Bulletmail (www.bulletmail.com) gives you a choice of more than 100 targeted, opt-in email lists not available elsewhere. This company also targets your market by email in a Net-appropriate manner. In addition, it includes an unlimited number of hotlinks in your email message that transport the consumer to your site offer and even your own email box. If you want to send emails using demographic information, then check out Targ-It (www.targ-it.com). This company's lists are all 100% opt-in, and more than 350 lists are available for purchase.

And here's an important point to remember: Don't do email marketing in a vacuum. Treat your mailings as part of an integral marketing program. Make sure that everyone in your organization is kept up-to-date with the information that you send so that they're fully prepared to respond to inquiries. Nothing looks worse to a consumer who has just received an offer than to contact your company and reach someone who doesn't have a clue what that customer is talking about.

Finally, keep in mind that 5% of your email addresses will become obsolete each month. Make sure that your mailing campaign collects all the bounced-back emails and places them in a database. Try to remail to these bounce-backs. Sometimes the email addresses are good but did not reach the recipient because of network problems or outages. If the messages still bounce back after the remail, remove the addresses from your mailing list.

Prevention is always better than reaction, so give the recipients in your database a way to notify you if their email addresses change by

CASE STUDY

SMARTERKIDS.COM

SmarterKids.com provides parents of children from birth to 14 years old with the information, advice, and tools that they need to find the best educational products and services for their individual children. SmarterKids.com uses a sophisticated, patent-pending product evaluation and recommendation process to analyze each product on the site. SmarterKids.com identifies which educational skills a product covers, how well it covers these skills, what educational approach it

takes, which learning styles it supports, how and when it is best used, and more.

When SmarterKids.com decided to do an email marketing campaign, it decided to rent a list from a third-party source. The company turned to PostMasterDirect.com (now called NetCreations [www.netcreations.com]), an opt-in email marketing site, to conduct the campaign. Companies that used PostMasterDirect.com's services saw an average of 5% to 15% click-through rates, and conversion rates of anywhere between 5%

sending them to a maintenance page on your Web site. On the maintenance page, users should be able to change their email address, update their personal profile, and perform other house-keeping items that can keep your email marketing database up-to-date.

Crafting Your Direct Email Message

Direct email is one of the most cost-efficient ways to advertise. If you're not careful, however, it could be one of the most costly advertising mistakes you can make.

First, consider the format of your email. Although more email reader programs now can display HTML, a large percentage of Net users (including more than 20 million America Online subscribers) can read only text messages, so consider using ASCII text only.

Next, keep your message simple and short. Deliver your most important information up-front. People don't have a lot of time, so you have to grab their attention in the first few lines of your message. People scan the subject lines of their emails first, so make sure the subject line of your message grabs the attention of the reader. If the subject line is compelling, they'll open your message.

Remember to include enough whitespace in your messages as well. Too much text will make the email look cluttered and unappealing. Also be careful with capital letters—don't overuse them in your message. Remember, in netiquette, using all caps is

and 20%, depending on the offer. For the past year, SmarterKids.com regularly has been sending mailings to PostMasterDirect.com members.

SmarterKids.com started mailing about twice a month to 100,000 opt-in email addresses. It usually sends out an offer that contains some sort of incentive for first-time customers, such as free children's CD-ROM with a purchase of a certain amount. SmarterKids.com pays PostMasterDirect.com

anywhere from 10 to 35 cents per name, depending on the list.

Seventy percent of SmarterKids.com's overall marketing budget is devoted to online marketing, most of which is allotted to email marketing. The agreement with PostMasterDirect.com is a large part of that email marketing strategy. Click-through and conversion rates are good enough that SmarterKids.com continues to rent lists from PostMasterDirect.com.

Direct Email Should Catch the Eye

When sending out a direct email piece, do *not* use the words "free" or "buy now" in your message. This is a sure way to get your email message sent to the trash bin. Take the time to explain your offer without the hype, and remember to play up benefits for the customer, not features. Consumers are not interested in what a product does (the features) but what it does for them (the benefits).

the equivalent of yelling. Finally, try to make your pitch easy to scan and read, and use wide margins with 64 characters or less per line. This helps make your message readable with many different email programs.

Finally, before you roll out your email campaign to a full list, test each element of your message one at a time to selected portions of your list. Test the subject line or headline. Select a test set of names, and see what the response is from your test sample of emails. Then test the body of the message, the layout, and even any P.S. at the end. After you've determined what works—that is, did you get the response you expected—then send your message to the full list.

When executing an email campaign you should keep these key rules of direct emailing in mind:

- **Identify yourself**—Let your prospective customers know who you are right up-front. If you've rented an opt-in list, remind them that they opted in. Include a sentence reminding them why they're receiving your email. Also, if you're mailing to a another business, send your email from either a real person in your company or at least an alias with a title.

- **Always provide a "from" address**—Give the recipient a valid address to which he or she can reply.

- **Keep the subject line short but descriptive**—The subject line is the outer envelope of an email campaign. This is the vehicle that decides whether your message will be read, so your choice of words—and the length of the heading—is critical. Keep the number of words in the subject line to no more than 35 characters.

- **Keep the message short**—A good rule of thumb is to keep this less than one page: Email is most effective when it's short and simple. After you introduce yourself, give a brief description of your offer. Capture the consumers' attention in the first two or three lines. Within the offer, give them a link to click, or refer them to the URL of the buying page. Keep the message within 500 words.

- **Provide value for their time**—Make it a compelling or a limited-time offer. Offer something that customers couldn't already buy from your site, perhaps an exclusive offer made only through your email. Offer coupons or a free sample. According to Forrester Research, two-thirds of consumers like free samples, but only one third of merchants offer them.

- **Be ready to apologize**—Customers sometimes forget that they opted into the list, or their tastes or needs might have changed. So, inform the recipients that they've chosen to hear from you. Many times people who opt-in to receive email from companies forget that they did so and consider messages from these companies as spam. If they complain or ask to be removed from your list, respond quickly and politely.

- **Make it easy to unsubscribe**—Place your unsubscribe instructions both at the beginning and at the end of your email message. Don't make customers call a phone number to unsubscribe; give them a link to go to quickly and easily. The unsubscribe process should be both fast and simple.

Using Email to Sell Services

Selling products isn't the only use of direct email marketing—you can use it to sell services, too. This type of email marketing is called electronic invitation services or invite sites.

Here's how it works: You create an email invitation and then send it to those on your mailing list. Recipients receive the invite and can either respond from their email program or click on a link embedded in the message to open a Web browser that takes them to the offer page.

On the notification page or in the email message—depending on the procedures of the invitation service—is a button to click for payment. The recipient enters a credit card number, which is transmitted over a secure server to the invitation service, where it's collected. The service cuts a check for the amount gathered and mails it to you. Some services charge handling fee or credit card processing fees, while others do all this for free.

For what services can these be used? Some services include seminars and workshops, PowerPoint training sessions, concert promotions, and services that collect an annual membership fee. If your e-business sells activities, tickets, bookings, or memberships, or if it requires that a customer prepay for the service, you may find an invitation service useful.

An example of such a service is Acteva (`www.acteva.com`). Companies selling services or events list their services on this site. Visitors can search for, find, and pay for services there. You can list your service in Acteva's database so that it's accessible to anyone who visits the site, or you can send email invitations (Acteva calls them "prevites") to your customers.

If you're a click-and-mortar company sending snail mail postcards to remind your customers of an upcoming event or service offer, or if you want to find new customers, you can use e-invites. Not only will costs drop, but you'll also be putting a Buy button in front of customers' noses. They don't have to call for a reservation or ticket, and because you get the cash before the event, you're relatively sure about attendance.

Best of all, you don't have to set up an e-commerce site with complicated code to take bookings, or sign up for a merchant account to get the money. In other words, you can use these sites' own commerce capabilities to handle your monetary transactions.

One final thought on permission marketing: Permission marketing is a powerful tool in your marketing toolbox to build customer loyalty and repeat business. Remember, though, that this means asking not what you can do *to* your customers, but what you can do *for* them.

CHAPTER 13

Marketing Opportunities of the Future

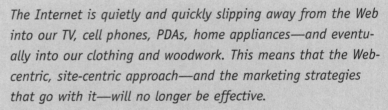

The Internet is quietly and quickly slipping away from the Web into our TV, cell phones, PDAs, home appliances—and eventually into our clothing and woodwork. This means that the Web-centric, site-centric approach—and the marketing strategies that go with it—will no longer be effective.

The proliferation of selling channels and the growing customer demand for personalization are marketing challenges that cannot be ignored. The goods and services that you sell must be packaged, marketed, sold, and serviced through a growing number of sales channels. This will be the determining factor in who wins or loses the e-commerce game. What your e-business sells must be channel-transparent—your goods and services sold through any Net-enabled device or channel of distribution—to the consumer and then must be configured to individual needs. In addition, price-competitive offers will come to them, and everything they own will be plugged into the Net. Consumers will connect to this digital network at any time, from anywhere to purchase anything, any way they'd like. As an e-marketer, you must be prepared for this.

In addition, the price of goods and services is being increasingly commoditized. The solution to this unrelenting commoditization is to add value to products and services by telling compelling stories tied to the product or service.

On his deathbed, Edmund Gween, a famous Hollywood actor, was asked if it was hard to die. He replied, "Dying is easy. Comedy is hard." I would apply that to e-commerce, too.

As I write this, dot-coms are having a miserable time. Most of their stocks are trading 50% to 80% off their highs, and many of them are trading below their IPO price. Gartner Group CEO Michael Fleishe recently predicted that 95% to 98% of dot-com companies will fail by 2002. Even the poster child of e-commerce, Amazon.com, may be headed for a fall. A noted security analyst predicted in June 2000 that based on cash flow reports and interest payments on its debt, Amazon would run out of cash by 2001.

But that's the problem with dot-coms. The majority of them *are* dot-coms, and they think like dot-coms. But as I said before, that type of thinking is passé. Any e-business that relies on a site-centric, Web-centric, PC-centric, U.S.-centric, and English-centric marketing strategy is doomed to fail or be quietly absorbed by more successful companies.

The terrain is shifting fast, and the business challenge—and marketing opportunity—for your e-business is now to sell anything, anywhere, any way, any time, at any price.

The Marketing Challenges

The Internet is quietly and quickly slipping away from the Web into our TVs, cell phones, PDAs, and home appliances—and eventually into our clothing and woodwork. In the near future, new technologies will make the Internet completely invisible to the user. Thus, the Web-centric, site-centric approach—and the marketing strategies associated with it—will no longer be effective.

Ultimately, all long-distance traffic over the Net will be fiber, and all short-distance traffic will be wireless. This means that any and all devices with a computer chip embedded in them can be connected to each other and can communicate with each other over the Net.

Will we all look like roving techno-geeks with Batman belts carrying an array of wireless net-enabled devices? Not really. All these devices will probably be collapsed into just a few devices that can serve as our digital wallet, address book, calendar, cell phone,

The Internet Is Not Like It Used to Be

The typical narrow view of the future of the Net is described as being 50% American, 40% European, 5% Japanese and Korean, and 5% the rest of the world. But that's not so. Be prepared for the rest of the world. Within three years, the developing world will represent more than 50% of the Net, and three years after that, the most widely used language on the Net could be Chinese. (Source: Nicholas Negroponte; *Time* Magazine)

email box, digital pager, and more. The capability to reach and market to consumers through these devices will give e-businesses the opportunity to sell goods and services whenever and wherever the consumer may be.

For example, consider our current willingness to use wireless technologies. Research shows that most car buyers are comfortable and experienced in using new interactive communication technologies in their daily life. Because most people spend a significant amount of time commuting in stop-and-go traffic every day, in-vehicle voice-operated Internet access might be a useful alternative to the passive radio. In Table 13.1, you can see how very few people object outright to accessing the Internet, at a reasonable cost, while driving.

Table 13.1

Interest in Vehicle Internet Access						
Price	Over $25	$25	$20	$15	$10	$5
Favor	8.3%	14.7%	23.1%	32.1%	37.5%	48.3%
Oppose	68.2%	47.9%	26.9%	19.7%	16.1%	9.4%
Don't Know	23.5%	37.4%	50.0%	48.2%	46.4%	42.3%

Source: CNW Market Research

The proliferation of selling channels and the growing customer demand for personalization are marketing challenges that cannot be ignored. The goods and services that you sell must be packaged, marketed, sold, and serviced through a growing number of sales channels. This will be the determining factor in who wins or loses the e-commerce game.

The bottom line is this: Your e-business must expand its view to include any and all of these possibilities, which will affect whatever marketing strategy you may have, whether it's clicks and bricks, flips and bricks, or wired and wireless. What your e-business sells must be channel-transparent—your goods and services sold through any Net-enabled device or channel of distribution—to the consumer and then must be configured to individual needs.

Challenges to any and all current marketing strategies are already underway, and as an e-business, you should prepare for them. The popular view of the Net that most e-businesses hold is quite narrow in focus. Will your company be prepared to market over a multi-channel Internet that will become invisible to the consumer, who will demand a more customized and personalized experience?

The next sections discuss just two examples that will shake up the current narrowly focused view of the Net and how it will affect your e-marketing efforts over the next one to two years: free riding and scan shopping.

The Free Ride

The first example of shaking up the current narrowly focused view of the Net is *free riding*. Free riding had been around since the inception of direct commerce, but with the development of the Net, it has taken on a whole new perspective.

In a nutshell this is how free riding works: Let's say that a consumer gets the *MP3* bug and heads over to his local Best Buy store to purchase an MP3 player. Because the MP3 thing is new to him, he seeks assistance from one of Best Buy's knowledgeable sales clerks. Maintaining a staff costs money for Best Buy, so the sales clerk's salary is reflected in Best Buy's prices. The consumer feels that he could get it cheaper at Buy.com (www.buy.com), so he goes home, looks up the MP3 player on the Net, and orders it.

What he has done, of course, is free-ride off Best Buy. He got advice from the sales clerk and maybe even the opportunity to demonstrate the different MP3 players. Consumers will do this with lots of products, especially those that people like to touch or try before buying, such as furniture or clothes. One downside to free riding, of course, is the inconvenience. The consumer has to leave the store, search the Net, and buy the product on the PC. So, up until now, free riding has been kept, more or less, in check.

That's about to change—and with that change comes a major marketing opportunity for your e-business if it can be where and when the consumer is ready to buy.

Competition Can Come from Anywhere

Your competition can come from anywhere or nowhere—all at the same time. Your e-business must expand its view of the market to more than one dimension. Consider financial institutions such as banks. They should take into account competition from nonfinancial institutions such as Microsoft and Intuit.

What's Free Riding?

The act of seeking sales assistance from a brick-and-mortar store on a product, then going to the Net to shop for and buy it at a better price.

What's MP3?

Technically speaking, MP3 is the file extension for MPEG, audio layer 3. Because MP3 files are small, they can easily be transferred across the Internet. MP3 files can be very controversial because copyrighted songs can be sold and distributed illegally off of Web sites.

I'm talking about m-commerce here. Allen Weiss writes in *Upside* magazine that the exploding wireless communications market will change the retailer landscape. Potentially, a customer armed with a Net-enabled wireless device could easily free-ride off a brick-and-mortar company by simultaneously using the store's service and looking at auction sites, buying groups, and online stores to purchase the product.

In the example with the MP3 consumer, if the sales clerk convinces him that a particular MP3 player is the one for him, he can pick up his wireless device and check the online merchants. If the price is right, he buys online.

How soon will this happen? It's happening now. Many e-commerce players are already going wireless. Online retailers such as Barnesandnoble.com and Amazon.com are porting to wireless devices, as are comparison-buying guides and services such as eCompare.com and DealTime.com. Will your e-business be accessible by consumers on the go from their Net-enabled devices?

Furthermore, if the wireless crowd is right, consumers won't have to deliberately comparison-shop for products from a brick-and-mortar store wireless. Price-competitive offers will come to them. Using GPS technology, companies could send customer messages based on who is using the service and where that individual is located. Let's say that you're in Tower Records looking to buy a new CD. While you're talking to the sales clerk, your cell phone rings and sends you a message about an auction for CDs going on at eBay, or even a special sale at CDNow. Using wireless m-commerce in this way lets an e-business market to consumers when and where they're ready to buy.

In this instance, there's no need for a Web site or a contrived URL. But there's a real need to learn how to market through Net-enabled devices.

Scan Shopping

The second example of shaking up the current narrowly focused view of the Net is *scan shopping*. You've seen those signs on vacant billboards along the highway with the words "Your Company Here"

Yahoo! Moves Closer to Being Wireless

Yahoo! recently created wireless versions of its auction, movie listings, and Web directory for delivering Internet content to mobile phones and other portable devices. The new services can be accessed on any mobile phone or device that supports Wireless Application Protocol (WAP) and can add to Yahoo!'s existing wireless offerings, which include email, stock quotes, news, and calendaring.

plastered across them. Now can you see your Web site on a can of peas?

Although primitive, a company called BarPoint (`www.barpoint.com`) is already putting scan shopping to use. A consumer can take a bar code number from a product, go to BarPoint's site, and enter it. BarPoint then provides complete and accurate information on that product. It even offers a BarPoint Shopper Web Clipping Application for the Palm VII. With it, you can get product-specific information right from the palm of your hand.

That's just price comparison—but can you buy? Yes you can. Motorola has joined a group of firms in a new venture to allow consumers to use their cell phones or PDAs to scan bar codes off magazine ads or products and connect to companies via the Net. Using a new technology being developed by the firms, consumers will not have to type in Web addresses (*URLs*) to get information or conduct a transaction. The technology will provide an open interface that will allow developers to create unique bar codes that contain instructions for executing tasks.

This means that "Web codes" can be embedded into products; printed in ads in newspapers, magazines, or posters; or even shown on television. Just scan a Web code into a bar code scanner-enabled device, and a command will be sent instructing the e-business to send information back to the user. This would allow consumers to order products, get additional product information, compare prices, get directions, or even pay bills.

For instance, a bookstore could run an ad in the newspaper for a book with a "purchase now" Web code at the bottom of the ad. When a consumer clicks on that code with a device, the book will be ordered instantly at the price advertised, using the consumer's personal data already stored on that device. In this example, there's no need for a URL—or even a Web site, for that matter.

The Marketing Opportunities

In the June 19, 2000, issue of *Time* magazine, the editors reported on the future of technology. They spoke of smart cars, uppity robots, and cybersex—pretty much of what we've all heard before.

What Is Scan Shopping?

Scan shopping is the use of specially encoded bar codes on products and in printed periodicals; when scanned with a special bar code reader, connected to a Net-enabled device, the consumer is sent directly to a Web page. Some companies offering this technology are Planet Portal (`www.planetportal.com`), GoCode (`www.gocode.com`), and Digimarc (`www.digimarc.com`).

What's a URL?

URL stands for uniform resource locator. It's the address of any resource on the World Wide Web, such as your Web store's home page: `http://www.your_business_name.com`.

However, the magazine did offer to the reader a vision of a digital future in which everything that was wired becomes wireless, and in which atoms are replaced by bits. The article spoke of micro-wireless devices implanted in our radios, cars, TVs, washing machines, car keys, pagers, and hundreds of other everyday devices, communicating with each other, and sending instructions to other devices on our behalf.

According to *Time*, these new smart devices will have wireless identification tags that look like product bar codes (Web codes, perhaps?) that act as tiny computers broadcasting their status to other devices in your home. For example, your prescription bottle of pills would sense that it is running low and would broadcast this fact to your medicine cabinet. Your medicine cabinet would be connected to your local drug store, which would deliver your prescription refill automatically and on the same day by a roving band of FedEx or UPS trucks.

This is a world in the not-so-distant future in which everything we own will be plugged into the Net. We will *jack in* to this digital network anytime, from anywhere, to purchase anything in any way we'd like. As an e-marketer, you must be prepared for this.

All this Buck Rogers technology makes great print material and sells a lot of magazines, but e-marketers must be more realistic. What we're interested in are potential markets of the future that we can understand and plan for now. Technology is, in itself, not a market. Technology *creates* market opportunities.

Products—and services, in a lot of cases—are quickly losing their intrinsic value. The price of goods and services is being increasingly commoditized, not necessarily because they are commodities, but because the technology of the Net is making them so. Price comparisons are too easy to do on the Net, and with the evolution of comparison-shopping agents, it's getting even easier.

The solution to this unrelenting commoditization is to add value to products and services by telling stories tied to the product or service. Telling stories—not selling goods or services—is the marketing challenge before us. After all, isn't that what a marketer does?

What Does It Mean to Jack In?

In William Gibson's *Neuromancer,* the digital world is defined as *cyberspace.* Gibson's characters in the book enter cyberspace by jacking in from any terminal devices connected to the digital network.

So, put on your future glasses, and let's explore some of these markets of the future that storytellers—that is, e-marketers—can exploit in the future.

Markets of the Future—Telling the Right Story

There's an old marketing strategy that says, "Sell the sizzle, not the steak." That's still true today. The new sizzle is the story that you tell about your product or service.

Futurist Rolf Jensen, director of the Copenhagen Institute for Future Studies, lists several markets of the future that storytellers— that is, marketers in business—can exploit in the future: Adventures for Sale, The Market for Togetherness, The Market for Care, The Who-Am-I Market, and The Market for Peace of Mind.

- **Adventures for Sale**—Travel, entertainment, and sports will be huge markets in the future. The potential here for telling stories for entertainment and educational purposes is virtually unlimited. Fantasy sport resorts that enable visitors to do things such as play ball with Willie Mays or play tennis with Tiger Woods already exist. You can even attend seminars at Disney World that teach adults how to create animated cartoons or cook exotic meals. Extreme adventures are available for adults who enjoy the outdoors. People will travel to remote corners of Sumatra and the South Pole to experience, adventure, and consume other people's myths and stories. People will also continue to live vicariously through extreme events such as the Olympics. And if you think that all these high-energy activities are only for the young, think again. The post-war adult population will not go willingly into that dark night. They will be active participants in life, looking for new adventures well after they retire. The trick here is to tell the right adventure story around your product or service.

- **The Market for Togetherness**—The need for interpersonal relationships is a very strong human motivator. Surround your product or service with a story of friendship and love, and consumers will be drawn to your offer. Guinness, for example, no longer sells beer—it sells relationships. To this end, it currently is opening a chain of Irish pubs around the

L.L. Bean Gets It Right

L.L. Bean has the Adventure Story and marketing strategy down pat. The company doesn't promote its clothing; it promotes what you can *do* in that clothing. The story is the adventure of the outdoors.

world to sell Irish-style togetherness. Jensen sees big opportunities for exploiting togetherness through such disparate areas as theme restaurants, coffee drinking, and Net connections. A market for togetherness will quickly appear on cell phones and PDAs when instant messaging catches fire.

Staging events is another form of storytelling that e-marketers can exploit. Staging live Webcasts, netmeetings, and chat sessions around special events such as middle-school dances, bar mitzvahs, and sweet 16 parties can become marketing events that lead to memories, friendships, and the sharing of good times connected to a product or service that you offer.

- **The Market for Care**—Showing how your company cares for people, the environment, and the life forms that we share on our planet is another future market segment with a strong story to tell. Selling products or services that center on caring for children, seniors, and animals and supporting humanitarian groups such as the Salvation Army and Greenpeace can brand your company as one that cares. The Body Shop and Ben and Jerry's Ice Cream—with their support of "green consumerism"—as well as McDonald's—with its Ronald McDonald House Charities (www.rmhc.com)—leverage the market for care.

To reach the market of care, wrap your offering with a story that sells on the metaphors of goodness, beauty, liberty, fair-

HOLLYWOOD STOCK EXCHANGE

The Hollywood Stock Exchange (HSX), launched in 1996 (www.hsx.com), tells a great story around a simple entertainment site. Visitors to HSX can buy and sell virtual "shares" in movies, celebrities, and musical artists with HSX's own currency, Hollywood Dollars. They can trade these hot entertainment commodities for free, build their portfolio, check out the latest news, chat with fellow entertainment buffs, and even win prizes.

Recently, HSX has made a deal with Lions Gate Films that lets its participants get a share of the box-office proceeds from an upcoming movie. HSX hopes that the move will help the site evolve into a vehicle for investments in films.

With HSX's latest deal, Hollywood Dollars become more like real cash. For example, HSX customers who buy shares in a current movie can redeem them later for money if the movie scores $20 million at the box office in its first four weeks. Specifically, a million Hollywood Dollars buys one Audience Participation Note. If the movie you selected hits $20 million, the film's producers will give HSX $20,000 to divide among note holders.

ness, justice, or equality, and the meaning of the universe and humanity's place in it.

- **The Who Am I Market**—People like to be different. They want to know that they are unique or of a certain class shared by others, and they want others to know it. This type of market can be reached by expressing consumer personalities— their needs and desires—through the story associated with your product or service. Take Louis Vuitton: His handbag is really no different than other handbags of comparable quality. But Louis Vuitton sells the story of the luxury lifestyle. His story is a global epic—the lifestyles of the successful and famous—that overshadows price.

  Personalization is another way to reach the Who Am I market. A successful brand must cater to individuals and niche communities without conveying the impression that it's part of a huge enterprise. Amazon is a prime example of this concept, with its personal product recommendations. Other examples are any businesses that let consumers place the word "my" in front of a company's brand, as in "my Yahoo!" and "my Excite."

- **The Market for Peace of Mind**—The dream of happier days gone by and the comfort of nostalgia have a strong pull on people. Romantic stories to sell idealized versions of the past insulate people against the "future shock" that we experience

For every additional $1 million that the movie makes, the "investors" get to split another $1,000.

Why would a film studio pay out cash to HSX subscribers? Lions Gate Films, the company behind the movie you selected, says that the deal is part of an overall marketing program. It hopes that the promise of cash will inspire HSX investors to spread word of the movie to boost its chances of hitting the $20 million mark.

For HSX, it's a step toward financing films through its site. HSX believes that if studios get used to including the HSX customer base in their film profits, they may eventually see value in tapping it for funding. And because the group of HSX customers has consistently predicted box-office hits so far, they would make smart investors.

Whether HSX will become a major force in film investing is yet to be seen. But it does show how an e-business can take a common commodity as an entertainment site, wrap it in a compelling story, and transform it into a unique product to attract customers.

Retaining Intellectual Capital

Which is better, the carrot or the stick? That's what's facing employers today. Should they monitor employees or trust them? With the frequency of job-hopping these days, companies are hard-pressed to keep a very valuable asset: their intellectual capital. Abilizer Solutions (www.abilizer.com) has one answer. It has attracted 70 companies with more than 2 million employees to use their Errand Portal, where workers can do everything from check stock quotes to plan family reunions and birthdays. The portal consists of five major channels: Life at Work, Family, Shopping, Personal Finance, and Home and Garden. Part concierge, part errand boy, part personal ads, Abilizer strikes deals with shopping and service sites, and then delivers them to employees.

every day. Banks previously sold peace of mind, which they abandoned in favor of stories about efficiency, technology, size, and profitability, Jensen says. Banks will return to selling peace of mind through services such as "private banking" and by building old-fashioned, wood-paneled branch offices. Software and technology that protect a consumer's privacy, such as Pretty Good Privacy (PGP), which encrypts email messages, and virus protection services for Net-enabled wireless devices such as McAfee.com (www.mcafee.com), are other examples of products and services that sell peace of mind.

Each of these future markets—and stories—should be explored by your e-business to see how they may fit into your product or service offering.

PART IV

Managing Customer Relationships

Connecting with the Customer

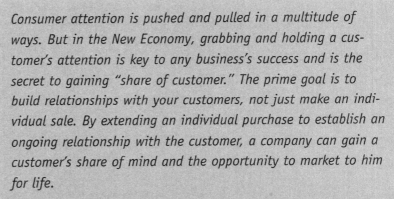

Consumer attention is pushed and pulled in a multitude of ways. But in the New Economy, grabbing and holding a customer's attention is key to any business's success and is the secret to gaining "share of customer." The prime goal is to build relationships with your customers, not just make an individual sale. By extending an individual purchase to establish an ongoing relationship with the customer, a company can gain a customer's share of mind and the opportunity to market to him for life.

In effect, the product a company sells is becoming the platform from which customer relationships can be built. Marketing becomes the central focus of the company, and building customer relationships and owning the customer is the goal.

One very powerful attention-grabbing strategy is to give the consumer the chance to get something free, such as money, merchandise, or services. In the case of sweepstakes and contests, keep in mind that you must structure them properly to ensure compliance with federal and state laws. Also keep in mind that community bonds are extremely durable and valuable to your company. When your company succeeds in creating a relationship with your customer, you cease being a seller and become a trusted advisor.

The New Economy has caused a major shift in the way companies relate to their customers. Relationships have replaced the sale as the goal of business. Negotiating individual market transactions is becoming less important than securing a lifetime relationship with the customer—in a sense, owning the customer. But as in life, you first must get a person's attention before a relationship can be forged. The key, of course, is to find the proper strategies for getting a customer's attention—and then holding on to that customer for life.

Getting to a customer early is one way of holding a customer for life. Apple did it by giving computers to elementary schools so that when the kids grew up and bought their own computers, they would choose Apple. McDonald's has a similar strategy: Get the kids to eat Happy Meals when they're young, and they'll continue to eat at McDonald's when they grow up.

These strategies may work fine for companies in the real world, but what about e-business? What works for them?

Jeremy Rifkin, a fellow at the Wharton School Executive Education Program and president of the Foundation of Economic Trends in Washington, sees information technologies morphing into "R-technologies," or relationship technologies. In his view, managing information with technology is giving way to managing relationships with it. New computer and software technologies such as the Internet allow for a rich web of interconnections and relationships between manufacturers, suppliers, and consumers that never before existed. These relationships can be exploited for gain by companies who understand the power of the relationship. Using R-technologies properly, an e-business can own its customers and benefit from their *lifetime value (LTV)*.

Business schools teach the importance of gaining as much market share as possible to make a company a success in the marketplace. Capturing share of market previously was the goal of every marketing professional. But today, the new marketing cry is, "Share of customer, not share of market."

Share of Customer, Not Share of Market

Holding a consumer's attention in today's world is difficult, to say the least, because consumer attention is pushed and pulled in a multitude of ways. In the New Economy, however, grabbing and holding a customer's attention is key to any business's success and is the secret to gaining share of customer.

The key is not to think in terms of an individual transaction, but to think in terms of the ongoing relationship that a transaction can create. By extending an individual purchase to establish an ongoing relationship with the customer, a company can gain a customer's share of mind and the opportunity to market to him for life. In effect, the product that a company sells is becoming the platform from which customer relationships can be built.

It takes more than one sale to reclaim the acquisition cost of a customer. Table 14.1 shows that an apparel retailer had to retain and sell to a customer for 12 months just to break even.

Table 14.1

One-Shot Customers Don't Earn Profits	
Average Profit Per Customer Per Six-Month Period	
Month 0	−$52 = Cost of customer acquisition
6 months	$21
12 months	$26 = Break-even point
18 months	$29
24 months	$30
30 months	$32
36 months	$33

As Table 14.2 shows, building a long-term relationship with a customer pays off in the long run.

Table 14.2

Repeat Customers Consistently Spend More	
Purchase History with Apparel Retailer	
6 months	$178
12 months	$234
18 months	$282
24 months	$332
30 months	$357

Source: Bain & Company and Mainspring Communications, 1999

Rifkin sees products as fixed items with set features and a one-time sale value, and should be thought of as platforms for all sorts of value-added services and upgrades. In his view, products have merely become vehicles for value-added services that create long-term relationships with buyers. A perfect example of this marketing strategy is Microsoft's Internet Explorer. Microsoft gave the Web browser away for free, then taking a leaf out of Netscape's marketing book, sold additional Microsoft Internet products and services like their NT Web servers to those businesses who built Microsoft IT solutions around the IE browser. Selling the product becomes more the cost of doing business than the sales objective of a company. It establishes a physical presence in the customer's home or place of business from which a company can begin an ongoing relationship with the customer. In the case of Microsoft's IE browser, the cost of doing business was giving the browser away for free.

An example that Rifkin uses is emWare (www.emware.com), a company that has created a lawn sprinkler system connected to the Net. The sprinkler itself is merely a platform for a range of upgraded services that can be integrated into the product. For a service fee, the sprinkler can be programmed to automatically contact the National Weather Service's Web site to check weather conditions and forecasts, and then turn the spray on and off accordingly. The sprinkler company makes money on the subscription services, not the product. In a way, the Gillette Razor Company used a similar idea many years ago when it gave away the razor and made its money selling the blades.

LEGO Connects Its Products to the Net

Danish toy maker LEGO Group sells a new toy that combines a computer brain with LEGO building blocks to build robotic toys. The product, LEGO Mindstorms (www.legomindstorms.com), can be connected to a PC, and commands can be downloaded via an infrared signal into the toy to expand the toy's capability. At LEGO Mindstorms, owners of the toy are given free "personalized" accounts where they can upload creations and discuss building ideas thus creating a sense of community between the toy owners—that is, the LEGO customers.

This shift from manufacturing and selling products to establishing long-term customer relationships brings marketing to the forefront of what a business is supposed to do. Marketing becomes the central focus of the company, and building customer relationships and owning the customer becomes the goal. Peter Drucker, the father of modern business practices, states this best: "The customer is the foundation of any business and keeps it in existence. Because it is its purpose to create a customer, any business enterprise has two—and only these two—basic functions: marketing and innovation."

In his book *Getting Everything You Can Out of All You've Got,* Jay Abraham makes the marketing task simple. He states that there are only three ways to grow your business: "You can find new customers, or … you can have your current customers buy more frequently from you, or … you can give your current customers more opportunities to increase the size of the purchases they make." In other words, grab a customer's attention and hold on for life!

Getting the Consumer's Attention

Before you can get a consumer's attention, you have to know who they are. According to a study from Media Metrix and consulting firm McKinsey, every online consumer falls into one of six e-shopping types: simplifiers, surfers, connectors, bargain shoppers, routine followers, and sports fans. Knowing what kind of customer you want to target will help win over consumers by giving them more of what they really want. Let's look at these categories one by one.

- **Simplifiers**—These types of shoppers are impatient but lucrative. Although they spend just seven hours a month online, they account for half of all Internet transactions. They like things simple and direct, and they like the convenience of Internet shopping. You can grab their attention by showing them end-to-end convenience and proving that they will save time by buying at your e-business.

- **Surfers**—These shopper types are consummate browsers and love to window-shop. They look at four times more pages than other Net users. They're drawn to new features and content. You can grab their attention by constantly updating your offering and your site.

- **Connectors**—These shoppers are new to the Internet and are less likely to shop online. But they can be reached. They are very brand-conscious and are drawn to brick-and-mortar brands that they know. Win them over by emphasizing affiliations with strong offline brands. These shoppers also enjoy connecting with others online. Community is big with them, so offer them a chance to chat with others like them on your site, or provide a service by which they can send free email greeting cards to their friends and family.

- **Bargain shoppers**—Their name says it all. They enjoy ferreting out bargains and have an unerring instinct for what's a good deal. Grab their attention with low prices. Be prepared to compete actively on price, offer auctions and classified ads, provide price comparisons, and get them involved in a community on your site where they can exchange shopping tips and stories with other bargain shoppers.

- **Routine followers**—These shoppers are information addicts who use the Net mainly for the information that it provides. They're attracted to news and financial sites. Get their attention by emphasizing news. Be first with new information and offer real-time data, and they will return again and again to your site.

- **Sports fans**—This type of shopper is a sports and celebrity enthusiast, who lives for the next score or the next tidbit of gossip. These shoppers are attracted to sports and entertainment sites. Grab their attention with updated sports and celebrity information, and help them connect with other fans through chat rooms, discussion boards, and email discussion lists.

In addition to the attention-grabbing strategies, another very powerful incentive cuts across all customer types to attract the attention of your target customer: the word *free*.

Nearly one fifth of U.S. households made a total of 130 million purchases online in 1999. Online participation in contests and sweepstakes nearly doubled from 27% in 1998 to 48% in 1999, and

Targeting Wireless Palm Pilot Users

One of the ways to grab the attention of wireless Palm Pilot users is to advertise. A number of online publications, such as *PalmPower* (www.palmpower. com), *PalmUser* (www.palmtop. co.uk/palmuser/index.htm), and *Pen Computing* (www. pencomputing.com/palm/), carry advertising, and you'll also find sections in traditional computing and mobile computing magazines.

Customers Can't Pass Up a Sweet Deal

Chocolate has a strong pull on people, especially if it's free. So, SmartCasual.com (www.smartcasual.com) sent out an email to its prospect list with "Mmmmm... chocolate!" in the subject line. The message informed the recipients that they could give free chocolates to a friend if they registered at SmartCasual's site. More than 20% of those who visited the site converted to opt-in registrants.

it is expected to grow even further in 2000. The pull of these contests and sweepstakes, of course, is the chance to get something free, such as money, merchandise, or services.

The word *free* is music to consumers' ears and definitely gets their attention. In fact, according to a study by Jupiter Communications and NFO Interactive in 1999, 45% of online purchasers claimed that they made their first purchase or transaction at a site because of a promotion.

The most popular promotions mentioned in the survey were these:

- Free shipping: 58%
- Limited-time discount: 35%
- Free gift with purchase: 33%
- Free coupons: 32%
- Free sweepstakes: 24%

Notice that the word *free* appears in four of the five popular promotions. First-time buyers are looking for free shipping, free products, cash, and rebates. But do these giveaways pay off, or do they just attract those who take but don't buy?

PC Data CEO Ann Stephens says that previous research by PC Data Online showed that 89% of Web surfing time is spent in search of free information, entertainment, or prizes. But that's changing. Stephens also says that a new type of giveaway Web customer is emerging—this type of customer is most likely to make a purchase more than previous users and also is more loyal. On average, these new giveaway customers are 40 years old, are 40% more likely than the average Web surfer to make an online purchase, and are 40% more loyal to an individual site.

Consider using some of these free promotions for your e-business to attract consumer attention.

Sweepstakes

Sweepstakes and contests are one of the most popular promotion gimmicks on the Net today to get a consumer's attention. Do a search on Yahoo! for "sweepstakes," and you'll come up with hundreds of sites listing tens of thousands of sweepstakes in which consumers can participate. What should you give away? How about a sample of your product?

By using your own products or services as a prize, you target people who are interested in them. Remember that you don't have to offer a large, expensive prize, such as a trip around the world or a new Porsche, to get a good response. But don't skimp on your prize, either. If you offer prizes such as coffee mugs, mouse pads, or T-shirts, your sweepstakes will get lost in the thousands of contests on the Net today.

You can run a sweepstakes monthly, weekly, or even daily. Announcing winners after each sweepstakes to all participants is great way to keep your e-business and its offerings in front of potential customers. But as with any good marketing promotion, you must plan the event carefully. To have a successful sweepstakes promotion, you should consider your promotion goals, know your target audience, design the structure of the sweepstakes, and then promote it on the Net.

Listing the rules on your site is very important in conducting a sweepstakes. Clear rules will not only inform the entrants of how the sweepstakes will be handled, but it also will keep you out of legal trouble.

At the bare minimum, you should do the following:

- Include the number of entries allowed (one per entrant or as many times as they like).

- Mention whether the sweepstakes is run daily, weekly, monthly, or just one time.

- Mention any restrictions or limits, such as age limits, whether it's open to U.S. residents only, and what states (or countries) can participate.

- Tell entrants when the sweepstakes ends and when the prize will be awarded.

- Detail any and all information required for entry, such as name, address, zip, phone, email address, and so on.

Create Your Own Sweepstakes

Dynoform (dynoform.com) lets you create personalized sweepstakes. And here's the good part: Its service is entirely Web-based. There's no software installation, and setup takes only a few minutes from the Dynoform site.

- Explain the entry method. Will entrants email their entries to you in response to your advertisement or posting? Or are they required to go to your Web site and fill out a form?

- Give entrants a full description of the prize that you're offering. Let them know exactly what they might win. For example, if they win a cruise or a weeklong stay in Disney World, is the airfare included?

- Make sure that you provide a way to contact you in case an entrant has questions about your sweepstakes.

Finally, display a set of the official rules that address in detail the elements that make up the structure of your sweepstakes. Every legitimate sweepstakes must have a set of official rules. The official rules should state exactly how the sweepstakes is structured and should give any restrictions or limitations about your promotion.

So what's the downside? How about hefty fines and even jail time? Keep in mind that although sweepstakes and contests can be an effective marketing tool, you must structure them properly to ensure compliance with federal and state laws.

Adhering to the law is extremely important here, and structuring your online sweepstakes to be legal is your first concern. And it goes without saying that before you run an online sweepstakes to promote your e-business, you should seek good legal counsel first. The key point to remember is that a sweepstakes is *not* a lottery. If your online sweepstakes is considered by law officials to be an unsanctioned lottery, you're breaking the law!

So what's the difference between a sweepstakes and a lottery? A sweepstakes invites eligible participants to register for a chance to win a prize. A drawing at the conclusion of the sweepstakes usually awards prizes. A lottery consists of a prize, chance, and consideration. It's the "consideration" part that makes lotteries illegal in most states. Although the definition of a consideration differs from state to state (you need that lawyer again), generally, consideration means that a willing participant is required to purchase something or pay for access to be eligible to enter the contest. Another exam-

Have a Pro Manage Your Sweepstakes

Sweepstakes Builder (sweepstakesbuilder.com) is one of the largest sweepstakes sites in the world. This company can build, maintain, and promote your sweepstakes for you for a fee.

ple of consideration might be the requirement of the participant to provide detailed consumer information to be eligible.

Finally, you must offer an alternative method of entry (AMOE). Allowing participants to enter offline via mail or fax is a form of AMOE. Why should you do this? Including an AMOE for your online sweepstakes might decrease the risk that a regulator will view a sweepstakes promotion as an illegal lottery.

Besides the risk of legal action, if you run your sweepstakes improperly, or if the participants feel that it was run unfairly, you risk a public relations nightmare that will be hard to overcome. Just because you are a small business, don't think that you're safe by flying below the "radar screen" of state and federal regulators. Also don't be lulled into a false sense of "safety in numbers." Seek legal advice, and run your sweepstakes properly.

Giveaways

Stuart Brand, creator of the Whole Earth Catalog, once said, "Information wants to be free." Online merchants have been using a variation of this idea for years: Give something free, and then sell something. This also is known on the Net as the Yoda Principle: "Give then take." Although this idea is not new to commerce (businesses have been using *loss leaders* for decades) it's the right formula for the Internet.

Giveaways also provide an opportunity to cross-promote with other noncompeting Web stores. You can offer one of your products or a compatible service free to other Web stores. For example, if a site sells auto accessories and you sell insurance products, you might offer a free comparison insurance quote. Or, if a site sells running shoes, you might offer a free pair of athletic socks with each purchase. The trick here is to get the customer from the other site to visit your site to get the free product or service. The partner Web store gets the sale, and you get additional visitors.

Besides giving away a product, information, or a service, offering discount coupons is another strategy to attract shoppers to your Web store. At first you might think of coupons as used only in the real world. And, yes, you can offer coupons on your site that can

What's a Loss Leader?

A *loss leader* is a product that a retailer sells below cost to get shoppers into their store.

List Your Freebie at FreeShop

A great place to list your incentive offer, free products and services, coupons, and other incentives is at FreeShop.com (freeshop.com).

be printed off and used in your real-world store. But if you're a pure Net-based e-commerce company, how can you make effective use of online coupons?

Why not offer them directly on your site? Here's how.

Iq.com (www.iq.com) has a product called Instant Action that is the digital equivalent of offline coupons. Using Instant Action, you can create any size "teaser" graphic that, when clicked, pops up an electronic coupon describing your offer. It might be an immediate discount on one of your products, or an offer of free shipping for a limited time. The consumer views your message in a small pop-up window and, when ready to take action, clicks a Buy button. The customer is sent directly to your site to take advantage of the offer. You can place your electronic coupon on your own site or on the banner ads that you place on other sites. Research by Forrester Research has shown that the average click-through rate for online banner ads with coupons is 20%, compared to .065% for standard banner ads.

Keeping the Consumer's Attention

On the Internet, your customer is just as likely to be your competitor's customer. As products become more commoditized and the choice of merchants to buy from expands, the type of loyalty once expressed in the real world becomes hard to find online. Loyalty is not so much to products anymore, but to value-added services and support.

CASE STUDY

S&H GREEN STAMPS

The veritable S&H Green Stamps has hit cyberspace. An old loyalty program—receiving little green stamps with each purchase at participating retailers then exchanging them for products in a catalog—has shed its skin and reinvented itself for the information age in a new company called S&H greenpoints.com.

In 1964, parent firm Sperry & Hutchinson printed more than three times as many green stamps as the U.S. Post Office did. The Green Stamps catalog was once one of the most popular publications in the country. In 104 years, the stamps have been redeemed for more than $10 billion in merchandise, from toasters to silver tea sets.

After many years, the poster child of loyalty programs pretty much fell off the radar screen. That is, until now.

Customer loyalty pays off in a big way. Table 14.3 shows how repeat customers make great ambassadors for your business.

Table 14.3

Repeat Customers Make Great Ambassadors Average Referrals Per Customer Since First Purchase	
First purchase	178
4 to 5 purchases	282
10 or more purchases	357

Source: Bain & Company and Mainspring Communications, 1999

You could build loyalty with incentive programs—literally buying a customer's loyalty—and a number of programs are available on the Net. Companies such as ClickRewards (www.clickrewards.com) offer ClickMiles—frequent flier miles—for shopping at your Web site. myPoints (www.mypoints.com) offers shoppers reward points in a similar fashion and offers completely customizable private label rewards program to e-businesses.

But according to Jupiter Communications, loyalty must go beyond points, and e-businesses must offer consumers compelling service and functionality to coax them online and develop deep relationships.

Take ePage (www.homepage.com), for example. The company's home page service offers a tool to e-businesses that personalizes customer Web pages to provide such customized information to

Free Report on Increasing Revenues

Creative Good offers a free report that shows how your e-business site can increase revenues by improving your customer experience. The report includes sections on strategies, tactics, and 31 e-commerce case studies on merchandising, email, navigation, search, checkout, and fulfillment. You can find it at www.creativegood.com/ survival.

Backed by new ownership, green stamps are being repositioned as digital currency with the launch of a Web loyalty program that aims to mesh the online and offline shopping worlds. Online shoppers can earn points purchasing from Borders.com, SmarterKids.com, and 60 other merchants, provided that they reach the sites through the greenpoints portal. Members can review account balances at the site, pool points with family members, and donate awards to charity.

Although there's no shortage of rewards programs already on the Net, a nostalgic boost may give greenpoints an edge. Dan Janal, author of *Dan Janal's Guide to Marketing on the Internet*, believes that with a stellar name, S&H can easily eclipse other companies that have been in the loyalty space for months.

the customer as product warranties, owner manuals, and purchase and customer service records—all part of on ongoing effort to keep customers informed and involved.

Another new service offered to e-businesses is from OrderTrust (www.ordertrust.com). This company's back-end loyalty program, called LoyalNet, is designed for easy use by online merchants, and the program is unthreatening and convenient for consumers worried about privacy and reluctant to carry even more frequent-purchase cards or to remember account codes. The company provided the loyalty program service quietly to existing customers for three years before offering it to any online merchant. Consumers simply register their credit cards with you, you send this information to OrderTrust, and OrderTrust tracks the consumers' activity every time that a purchase is made—online or offline—from any participating merchant. Neither merchant nor consumer needs special technology, cards, or account codes. OrderTrust acts as a trusted third party that serves as a virtual privacy firewall between you and the consumer, conveying only the appropriate purchase information.

Another way to maintain an ongoing relationship with your customers is to keep up an ongoing dialogue. Newsletters, polls, and surveys are a great way to keep your name in front of your customers and prospects. Using surveys and polls, you can ask consumers what they need and how your company can meet those needs.

But one of the best and most compelling ways to keep customers loyal to your e-business is to offer them the opportunity to participate in a community. We'll examine this next.

Community Bonding

Other than serving as a source for information, the Net provides the framework for the creation of communities on the Web. *Netizens* can interact with and participate in just about any kind of community niche that you can think of on the Net. They can participate in discussion lists, newsgroups, chat rooms, bulletin boards, and instant messaging services based around topics of discussion that interest them.

What's a Netizen?

A *netizen* is any Internet user, a citizen of cyberspace.

Community is a very important and powerful element on the Net and is being applied increasingly to consumers. Like-minded individuals are drawn to consumer communities because of a shared interest in a particular commercial endeavor, activity, or pursuit. Rifkin sees establishing consumer communities of interest as one of the most effective ways to capture and hold consumer attention and to create lifetime relationships with them.

So how do you create these consumer communities of interest?

In their book *Customer Bonding*, Richard Cross and Janet Smith list four critical stages in the creation of consumer communities. Stage 1 is *awareness bonding*. First, you have to make the consumer aware of your company's product or service, and then convince him or her to make the first purchase. Stage 2 involves *identity bonding*. Through use of your product or service, the customer begins to identify with your company's product or service and incorporates it into his sense of self. In a way, it becomes one of the ways in which the customer differentiates himself in the world. Wearing 501 jeans or owning a Rolex watch are examples of this.

Stage 3 is relationship bonding. Your company and the customer move from a one-time sales relationship to an interactive one. This is where relationship technologies begin to play an important role. You begin to establish a one-to-one dialogue with your customers, being conscious of their wants and needs and tending to them. This creates customer intimacy. Stage 4 involves community bonding. Your company brings your customers into relationships with other customers based on their shared interest in your company's products and services. Your task now is to create communities for the purpose of establishing long-term commercial relationships and optimizing the lifetime value of each customer.

The key to creating communities of interest, of course, is to bring customers together to share their common interest in your company's brand. In effect, by buying your product or service, your customers gain the opportunity to interact with and be entertained by each other. In their book *Unleashing the Killer App*, Larry Downes and Chunka Mui say this is the process of "creating communities of value by valuing community."

Finally, keep in mind that community bonds are extremely durable and are very valuable to your company. To break them, your competitors must persuade your customers to actually disregard social ties among friends, colleagues, or family that they have formed within the community. In essence, you own your customers.

When your company succeeds in creating a relationship with your customer, you cease being a seller and become a trusted advisor. And as long as you maintain that trust, you will benefit from the lifetime value that your customer represents. In effect, you become a new intermediary. And, if you remember, this is a prime way to overcome the commoditization of your business.

CHAPTER 15

Servicing the Customer

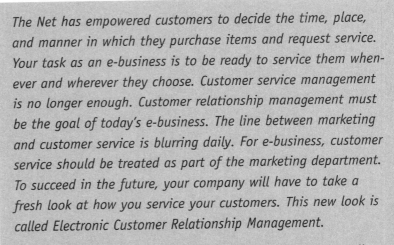

The Net has empowered customers to decide the time, place, and manner in which they purchase items and request service. Your task as an e-business is to be ready to service them whenever and wherever they choose. Customer service management is no longer enough. Customer relationship management must be the goal of today's e-business. The line between marketing and customer service is blurring daily. For e-business, customer service should be treated as part of the marketing department. To succeed in the future, your company will have to take a fresh look at how you service your customers. This new look is called Electronic Customer Relationship Management.

Email and FAQs are not enough. The Net is an instant medium and an instant medium requires instant answers. People still prefer interacting with other people—not technology. Customers enjoy and want the personal attention and feedback received from a live customer service representative. Luckily, the technology of live customer contact is developing fast and offers your e-business several customer service applications that you can apply today. If your goal is to attract a loyal customer with the opportunity to market to them for life, then personalized customer service and the technology to do it should be high on your marketing agenda.

In a way, e-commerce is payback for years of less than satisfactory customer service in the real world. For once, customers are delighted to find a shopping environment in which their needs are given top priority. The days of "Allow six to eight weeks for delivery," "Press 1 for this and 2 for that—then hold for the next customer service agent," and "We will sell your personal information to whomever we wish," are over.

Online shoppers are voting with their fingers on their mouse and are gravitating to companies that make customer service and satisfaction job one. Customers have regained the power that enables them to expect and ask for a decent level of service. To succeed in the New Economy, companies need to understand that the service problems of their customer are not minor inconveniences, but terribly annoying, inconvenient, time-consuming problems. People live busy lives and every second counts. The last thing they need is to enter a long-winded dialogue with a company whether through email, phone, or fax to solve a customer service issue.

Waiting patiently for service in the real world might be the norm, but the credo of the online customer is "I want it and I want it now!"

The Net has empowered customers to decide the time, place, and manner in which they purchase items and request service. Whether you're a click-and-mortar e-business or a pure dot-com, your competition is just a mouse click, phone call, or street corner away. Not only must your e-business sell through all channels of contact but service through multiple channels as well.

Customer service management is no longer enough. Customer relationship management is the goal of today's e-business.

e-CRM—Electronic Customer Relationship Management

The quickest way to e-commerce failure is not delivering on what you promise. Your promise to your customers is a good product or service, at a fair price, delivered promptly. But your responsibility to the customer doesn't end there. What you do or do not do after the sale determines whether your customer returns and buys from

Barnes&Noble Same Day Service

Barnes&Noble has instituted same day service on more than 800,000 books and CDs in New York using local delivery couriers. Not to be outdone, Amazon invested $60 million in same day delivery of books, videos, and music from Kozmo.com.

you again. Here's another important point. It's five times more expensive to get a new customer than it is to keep an existing one. So retaining loyal customers impacts your marketing budget considerably.

The line between marketing and customer service is blurring daily. For e-business, customer service should be treated as part of the marketing department. In many ways maintaining good customer relationships through excellent customer service is one of the best ways to gain the loyalty of your customers and their permission to market to them. According to the April 2000 "eMarketer eCommerce: B2C Report," the biggest reason customers gave for returning to shop at a Web site was "level and quality of customer service," at 63%.

So, how are e-businesses doing? Not so well. A recent report, issued by consulting firm Shelley Taylor & Associates, studied 100 online stores in the United States and the United Kingdom. While a few sites got top marks for their capability to handle checkout, post-transaction communication, and returns, the majority of them fell short. Many of the e-tailers surveyed simply did not keep their customers informed.

A report from market analysis firm Datamonitor paints even a gloomier picture. They reported that Internet retailers lost about $6.1 billion in online sales last year from transactions that were abandoned by consumers but could have been salvaged with decent customer service. If this trend continues, Datamonitor forecasts a cumulative loss of more than $173 billion in potentially salvageable sales over the next five years. Steve Morrell, a Datamonitor consultant, said, "The average company could have improved its online sales figures by almost 35% last year if it had provided better online customer service for potential customers. This will be particularly important for dot-com companies who are now realizing that they have to produce a profit, and soon."

Morrell also said "Companies wishing to do e-commerce must provide e-service, otherwise, they will cast away significant amounts of revenue and long-term customer relationships."

To succeed in the future, your company will have to take a fresh look at how you service your customers. This new look is called

Electronic Customer Relationship Management, or *e-CRM*. e-CRM is not just the ability of your customers to communicate via email. The integration of all channels of contact—voice, fax, email, and Web interactions—gives your customer the ability to communicate and interact with your e-business anytime, anyway, and anywhere.

These interactions take the form of online help, email, live text chat, fax backs, call backs, voice over a Net connection, as well as traditional inbound and outbound telephone contact. Multiple channels of contact ensure quality customer service with quick response to customer inquiries, giving customers the ability to control their service needs.

The integration of communications channels for service not only helps your customers reach you but also helps you correlate and track all customer contact within your company. Lawrence Byrd, vice president of marketing at Quintus (www.quintus.com), an e-CRM company on the Net, uses this example: How do you respond to customer query that says, "I'm phoning you today about yesterday's email concerning last week's Web transaction that I faxed you about?"

That's why the integration of the channels of contact is essential to good customer care. A report by Forrester Research suggests that modern customer service departments must be flexible and able to handle the multiple ways customers want to contact them. And the numbers support this. In 1997, about 97% of all interactions between customer and business were through telephone. In the year 2000 that figure will be 60% and will continue to fall to 5% by 2003.

But keep this in mind. Using technology to open up multiple lines of communications is fine but it doesn't replace the human element. After all, behind almost all channels of communication is a human customer service representative. Training that rep to properly service your customer is of prime importance.

Live Customer Service

The speed of doing business online has created the expectation of speedy customer service. Unfortunately, the most popular form of communication being used by e-businesses is email links and FAQs

Improve Your Auto-Response Emails

Don't have a standard auto-response. Customize it. Mention the person who writes you by name. Give them a trouble ticket number. Add their problem to the auto-response, and tell them in the message that it's an auto-response. And remember to get out the auto-response within an hour of your problem receipt.

(Frequently Asked Questions) on their Web sites. The track record of companies who respond to email in a timely manner is far from adequate and FAQs cannot answer all customer questions. Besides, some people simply will not go to the FAQs section or spend time hunting around for the online help section of a site. If you believe that service helps sell, then relying solely on FAQs or email for customer service is an inadequate way to build customer loyalty and develop a truly personalized relationship with your customers.

For instance, imagine walking into a store with no sales person in sight. You need a question answered. Now imagine you had to write down your question, slip it into an information box, and then keep checking back each day to see if your answer had arrived. Not a way to endear customers to your business, right? Well, that's exactly what companies on the Net who offer email as a customer's only way to communicate with them online are doing.

The Net is an instant medium and an instant medium requires instant answers. In addition, people still prefer interacting with other people—not technology. Customers enjoy and want the personal attention and feedback received from a live customer service representative. Which would you rather do? Communicate through a faceless piece of technology, such as email, to confirm the shipment of a gift two days before your wedding anniversary; or interact with a live human being for the information?

Robert LoCascio, CEO and founder of LivePerson (www. liveperson.com), which provides technology that facilitates real-time sales and customer service for companies doing business on the Internet, states that a Web site is not a vending machine, although many e-businesses think so.

A vending machine sells simple products with zero need for human interaction. When buying a can of Coke from a vending machine, you do not need to speak to anyone. Drop your coin into the slot and you know exactly what you're going to get. On those occasions that you don't get what you expect—like losing change in a soda machine or when the candy bar fails to fall from the dispenser—there is seldom any recourse. Most online products cannot be treated as vending machine merchandise. Even when buying books or CDs, there are many occasions for the need to

Improving Your Customer Service

Each customer question, no matter how trivial, helps build your knowledge database of customer service response. By storing these questions in a database, you can analyze and anticipate customer questions providing better service in the future.

speak to a customer service rep to clarify shipping dates, availability, and returns policies. And with the majority of shopping carts at online stores—including book and music stores—being abandoned during the checkout process, it seems that customers have questions that go unanswered.

According to a recent study by Forrester Research, 41% of online customers say they would be more likely to check out and actually buy something if they could consult or interact with a human being during the process.

Another important feature of real-time customer service is that it enables customers to communicate with an e-business at critical moments, particularly at the point-of-sale. It creates an opportunity for customer service representatives to answer questions on products and policies as they arise, aid consumers in finding what they're looking for, or suggest alternatives.

Nothing can replace a live contact and unlike email management systems, most live customer service solutions can be implemented relatively quickly. Typically, all that's required is a link placed on your Web site. Once clicked, a pop-up window appears within which your customers can begin a text-based conversation with live customer service representatives.

Luckily the technology of live customer contact is developing fast and offers your e-business several customer service applications that you can apply today.

Click-to-Chat

The first problem to overcome for live customer service is one of connectivity. Most people purchasing goods online are doing so from home on the same line as their telephone. If they have a question while on a site, they have to disconnect to call the company's customer service number.

With click-to-chat, that's not necessary. LivePerson (www. liveperson.com) is a good example of this click-to-chat technology. (See Table 15.1 for others.) Clicking the LivePerson link placed on a Web page launches a chat window where a customer service operator initiates a secure one-on-one text chat with the user. LivePerson requires no hardware or software installation on the part of your e-business. The application rests on LivePerson's server so there is no need to install the application on yours.

Table 15.1

Click to Chat Service Companies	
Company Address	**Service**
eTetra.com (www.etetra.com)	Web-based software enabling real-time, interactive communications with online customers.
HumanClick (www.HumanClick.com)	Offers instant messaging chat service that connects Web site visitors with live sales person and customer service agent.
International Business Systems (www.liveassistance.com)	Produces LiveAssistance, a Web call center (in-house or outsourced) that offers communication through text chat.
Talk to a Person (www.talktoaperson.com)	Allows a customer to chat instantly with sales and customer service staff.
LivePerson (www.liveperson.com)	Offers a chat window where a customer service operator initiates a secure one-on-one text chat with the user.

CASE STUDY

LANDS END

Lands End brings a long tradition of effective catalog retailing to the Web and succeeds equally well in delivering a positive online user experience. The site is sparse on graphics and careful in its authoring of text.

Lands End also brings a tradition of good customer service to its Web site. Lands End informs customers of the variety of ways to contact them, the nature of their guarantee, their policies and procedures—even size charts to help customers choose clothing that will fit. But their best innovation is their use of customer service interactive technologies.

Lands End offers not one, but three ways that a customer can have a live interaction with a service representative.

Customers can choose to open a chat window through which a text-based interchange can take place with a Lands End customer service representative or an instant call back can be requested. Through the text chat window,

Using technologies like LivePerson allows your service representatives to provide shoppers with links that immediately transport them to products of interest during their online inquiry. This is a win-win situation for your e-business and shoppers alike. It gives your company a proactive sales tool, while allowing shoppers to find what they want quickly and with less hassle.

A company that uses this kind of technology is Lands End (`www.landsend.com`). The technology provided by Webline Communications (`www.webline.com`) includes an online chat window for customer service as well as a feature that allows two Lands End customers to link their browsers and shop together. You can't get any closer to a virtual brick and mortar experience than that.

According to Robert LoCascio at LivePerson, implementing such a solution is a small price to pay for increased customer satisfaction, loyalty, and the higher sales that result.

Instant Messaging

Another form of live customer contact is called instant messaging (see Table 15.2). Instant messaging technology, popularized by both America Online's Instant Messenger and ICQ software (`www.icq.com`), is a growing hit among consumers as a cheap—read free—and easy way to communicate. *Instant messaging (IM)* is a small application that resides on the consumer's computer desktop. With it, consumers can send messages through a small pop-up window instantly to anyone who has the application and who's online at the time.

Shop with a Friend

Cahoots puts Web surfers in touch with each other when visiting the same Web sites. Unlike instant messaging technology that lets people chat with others they know, Cahoots (`www.cahoots.com`) is designed to let strangers know about a site's content or products.

customers can ask any question they desire while on the Lands End site and receive an immediate text reply in real-time. If they would rather speak over the phone, they can use the instant call-back option. If they have a separate line connected to the Net, they can ask questions of the service representative while viewing their site.

But it gets better. If a customer has a direct connection to the Net and has a microphone on their PC, they can talk directly to a service representative over their Internet connection.

Lands End shows that with the current interactive technology of the Net and a commitment to customer service, an e-business can duplicate—or even exceed—the kind of customer service that only brick-and-mortar stores could do in the past.

Now the idea is taking hold among businesses. Software makers Novell, the Sun-Netscape Alliance, IBM subsidiary Lotus, and others are building new IM software tailored for business use with new features such as increased security and audio and video capability.

The problem, however, is that unlike click-to-chat applications such as LivePerson, a shopper must have the IM application installed to talk to you. Instant messaging is still in its infancy but could become an important communications tool like pagers, cell phones, and voice mail. IBM and Sun-Netscape executives said they've heard of executives negotiating contracts and company acquisitions through instant messaging. According to Giga Information Group analyst Rob Enderle, "It represents one of the strongest opportunities to apply technology in a way that makes companies more competitive."

Table 15.2

Instant Messaging Service Companies	
Company Address	**Service**
ICQ (www.icq.com)	Chat in real-time with customers, and launch peer-to-peer applications with them.
AOL Instant Messenger (www.aol.com/aim)	Chat with customers when they are online.
Jabber (www.jabber.com)	Commercialized open source, XML-based instant messaging platform.

Case in point is EXP.com (www.exp.com), an online advice Web site. They use IM to pair consumers with third-party experts and to communicate with customers. About one-third of the site's interactions between consumers and experts takes place via instant messaging. But other companies are getting into the act. With more businesses using the technology, firms such as Lotus, Novell, and the Sun-Netscape Alliance are building their own instant messaging software with security features. John Patrick, IBM's vice president of Internet technology, said businesses are demanding more security, so software companies are encrypting the messages that go over the public Internet.

Both Lotus and Novell plan to add audio and video in future versions of the software. And later this year, the company will add translation software that supports eight languages, including German and Chinese, so that a message typed in Chinese can be read in English by the recipient.

Another variation of IM is Instant Call by Global Online Telephone (www.globalonlinetelephone.com). Email marketers—B2B marketers in particular—could greatly benefit from IM technology. Using Instant Call, the usual email promotion is sent but with the additional enhancement of an embedded link that gives recipients the option of receiving an immediate phone call from a sales or service representative. When the recipient clicks the link, he or she is taken to an easy-to-fill-out form. As soon as the consumer completes it and clicks the "Call Me!" button, they are immediately phoned and quickly hooked up with a sales or service representative.

Live Voice

The best form of communication, of course, is real-time voice. Thanks to the Internet, telephony is on the verge of a revolution. Recent developments in Net technology give companies the capability to add real-time voice communications with their site visitors.

Live voice interaction is a powerful tool for turning shoppers into buyers. Although text-based interactions are effective, they can't replace live-voice conversations, which are far more personal. Live voice humanizes the online experience and greatly accelerates the selling process. In fact, according to Jupiter Communications, online shopper desire for human contact leaps once the purchase price exceeds $50.

One such service is HearMe (www.hearme.com) (see Table 15.3 for others). Their HearMe e-commerce solution provides both click-and-talk and phone call back capabilities, providing flexibility for both the customer and your customer service center. In addition, their application allows for multiparty conversations that allow customers to be transferred from one agent to another and agents to conference in expert help. A similar service is called Lipstream (www.lipstream.com). Lipstream has built a very simple, scalable

WAP Mobile Phone Call Backs

NetCall (www.netcall.com) let's customers on the Net instantly connect to someone they can talk to whether from the Web, WAP, or digital TV, at any time, in real-time.

voice service that enables people to talk to one another one-to-one or one-to-many, live on the Internet.

Table 15.3

Live Voice Service Companies	
Company Address	**Service**
HearMe (www.hearme.com)	e-Commerce solution provides both click-and-talk and phone call back capabilities, providing flexibility for both the customer and your customer service center.
Lipstream (www.lipstream.com)	Offers a very simple, scalable voice service that lets people talk to each other one-to-one or one-to-many, live on the Internet.
Net2Phone (www.net2phone.com)	Provides services that enable high-quality, low-cost telephone calls over the Internet, which enables customers to call individuals and businesses worldwide using their personal computers or traditional telephones.
Vocalcommerce.com (www.vocalcommerce.com)	Features voice over IP program. Adds Web-to-telephone functionality to Internet sites.
Instant Call (www.instantcall.com)	Web call back service from USA Global Link. Customers click a button to instantly receive a free phone call. No software or hardware required.

A variation on this technology is from E-call (www.ecall.com). With E-call, any e-business can accept voice-generated feedback and technical-support calls directly from customers without having to use an 800 number. Their technology provides free voice communications over the Internet in a real-time intercom mode or via instant voice mail. If the recipient is offline, messages are stored for later retrieval.

Even though many Net users have slow connections, don't have microphones, and have non-duplex sound cards that hinder the use of voice/chatting over the Internet; if your goal is to attract a loyal customer with the opportunity to market to them for life, then personalized customer service and the technology to do it should be high on your marketing agenda.

Managing Returns for Customer Retention

The old adage goes, "A satisfied customer tells no one. A dissatisfied customer tells 10 friends." And on the Net, a dissatisfied customer can tell thousands of other consumers about a bad shopping experience. One of the worst problems of a disgruntled customer is dealing with his or her returns.

For companies selling goods on the Net, dealing with returns is one of the ugly facts of life. This is true for both B2C and B2B companies. But it's not just the logistics problem of handling returns. The returns process itself is costly. Figures from the U.S. Census Bureau show that customers returned an estimated $62 billion worth of merchandise in 1997—the most recent year for which numbers are available—resulting in $10–$15 billion in losses to retailers.

Forrester research paints a similar picture for online retailers. It estimates that e-tailers will have to deal with $11 billion worth of returns by 2002 resulting in $1.8–$2.5 billion in losses. About 9 out of 10 online shoppers say return policies influence their decision in dealing with particular e-tailers, according to research by BizRate (www.bizrate.com) and the Boston Consulting Group (www.bcg.com). The absence of good return mechanisms was the second-biggest reason shoppers cited in Boston Consulting's research for refusing to buy clothing on the Web, after inability to see and feel the merchandise.

This headache to e-tailers has created an opportunity for a new kind of service on the Net, one that can help your e-business manage its returns easily and less expensively.

Pay Your Customers to Complain

Even negative feedback is useful in running your business. Sometimes it's better than positive feedback. So, run a complaint contest to elicit feedback on your site and service.

Mark Hilinski, vice president of sales and marketing of the Return Exchange (www.returnexchange.com), says that returns are normally counted as part of the cost of doing business. They should be viewed as a business-building opportunity. The Return Exchange offers a one-stop solution to a company's returns problem. They provide a plug-in that allows e-tailers to use its service as the Returns button for their Web site. After clicking the Returns button, a customer fills out an online form and sends the form along with the merchandise to be returned to the Return Exchange's warehouse—not the merchant.

Upon receipt, the merchandise is inspected and prepared for one of three methods of disposal: the product can be returned for credit to the manufacturer, the product can be repackaged and put back in inventory, or the Return Exchange can put it up for auction on their auction site called FinalCall.

The Return Exchange is not the only company getting into the returns space. Return View (www.returnview.com) offers e-tailers a virtual solution to managing returns including automated returns authorization, reporting, shipping, receiving, restoration, and resale.

Even the brick-and-mortar crowd sees an opportunity in the returns arena. Third parties are circling the opportunity to assist e-tailers as 7-Eleven already does in Japan, says James Vogtle, e-commerce research director at Boston Consulting. Jim Amos, president and CEO of 4,100-site Mail Boxes Etc. (www.mbe.com), expects total returns of online merchandise, mainly from consumers, to grow 300% to $10 billion by 2004. His company aspires to be "a bridge between the physical and virtual world," offering instant credit card or merchandise credit.

Clearly, it's only a matter of time before both UPS and FedEx see the opportunity and enter this space and offer their vast knowledge and logistical resources as services to e-tailers.

CHAPTER 16

Protecting Customer Privacy

One of the quickest ways to turn off customers is to send them unsolicited email. An even quicker way is to give them the impression that you're violating their privacy. There's also the growing trend of government investigating the business practices of e-business as it pertains to consumer privacy. This is not good for e-businesses that want to target their offers, connect with their customers, and build a lifetime relationship with them. e-Businesses need to know what the privacy equation is in order to convince consumers and customers to give up their personal information. The FTC calls the principles of this privacy equation the fair information practices. They are notice, choice, access, and security. Your company needs to adhere to them when creating and implementing your privacy policy. Using the services of third-party privacy seals is a good way to gain the trust of consumers because these third-party consumer privacy protection organizations certify your privacy policy. But if the government gets more involved because self-regulation of the industry does not work, then its intervention could close off marketplaces to many companies on the Net. The Children's Online Privacy Protection Act or COPPA is one such example and could be the start of more laws established to protect a consumer's privacy. Consumer privacy issues and concerns can have a drastic effect on your ability to market to, connect to, and create an ongoing relationship with your customers. All of which is critical to your e-business success in the future.

The Internet is a great medium of commerce. With it, you can create new marketing methods, tap new markets, and target potential customers with electronic ease. And the Internet also can get you sued by millions of consumers for violating their privacy!

If you thought spamming consumers with unwanted email was a blight on your company's reputation, consumers are even more upset over the incessant abuse of their personal privacy—not to mention the government investigations of the business practices of e-businesses. But gathering a certain amount of information is necessary for companies to personalize and better serve their customers. After all, how can you connect with a customer if you know little or nothing about them?

There has to be some kind of balance between protecting a consumer's privacy and the need for your business to target and personalize your offers to your customers. The funny thing about the privacy issue is that it's primarily focused on the B2C marketplace. In the B2B arena, privacy is pretty much a non-issue. Consumers might be afraid of filling out pages and pages of personal information on a Web site, but B2B customers are glad to share their information because it makes things go more smoothly for them in their work lives.

But that's no consolation when the federal government starts looking into your business practices as in the case of Yahoo! and Amazon. In early 2000, the U.S. Federal Trade Commission launched investigations into the consumer information practices of Internet powerhouses Yahoo! and Amazon.com. In addition, the FTC launched a high profile investigation of online advertising agency DoubleClick (www.doubleclick.com). The contention here is DoubleClick's capability to track a consumer's surfing pattern on the Net and link specific personal information with accumulated data on that specific individual.

These actions by the FTC serve notice that it appears to be taking a much stronger interest in online companies' business practices. Although the federal government continues to urge U.S. companies to regulate themselves regarding customer privacy, increasing governmental intervention into online companies has caused many industry observers to note that Internet privacy legislation might be inevitable.

Consumers Are Not Happy

The Internet industry might think that self-regulation is the best way to handle online privacy, but consumers do not.

According to Odyssey L.P.'s January 2000 Homefront study, online users overwhelmingly support government intervention to set standards for how companies can use personal information gathered through the Internet and the Web. Of the online households polled, 82% agreed strongly or at least somewhat with the statement "The government needs to step in and regulate how companies can use personal information."

It seems that online consumers are not convinced that the privacy polices posted on e-business Web sites are adequate enough or actually followed by the company. That kind of attitude is not good news to e-businesses that want to target their offers, connect with their customers, and build a lifetime relationship with them.

To throw more gasoline on the fire, Enonymous.com (www. enonymous.com), a Web ratings firm that rates the privacy polices of Web sites, surveyed 30,000 Web site's privacy policies early this year and rated each one with the best privacy policy. They found that only 6% of the top 50 trafficked sites and only 8% of the top 100 sites had the best privacy policies posted. The best policies stated that the company would not contact the user without specific permission and would not share personal identifiable information with anyone.

Enonymous.com also found that only 26% of the companies surveyed in the top 50 and only 22% in the top 100 had privacy policies that stated they would not contact the user without specific permission and share personal identifiable information only with explicit permission. The remaining Web sites did not state clearly what kind of control the consumer had over personal information submitted to the site.

Consortium Pushes Net Ethics

The Personalization Consortium was founded by 26 companies that represent a mix of established and startup businesses, ranging from American Airlines and KPMG Consulting to DoubleClick and E.piphany. The objective of the consortium is to promote responsible use of rapidly developing personalization technology. The consortium's initial guidelines for personalization technology include providing consumers access to their personal information, "responsible" linking of online and offline information, and criteria for opting in or out.

Table 16.1

Consumer Willingness to Allow Shared Information Between Sites	
Share Information Concerning...	**Acceptance Rate**
Promotions I respond to	56%
What ads I click on	52%
A short survey about my attitude towards the Net	50%
Products I buy on the site	48%
My hobbies and special interests	47%
My age	41%
My level of education	37%
My name	30%
My mailing address	17%
My household income	14%
My salary	13%
My credit card number	1%
None of the above	29%

Source: Cyber Dialogue

In a study of 1,500 Web users, Cyber Dialogue (www. cyberdialogue.com) found that while 80% of people didn't mind providing personal information to receive customized information from a site, 49% of surfers felt that sites sharing this information with others is a violation of their privacy.

It seems that consumers are sensitive to what is done with their personal information but it doesn't mean they're against giving it if the circumstances change—including getting something back for the information. (See Table 16.1.)

Still, e-businesses need to know what the privacy equation is to get the cooperation of consumers and to get customers to give up their personal information. And the principles of that privacy equation include the *fair information practices.*

The Fair Information Practices

In the FTC's year 2000 online findings, it found that although 90% of e-businesses have some kind of privacy policy, only 20% had implemented all four recommended fair information practices of notice, choice, access, and security.

The first two practices of notice and choice are fairly common in the privacy practices of e-businesses. Most Web sites give the consumer notice that they are collecting information and tracking their behavior and then give them a choice to avoid such tracking.

What's missing—and this is what the government is closely watching and where legislation will come from—are the last two practices. Giving consumers access to data collected on them and providing them with the security that the data is kept private.

A good privacy policy should give consumers the ability to check the files that others keep on them and to change anything that is wrong. For example, Yahoo! tracks visitors' search patterns by keywords. Privacy advocates believe that a consumer should be able to go into Yahoo!'s database and work with their profile. They want consumers to be able to remove certain search words in their profile that they deem of a personal nature, such as adult entertainment, sex, or marijuana. Consumers should be able to erase these words from their search profiles. In addition, privacy advocates believe that a consumer should be able to go back to a form that they filled out years ago detailing their name, address, household income, and so on and delete it.

But that's no easy task and it can become very expensive for an e-business to implement. Still, there are online companies that have taken the challenge and provide consumers with access to their information. One such company is BeFree (`www.befree.com`). Besides being a management company for merchant affiliate programs, it distributes software that helps online businesses tailor their content to the user's interest. BeFree requires companies that use the software to inform customers how it works, and also gives customers a way to opt out of the tracking. But the company also goes one step farther, by giving users access to the information gathered on them.

Giving Consumers the Power

Dash.com (`www.dash.com`), a comparison-shopping agent, looks over the shoulder of a consumer while he or she shops the Net. It compares the offers that a consumer is looking at with other online store offers in its database showing better deals when available. Dash.com collects an extensive amount of information on a consumer's shopping behavior but it also lets customers see, in real-time, what information the company has collected about their shopping habits. They can delete or change any of it whenever they see fit.

An example of this is SuperGo.com (www.supergo.com), an online bicycle store. When a consumer clicks SuperGo.com's privacy statement link, he goes to another site set up by BeFree, which then discloses on one page the information compiled about the user's behavior on SuperGo.com from all the sites using BeFree's software.

The Acxiom Corporation, which sells information on tens of millions of United States households, released technology last year that allows companies with vast amounts of consumer data to sift through it quickly and present it for review or editing by consumers or a sales staff. The technology, called AbiliTec, solves the access issue for companies that collect data on consumers from several sources such as mail order operations, retail stores, or their online store.

All this reflects the desire of consumers to protect their privacy while at the same time wanting to be known by the e-business, wanting to be greeted at the door by name, and expecting a level of personalization that approximates what they get at the corner store. However, at the same time they want control of their personal information.

A new ripple enters in the privacy area and one that can impact your e-business's capability to collect information on consumers.

Companies such as Persona (www.privaseek.com) offer free software that gives Internet users control over how their personal information is used by the Persona-empowered sites they visit. By creating a persona, consumers can provide only the types of personal information they would like to share with the sites they visit. Persona's partner sites use this permissioned data to provide personalization and enhanced services to Persona users.

Another company called Advercast (www.surfsecret.com) offers a software tool to consumers called SurfSecret that blocks sites from tapping into the data stored on cookies in the user's browser. The bottom line with these new entrants to the privacy debate is that the consumer is gaining more and more control of not only the transaction but also how and when his or her personal information is collected and used.

Paying Consumers for Their Information

Why not pay consumers for their information instead of just asking for it? That's what mValue.com (www.mvalue.com) does. It pays consumers cash to share their personal information with selected Web sites.

Privacy Seals and Government Regulation

When it was revealed that online advertising agency DoubleClick was combining data it collected on Web users with demographic information culled from a direct marketing company it recently acquired, without telling the consumer, it brought about an FTC inquiry, several state investigations, and a number of lawsuits. The DoubleClick issue caught the eye of the federal government and prompted calls from privacy advocates for stringent legislation to protect the privacy of online consumers.

Now, for e-businesses, self-regulation is far more desirable than government regulations that could hinder a company's capability to serve its customers and build relationships. So a number of privacy protection organizations have appeared to help soothe the concerns of online consumers. And they do this by offering third-party privacy seals to e-businesses.

This is a good way to gain the trust of consumers because these third party consumer privacy protection organizations certify your privacy policy. In recent years a number of different online organizations have offered privacy seals to companies that meet their guidelines.

There are two types of privacy seal programs. One has strict guidelines that prohibit sites from sharing consumer information they collect with other business partners or from using it for direct marketing programs. Other privacy seal programs award their stamps-of-approval to sites that simply stick to whatever privacy promises they made. Those promises could include passing on personal information to advertising networks or other businesses as long as they spelled it out in their posted privacy statement.

The oldest and most well known privacy seal program is TRUSTe (www.truste.org), which was started in 1997 by the Electronic Frontier Foundation. TRUSTe has more than 1,300 companies participating in its privacy seal program, including names such as AOL, eToys, and myPoint. To display the TRUSTe seal on your site requires a TRUSTe audit and an annual fee of $299 to $6,999 depending upon your e-business revenue.

e-Businesses can display the TRUSTe seal and share consumer information with other businesses as long as they state this fact in their privacy policy. The same holds true for the Better Business Bureau's (www.BBBoline.org) privacy policy program. It has attracted almost 300 members including AT&T, American Airline, and Dell Computers).

At the other end of the spectrum, there's Secure Assure (www.secureassure.org). It not only offers an audit program but requires members to adhere to a stringent privacy guideline stating that the e-business will never share a consumer's private information with a third party. It currently has almost 200 member sites.

The advantage of having a third-party seal on your Web site is that the consumer doesn't have to read through an extensive privacy policy to see what kinds of controls there are on his or her personal information. Should your e-business pay to join these types of programs? That really depends on the credibility these seals have in the eyes of consumers. Organizations such as BBBOnline and TRUSTe, for example, have never withdrawn an endorsement from an approved site. Since these privacy assurance companies are relatively new, only time will tell how credible they will be in the eyes of the consumer.

To thwart criticism of its inability to regulate its members, TRUSTe filed an antiprivacy brief in June 2000 against eToys. TRUSTe says that eToys—while in Chapter 11—is violating its online agreement by trying to sell its customer data to third parties to raise cash for operations.

If consumers lack confidence in these third-party seals, this opens the door to government intervention. And the camel's nose is already in the tent in the case of COPPA—a regulation that your e-business must follow.

The Children's Online Privacy Protection Act (COPPA) was enacted in late 1998 and became effective in April of 2000. COPPA bars the online collection and use of personally identifiable information from children under the age of 13 unless verifiable parental consent is provided.

New Privacy Protection Standards for e-Business

New privacy software from Tivoli Systems, a division of IBM, promises to enable e-businesses to seamlessly enforce privacy policies over the Web. Dubbed the Tivoli SecureWay Privacy Initiative, the software provides an access control solution that is designed specifically to help e-businesses protect consumers' personally identifiable information over the Net.

The Government Gets Serious

In 1999 the FTC charged that GeoCities—acquired by Yahoo!—misled adults and children as to how personal information collected at the Web site would be used. While GeoCities denied any wrongdoing, it did agree to obtain signed parental permission forms before collecting information on children under 13.

What's the penalty for breaking this law? There have been reports that the FTC might seek up to $11,000 per COPPA violation. It does not take a mathematician to figure out that penalties can really add up.

Not surprisingly, many e-businesses no longer cater to children under the age of 13. Here's a case of government intervention closing off a marketplace to many companies on the Net. But that's not all. This might only be the beginning of the story. In a recent survey, 96% of parents said that there should be similar COPPA protections for teenagers 13 years of age and older.

The threat to e-business is not only in the U.S. In Europe, the European Data Protection Privacy Directive came into effect in October of 1998. It mandates that member-countries must ensure that data transferred outside the European Union is protected and it bars the export of data to countries that do not have comparable privacy protection. And although the United States has been negotiating a *safe harbor* provision to allow continued data flow from Europe to the U.S., certain European members are concerned that the safe harbor provision does not provide for individual redress for privacy violations.

It all boils down to this: Consumer privacy issues and concerns can have a drastic effect on your ability to market to, connect to, and create an ongoing relationship with your customers—all of which is critical to your e-business's success in the future. A lot of thought should be given to your privacy policy and how you communicate it to visitors and customers to your site.

How to Create a Privacy Policy

Your best success tool for your e-business is customer loyalty. From loyalty stems relationships and from relationships come steady sales. Customer loyalty is one of the best barriers to your competition that a company can have. But customer loyalty comes from one thing—trust. And trust comes from being open and honest with your customers.

Telling your visitors and customers how you will use their personal information that you gather on your site goes a long way in building this trust. So, creating a good privacy policy should be first on your list to building customer loyalty.

You build a privacy policy by following the four fair practice principles of notice, choice, access, and security.

Notice

Inform the visitor that you are collecting information. If you think your company is not collecting information from visitors to your site—think again. You are. Most Web sites maintain logs that contain some amount of information on every visitor to the site. Most of this information is not identifiable but some of it can be under certain circumstances. If you maintain a site log, you're collecting information. Your privacy policy should disclose the collection and use of this site log data.

A common error in most policy statements is the one that states that information will not be disclosed to anyone. That's not

has figured that one out. At SmartKids.com, parents can create profiles of their children and alter them as they see fit. Parents can tell SmartKids.com's computer what a child's interests are and change them whenever their child's interests change, thus always presenting the buyer with a choice of relevant products.

As for their privacy policy, SmartKids.com touches all bases. Customers are informed as to what information is collected and how it will be used. Customers are given the ability to edit or delete information that SmartKids.com might have and also gives them the option to opt-in or out of any promotional marketing. They are also a member of a third-party privacy seal company called TRUSTe.

necessarily true. Companies make routine disclosures of personal data to their lawyers, auditors, computer service companies, and sometimes under subpoena. None of these disclosures are terribly bothersome, but they should be mentioned in the privacy statement. Nothing should be treated as obvious in a privacy policy statement. Tell the whole story. Consumers will appreciate it.

Finally, make sure regular folks can read your privacy policy. Leave out the legalese and tell it in straight, easy to understand language. Remember to be clear and concise and state everything you will and will not do. Also, make it easy to find. Place links to your privacy policy on your home page and all major sections of your site.

Choice

If you're planning on using a customer's data for marketing purposes, give them the choice to participate or not. Do not automatically subscribe a visitor to your newsletter or send them email promotions without asking permission first. Have them choose to opt-in to any ongoing communications with your company. This means keeping the "Would you like further information from our company?" box unchecked and have the customer or visitor manually check the box himself. Then give them the option to easily opt-out later.

Also, if you are tracking their behavior on your site, let them know that. Let them choose when and where they go on your site. You should always ask permission to gather information and market to customers using the information you have collected.

Access

Give your customers a way for them to view, edit, and update the information you collect on them. Give the customer the ability to correct false information. Not only will this keep you up-to-date on their desires and needs for personalization programs but also will give them the security that they have control over the information they provide to your company.

DMA Can Help Build a Privacy Policy

Members of the Direct Marketing Association (DMA) can go to the organization's Web site and find tools that help them develop a privacy policy for their Web site. But this is only a starting point. The privacy policy generated by its automatic policy generator is weak and limited. It won't hurt your company to exceed the DMA's privacy policy standards.

Security

State that any and all information you keep on your customers is kept secure and that no other party has access to it. In addition, state how a customer's data is secured inside your company, who will have access to it, and the controls you have on that access. If you're keeping personal credit histories and credit card numbers on file, how are those numbers being protected from hackers?

Finally, stay on top of privacy trends and regulatory issues so you can further strengthen your privacy policies. A good Web site for this is the Electronic Privacy Information Center at `http://epic.org`.

Building trust with your customer is job one in the New Digital Economy. And your customer is your most precious resource.

Ready Reference Guide

This Ready Reference Guide has been designed to help you locate Web addresses you will need for developing a successful e-marketing strategy for your e-business. It is divided into several main sections similar to the divisions of the overall book. Use this guide to seek out more information on the given topic areas, follow up on examples, or find that URL for the Web site you read about in the book.

Positioning Your Business in the New Economy

New Economy Index

www.neweconomyindex.org

This site provides a set of economic indicators specifically geared to the New Economy, gathered from both private and public sources.

Fingerhut

www.fingerhut.com

This company optimized their system for third-party fulfillment and now their warehouses are hopping 24 hours a day fulfilling orders from eToys, Wal-Mart, and other clients such as TurboTax and Pier One.

Autobytel

www.autobytel.com

By extending their reach through affiliation, Autobytel can offer its customers a one-stop shop for their car buying needs. They will not only sell you a car, but through affiliations with more than 100 banks will help you finance it as well. They also offer one-stop auto insurance quotes from the nation's top insurance companies.

Netpliance

www.netpliance.com

For $99 and a small monthly service fee, consumers can have a Web and email browser that's always on whenever they need it. They can check their email or surf the Web without the need of a PC.

WebTV

www.webtv.com

Consumers can check email and surf the Web between commercials, and even play along and interact with their favorite game shows such as "Jeopardy" or "Who Wants to Be a Millionaire?" with this inexpensive Net appliance that hooks up to your television.

NetByTel

www.netbytel.com

Enables companies to open up a whole new market and bring their online products and services to any consumer using any telephone, anywhere. Companies using NetByTel's technology can speech-enable their Web site so a customer can call from anywhere and transact business over any wire line or wireless telephone.

OnePage

www.onepage.com

Lets you create a tailored Web page, pieced together from many other Web sites.

FireDrop

www.zaplet.com

Their Zaplets transform email messages into commerce engines, can commerce-enable wireless devices such as Palm IVs and Nokia cell phones, and could make the current e-commerce Web site an evolutionary has-been.

Cybergold

www.cybergold.com

One of the first online marketing incentive companies to allow individuals to earn and spend money on the Internet.

InternetPhone

www.eurocall.com/e/ip5.htm

Using their service, consumers can download software that allows them to make long-distance calls to any phone in the world—free of charge.

Hotmail

www.hotmail.com

The originator of Web-based email and the leader in its space. By providing free Web-based email accounts to consumers, Hotmail has attracted tens of millions of active email accounts.

Netcentives

www.netcentives.com

Offers customers frequent flyer miles for spreading the word about its service or generating new sales.

MyPoints

www.mypoints.com

Consumers can earn Points that can be used to purchase rewards by simply reading email, shopping online, or visiting Web sites.

Mirabilis ICQ

www.mirabilis.com

Gave its service—instant messaging—away for free to anyone who would download it. By giving away the product, ICQ grew its subscriber base faster than any company in history. ICQ soon became the standard of instant messaging.

The Knot

www.theknot.com

A one-stop shop for shopping for a wedding. At The Knot you can plan and schedule your nuptials; send out invitations; register your china, silverware, and other wedding gifts; and find and book your honeymoon.

MyGeek

www.mygeek.com

Consumers tell merchants what they want to buy, merchants respond with bids, and the consumer picks the best deal. With MyGeek, the buyer is in control of what he or she wants to pay.

Vstore

www.vstore.com

Gives any Web site the capability to have their own online store right on their Web site. Vstore provides the products, design, marketing tools, and technology—all for free. And they do all the fulfillment and customer service.

Quotron

www.turnaround.com/ww_done/clients/citicorp/

An example of an infomediary, Quotron provided information about security prices to brokers. It had no proprietary access to this information. Quotron merely captured the security transaction information and recycled it back to the brokerage houses that generated it in the first place.

Candor's Birthday and Anniversary Reminder Service

www.candor.com/reminder/

An example of a service that reminds you about upcoming birthdays via email.

My Wish List

www.mywishlist.com

Enables consumers to create a shopping list of products that they want and direct friends and family to the site to view their list.

Your Registry

www.yourweddingregistry.com

Creates a custom gift-list registry for any occasion, then offers to purchase the gift from a variety of stores.

The Perfect Present

www.presentpicker.com

Lets a consumer choose a gift based on profession, lifestyle, age, or sex.

Deja.com

www.deja.com

Offers consumers reviews and recommendations on any number of products in a variety of categories.

Priceline

www.priceline.com

Pioneered a unique e-commerce pricing system known as a "demand collection system" that enables consumers to name their own price on a variety of products and services while enabling sellers to generate incremental revenue.

uBid

www.ubid.com

Operates an online auction for excess merchandise, offering close-out and refurbished products to consumers and small- to medium-sized businesses.

MobShop

www.mobshop.com

Aggregates demand for computer hardware and software, PDAs, home electronics, sporting goods, luggage, and more. As more consumers buy a product, the lower the price goes.

Respond.com

www.respond.com

An example of companies that have given consumers the power to negotiate the price they pay for products and services.

iShip

www.iship.com

Lets consumers price, compare, track, and manage shipments over the Internet. Consumers can see what kind of deal they received on shipping or do their research ahead of time to make sure they're charged a reasonable shipping rate by the e-tailer.

Digisolve

www.cemptor.com

Provides free complaint resolution services and statistical information on e-tailers such as the number of complaints logged against a company along with the average time of resolution.

MRO.com

www.mro.com

Good example of an exchange that supplies businesses with products for maintenance, repair, and operations.

iMark

www.imark.com

Focuses on selling used industrial equipment in an auction format between businesses.

iProcure

www.iprocure.com

Provides instant access to millions of industrial parts and supplies.

ChemConnect

www.chemconnect.com

Connect buyers and sellers worldwide on everything from raw chemicals to finished plastics and resins.

PaperExchange

www.paperexchange.com

Offers a marketplace for everything from cardboard to fine office paper.

Covisint

www.covisint.com

Five major automakers—General Motors, Ford Motor, DaimlerChrysler, Renault, and Nissan Motor—formed this automotive Internet Exchange. Covisint is touted by the automakers as the largest Internet business ever created.

Ask Jeeves

www.ask.com

Ask Jeeves provides its natural language search technology to other Web sites and companies such as Wal-Mart and Chrysler. In Chrysler's case, it lets the automaker provide better responses to online customer inquiries.

Staying Up to Date in e-Business

The Standard Intelligence Store

www.thestandard.com/research/store

Enables you to browse a variety of research reports all in one place. Report topics range from e-commerce and marketing to Web usage and auctions.

Jupiter Communications

www.jup.com

A research firm that focuses entirely on the Internet economy. Jupiter provides its business-to-business and business-to-consumer clients with comprehensive views of industry trends, accurate forecasts, and today's best practices, all backed by their proprietary data.

Forrester Research

www.forrester.com

A research firm that covers many of the same areas as Jupiter, such as research and analysis on the impact of the Internet and emerging technologies on business strategy, consumer behavior, and society. Their research spans consumer, business-to-business, and technology marketplaces.

The Right Site

www.easidemographics.com

Use their search interface to narrow your search by geography (ZIP codes, regions, and so on) and type of data (quality of life, income, and so on) for detailed market-specific statistics and reports.

eMarketer

www.e-land.com

Although not as proprietary or in depth as analysts such as Jupiter and Forrester, eMarketer is a comprehensive, objective, and easy to use resource for any business interested in the Internet. And it's free.

WebCMO

www.webcmo.com

Another free information source for market research. The marketing information they offer is not about what people have bought, but why people choose a product and the different market segments they belong to.

Cyber Atlas

cyberatlas.Internet.com

Gathers online research from the best data resources to provide a complete review of the latest surveys and technologies available.

NUA

www.nua.ie

Offers a compendium of news articles, reports, and surveys on all facets of the online world.

Deep Canyon

www.deepcanyon.com

Provides market research to help companies on the Net make informed strategic decisions.

Inc.com

www.inc.com/research/details/
0,3470,AGD1_CNT49_RSC15654,00.html

You can access more than 11,000 public, private, and international companies from Inc.com. Using their search facility, you can find basic company information, financials, key executives, key competitors, and home page addresses.

Hoover's Online

www.hoovers.com

At this site you can find the income statements and balance sheets of thousands of public companies. The service is not free but Hoover's Online lets anyone download free half-page profiles of many (mostly public) companies.

Inc. Top 500

www.inc.com/500

Inc. Magazine lists the fastest-growing companies in the country and provides information on thousands of privately held companies that have made the list in the past eight years. This information includes revenue information, profit-and-loss percentages, number of employees, and Web links.

NewsDirectory.com

www.newsdirectory.com

Find the latest news on your competitors. This site lists more than 2,000 newspapers, business journals, magazines, and computer publications. You can search any number of periodicals to locate news stories on your competitors. Some of the periodicals are more easily searched than others, and some charge fees.

Deja.com

www.deja.com

At Deja.com, you can search on keywords such as the name of your competitor or the product or service that you offer and see what the Net community is saying about them. Other places to check out include Remarq (www.remarq.com) and Liszt (www.liszt.com), a searchable directory of email discussion groups.

Patent and Trademark Office

www.uspto.gov

You can get a good idea on whether or not someone has filed a patent on a product or business methodology that your company is considering.

SurveySite

www.surveysite.com

SurveySite invites 8 to 10 people from around the Net or from a client's customer base for a specified period of time (90 minutes to two hours) in a specialized chat room. Their controlled chat room environment allows participants to view text, graphics, sounds, jingles, video, or multimedia for evaluation and testing.

Strategic Focus

www.sfionline.com

An online focus-group company that has been doing online focus groups since 1997 and offers companies an extensive screening and identification process.

Vividence

www.vividence.com

One of a new breed of Web-based survey groups that evaluates Web sites through online user testing. Vividence has a stable of nearly 100,000 online testers to view and comment on a company's Web site.

Active Research

www.activeresearch.com/products/ara_4c.htm

Their service is called ActiveFlash and is a custom Web survey service available for companies offering products or services within a large number of categories such as consumer electronics, home appliances, sporting goods, and so on.

OpinionLab

www.opinionlab.com

A different, more targeted, real-time approach to surveying a site visitor. Companies that subscribe to the OnlineOpinion survey service place a small OnlineOpinion icon on any page of their Web site, which invites consumers to voice their opinion on what they see or read.

Insight Express

www.insightexpress.com

Lets you create an online survey in minutes, choose your target audience, and receive feedback in hours. Through strategic relationships with Web sites and database companies, they can make your company visible to more than 70% of the entire Internet.

Protecting Your e-Business and Your Brand

CyberSource

www.cybersource.com

A provider of e-commerce transaction services and an early pioneer in the area of Internet fraud detection.

No Chargebacks

www.nochargebacks.com

A system that provides merchants access to a database of credit card numbers that have charged back transactions to mail order or Internet businesses.

CyberIntelligence's iDefense

www.idefense.com

Employs an entire group of intelligence analysts charged with identifying and fighting hacker attacks. For a yearly access fee, you can access the latest information on any computer virus, DoS attacks, or cyber-terrorists, as well as a full assessment of your e-business's current security infrastructure.

Elron Software

www.elronsw.com

A supplier of monitoring software for corporate email and Internet accounts.

MarketPlace Domain

www.marketplace.mp

Offers a new top-level domain (TLD) name with a suffix of dot-MP. The plan is to use the new TLD as a trademark-centric domain for those companies wanting to assure users that the Web site is real. MarketPlace Domain says it will eliminate the need for search engines and keyword searches for a company.

eWatch

www.ewatch.com

A clipping service that can provide you with up-to-the-minute notification of what's being said about your company in cyberspace.

MarkWatch

www.markwatch.com

MarkWatch provides the broadest coverage of Internet media for any company wanting to protect the abuse or use of their trademark on the World Wide Web.

WebClipping

www.webclipping.com

Services that monitor discussions about companies on the Net.

ePinions.com

www.epinions.com

Offers professional and volunteer-supplied reviews of consumer goods.

ConsumerReview.com

www.consumerreview.com

Offers frank opinions about products, services, and vendors from consumers that are either disappointed or delighted.

Shopserve.com

www.shopserve.com

This site enables consumers to post raves and rants about their experiences at stores, both on and offline. These sites could be monitored for these places are where consumers can get frank opinions about products, services, and vendors from consumers that are either disappointed or delighted.

Feedbackdirect.com

www.feedbackdirect.com

Using this site, consumers can initiate the customer service process with thousands of companies across more than 14 vertical categories. Using their service, consumers can fill out forms and fire off complaints and suggestions to e-businesses like yours.

Yodlee

www.yodlee.com

Helps consumers consolidate and manage personal accounts and interests in one place.

CallTheShots

www.calltheshots.com

Offers a technology that enables Web sites to deliver a personalized and customized user browsing experience.

Moreover.com

www.moreover.com

Provides news from a variety of sources in hundreds of carefully monitored categories, and custom news feeds for business applications.

Octopus.com

www.octopus.com

Allows individuals to customize and share their own news and information Web pages.

OnePage.com

www.onepage.com

One of several new companies creating a new way to view content on the Web. Rather than treat the Web as a collection of sites and pages, they literally scrape the content from Web pages, reorganize the content according to the wishes of the consumer, and serve it up in smaller components.

OpenTV

www.opentv.com

One of the leading worldwide providers of software that enables digital interactive television.

Pumatech's Browse-it

www.pumatech.com

This company provides services that chew up Web sites built for PC browsers and spit out versions reformatted for display on Net-appliances such as phones, set-top boxes—even voice-enabled Net gateways.

Selling Anywhere

EZsize

www.ezsize.com

EZsize sets up a pavilion at a brick-and-mortar store and consumers can measure their bodies in 3D. They then plug their measurements in the pavilion and order clothes that fit.

BarPoint

www.barpoint.com

Enter any barcode number of any product directly onto the BarPoint.com site and you can find all types of information on the item, check prices, read reviews, and, if you want, purchase it from one of more than 350 affiliate merchants.

Drugstore.com

www.drugstore.com

Drugstore.com and the click-and-mortar drug store RiteAid have integrated their services so that customers can place their prescription online and pick it up at the local RiteAid drug store.

Ecount

www.ecount.com

They have a Web certificate shopping card that's good at any brick-and-mortar merchant. If the recipient of an online Web certificate wants to make an offline purchase, Ecount issues a prepaid plastic card (that acts like a debit card) to use.

Dropzone1

www.dropzone1.co.uk

Dropzone1 is signing up petrol stations and corner shops across the U.K. that will accept delivery on behalf of online shoppers, who then pick up their packages on the way home from work.

UnderGroundOnline

www.ugo.com

This media distribution company has decked out two mobile Web assault–type vehicles that hit events such as skateboard competitions, concerts, and comic book conventions to reach its target market of 18 to 34-year-olds.

OpenTable.com

www.opentable.com

They are developing a massive nationwide network that will eventually handle tickets to restaurant tables in every major city.

Greatfood.com

www.greatfood.com

Part of 1-800 Flowers, this was one of the first pure dot-coms to launch a netalog. Its printed netalog was used to drive new traffic to its Web site.

Virgin Entertainment

www.virginmega.com

They distributed 10,000 Virgin-branded Web players to qualified consumers who can use them to buy CDs and videos from Virgin's online store.

GeePS.com

www.geeps.com

Provides a wireless shopping portal. Merchants can pinpoint a consumer's location and present offers to them as they pass by their establishments while either driving, strolling, or shopping.

NetByTel.com

www.netbytel.com

Brings e-commerce home to the common telephone. The company offers an automated, speech-enabled interface to e-commerce Web sites so that a customer can call from anywhere and conduct business over wired or wireless phone.

FreeTranslation.com

www.freetranslation.com

Offers a quick and simple translation of your offer. And it's free.

US-Style.com

www.us-style.com

They will handle the front end of your e-business if you are marketing to customers in Japan. They provide not only translation, but also cultural relevance.

VeloMail

www.velomail.com

A free email service that gives you the ability to write and receive emails in 40 languages.

Selling Anything

EXP.com

www.exp.com

One of a new type of e-businesses: expert services. It wants to be the next killer app of the Net, with person-to-person Q&A. It specializes in connecting people who have questions to people who can answer them.

CNET's Search.com

www.search.com

A perfect example of a comprehensive search service and an infomediary. True to the definition of an *infomediary*, most of the search engines that they offer really don't belong to them. Search.com links users to specialized engines on Web sites all around the Net, searching more than 700 different engines with one search.

Personics

www.personic.com

A B2B trading hub that links human resource departments, recruiting companies, and electronic job boards. Personics does not seek résumés from individual job-seekers. Rather, it aggregates data from individual job sites as well as from recruiting and staffing companies to create a central marketplace.

Delphi

www.delphi.com

Delphi has hundreds of thousands of discussion boards run by individuals on every conceivable subject. The company also provides live chat for each of the boards on its site.

Bot Spot

www.botspot.com/search/s-shop.htm

You can keep track of the price at which your competitors are selling the same products by using shopping bots. You can find a list of them at Bot Spot.

Frictionless Commerce

www.frictionless.com

This shopping bot not only will present the price of a product, but it also will include other offer information, such as shipping and handling fees charged for the product, merchant satisfaction guarantees, and return polices—that is, it will provide the full selling position of each merchant.

BiddersEdge

www.biddersedge.com

Let's shoppers compare prices for specific items at more than 80 auction sites.

AuctionWatch

www.auctionwatch.com

It specializes in boutique auctions, searching more than 300 boutique auction sites for products such as antiques and art, collectibles, and entertainment items.

Vertical One

www.verticalone.com

This company consolidates, organizes, and presents Internet users' personal account information with one master password, providing consumers with a single, easy-to-access interface for personal account information such as bank and brokerage statements, credit card balances, voice mails, emails, household bills, and travel award programs.

Third Voice

www.thirdvoice.com

It lets anyone who downloads its browser plug-in to post comments on any Web site. These comments can be viewed by anyone with the company's browser plug-in. The only way to see these comments is to use the Third Voice plug-in.

Selling Anytime

mySimon To-Go

www.mysimon.com/consumer_resources/mySimon_To_Go/index.anml

This company allows consumers to comparison-shop the Net while cruising their favorite brick-and-mortar stores. They can find out whether that hyped bargain at Best Buy is as good as it seems by running a quick comparison on their mySimon To-Go–enabled Palm Pilot.

PlanetRx.com

www.planetrx.com

Using ScanCart, their new handheld scanning device, you can load your PlanetRx shopping cart with all your favorite products from home. Just point it at an empty shampoo bottle or toothpaste tube, and it reads the bar code. Then upload the data into the PlanetRx shopping cart on the Web site.

RocketBoard

www.rocketboard.com

This company is giving its keyboard away for free. Each keyboard has 18 keys that link to more than 300 online merchants.

iChoose

www.ichoose.com

It created the iChoose Alert, a small, downloadable applet or software program that's installed on a consumer's computer. When the iChoose Alert icon spins on the taskbar, this signals the consumer that it's looking for a better deal on the product in the shopping cart. If the icon flashes, iChoose found a better deal, and it presents it to the consumer.

BeFree

www.befree.com

An affiliate solution provider that provides a service to track your affiliate program. Affiliate solution providers provide a combination of the network, software, and services needed to create and track an affiliate program.

Linkshare

www.linkshare.com

An affiliate solution provider that provides a service to track your affiliate program.

Commission Junction

www.cj.com

Another affiliate solution provider that also provides a service to track your affiliate program.

WebSponsors

www.websponsors.com

A results-based advertising network advertiser and affiliate. The sole purpose of this program is to provide reach to millions of new and different buyers for advertisers' products and services.

DirectLeads

www.directleads.com

Examples of pay-per-lead affiliate networks.

Barnes and Noble

www.bn.com

Offered the first email affiliate program through an affiliate solutions company called BeFree (www.befree.com).

Affiliateselling.com

www.affiliateselling.com

Has a list of the top 50 affiliate programs on the Net.

TRUSTe

www.etrust.com/wizard

You can create a privacy policy by using their wizard.

Selling Any Way

Dealtime

www.dealtime.com

This shopping bot can be accessed directly from the consumer's desktop, which enables them to start price comparisons instantly while they are browsing any leading online store without leaving the merchant's Web site.

RadicalMail

www.radicalmail.com

Delivers streaming content directly into emails without requiring a plug-in. There are no executable files and no lengthy downloads, and the email recipient requires no software.

Respond.com

www.respond.com

Connects shoppers with merchants using email. Customers submit requests in their own words, and Respond.com forwards these requests to the appropriate merchants. Merchants then send personal responses to shoppers through Respond.com. Shoppers then contact the merchants to negotiate a purchase.

Pointcast/EntryPoint

www.entrypoint.com

One of the first players on the Net to introduce a push technology. Pointcast pushed content to Net users in the form of news, weather, sports scores, and stock quotes.

FashionTV.com

www.fashiontv.com

Provides Internet viewers runway shows, photo shoots, fashion news, seasonal collections, and events in the fashion industry from around the world.

iNexTV

www.inextv.com

Provides streaming video programming for the Internet.

CinemaNow

www.cinemanow.com

Both of these companies demonstrate full-blown streaming video with elements of interactivity.

FileFury

www.filefury.com

Allows users to share files of any type, and search over other computers.

iMesh.com

www.imesh.com

This Web site allows users to search for and exchange various file types directly from the desktop without needing to set up a Web site or upload files to a server.

Centrata

www.centrata.com

This company is creating the world's largest virtual hard drive and most powerful virtual computer using PCs connected to the Net. Centrata has a unique business model that will enable the hundreds of millions of computer owners with Internet access to sell their unused computer resources over the Web.

Lightshare

www.lightshare.com

It's offering a service that will allow individual computer users to sell digital goods directly from their computers rather than going through centralized servers from companies such as eBay or Amazon.com.

eCount

www.ecount.com

eCount lets Net consumers conduct secure online transactions at any online store through the use of prepaid personal accounts.

RocketCash

www.rocketcash.com

Allows kids to purchase goods online without their parents' credit cards. Parents—or anyone, for that matter—who want to extend a prepaid purchasing limit to another party can set up an account at RocketCash.

PayPal

www.paypal.com

Provides account holders with a means to send money instantly and securely to other account holders for free.

eCommony's Pay2Card

www.pay2card.com

Enables Web sites to provide their customers with P2P transaction processing.

ProPay.com

www.propay.com

They offer secure payment services between consumers. With these P2P payment services, any consumer can become a seller—or a merchant—and can set up business on the Net.

Selling at Any Price

Mercata

www.mercata.com

Mercata lets consumers band together to get the lowest price on a product by using group purchasing power. This could revolutionize the power structure between buyers and seller.

TradeOut.com

www.tradeout.com

At Tradeout.com, companies with excess inventory can list it at auction for other companies to buy. Geared primarily to businesses, the average transaction at TradeOut.com is $20,000.

eWanted.com

www.ewanted.com

Lets buyers post what they want sellers to bid on.

NexTag.com

www.nextag.com

Offers online negotiations for computer products, software, and consumer electronics.

Priceline

www.priceline.com

Pioneered the "name your price" selling method in April 1998, when it launched its service enabling consumers to name their own price for leisure airline tickets.

HaggleWare

www.haggleware.com

It uses electronic salespeople to provide product information and pricing decisions that match buyers and sellers in online negotiations. You could haggle-equip your company Web site with the company's unique online negotiation technology.

Expedia

www.expedia.com

Lets consumers request their own prices for hotel rooms.

eCollegeBid.org

www.ecollegebid.org

Lets students set their own tuition and see if a college is willing to match it.

Fair Market

www.fairmarket.com

Gives merchants the ability to add an auction component to their site.

BillPoint

www.billpoint.com

Sellers who sign up for BillPoint can accept Visa debit or credit cards for their sales. This is as close to a person-to-person payment solution as any site so far has reached. Visa benefits by encouraging more people to use their Visa cards online for purchasing products at eBay.

The Consumer Product Safety Commission

www.cpsc.gov

Has partnered with two of the biggest online auction sites—Amazon and eBay—to protect people from buying dangerous second-hand products via online auctions.

Concurrent Commerce Technologies

www.concomtech.com

This company has patented a concurrent dynamic pricing system that lets merchants and manufacturers sell their goods in three or more dynamic pricing methods concurrently. Using CCT's technology, a merchant can dynamically price-enable any product offered on the Web site.

Promoting Your Business in the New Economy

notHarvard.com

www.notharvard.com

It builds compelling eduCommerce courseware for online stores.

iSyndicate

iSyndicate.com

It aggregates free content from more than 500 different providers in categories such as Top News and Weather, Sports News, Business and Finance, Entertainment and Lifestyles, Technology, and Health News—even Fun and Games. News providers include CNet, *Rolling Stone* magazine, CBS Market Watch, and Sporting News. And most of the content is free to use on your Web site.

Screaming Media

www.screamingmedia.com

With Screaming Media, you can display news stories based on any keyword that you choose. The story headlines and full stories are integrated into your site pages.

Pop2it

www.pop2it.com

This company helps content publishers link their articles to related products and services.

Flyswat

www.flyswat.com

Lets Web surfers click on what are called *flycons* attached to any word on a Web page or a computer screen and get a choice of links related to that information. These links let them go directly to the Web page they need. Flycons can be used within a Web site, email, word processing, or any Windows application.

Online Shopping Site

onlineshopping.about.com

Visitors can join in discussions, vote in polls, and participate in live chat sessions on the topic of online shopping connecting to the reader.

Build Your Own Community

www.buildacommunity.com

Offers software that lets you build guestbooks, discussion forums, polls, and many more interactive features including start pages for visitors that direct them right to your site.

Lands End

www.landsend.com

Provides live customer service through a chat interface.

Recommend It!

www.recommend-it.com

It supplies a service where you can ask visitors to your site who like what you offer to email your URL to a friend along with his comments.

The Mail Abuse Prevention System

www.mailabuse.org

It runs the Realtime Blackhole List (RBL), which is a compiled a list of *IP addresses* of known spammers, and offers this list to subscribers. Using the RBL list, these administrators reject any email that originates from those IP addresses.

The Direct E-Mail List Source

www.copywriter.com/lists/index.htm

A directory of voluntary email marketing lists. This is a resource for opt-in lists, newsletters, email discussion lists, advertiser-supported email services, and email list brokers where you can advertise without spamming.

Message Media

www.messagemedia.com

They will build and manage your opt-in email lists and send customized messages when needed; they can send email messages in either text or HTML formats.

NetCreations

www.netcreations.com

NetCreations works with more than 250 partner Web sites that ask visitors if they'd like to receive mailings on certain topics. NetCreations uses a "double opt-in" process and you can choose from more than 10 million opt-in email addresses in more than 3,000 categories.

Bulletmail

www.bulletmail.com

It gives you a choice of more than 100 targeted, opt-in email lists not available elsewhere. This company also targets your market by email in a Net-appropriate manner.

Email Marketing News

www.emailmarketingnews.com

A monthly email newsletter covering subscription email lists, opt-in email, corporate email marketing, advertising in email, email ad techniques, metrics, methods for countering spam, and evolving standards.

Acteva

www.acteva.com

You can list your service in Acteva's database so that it's accessible to anyone who visits the site, or you can send email invitations (Acteva calls them "prevites") to your customers.

GoCode

www.gocode.com

Offers a hand-held scanner to hyperlink print media to be viewed on a PC.

Digimarc

www.digimarc.com

Provides Scan Shopping to read specially encoded bar codes on products and in printed periodicals that, when scanned with a special bar code reader connected to a Net-enabled device, send the consumer directly to a Web page.

The Hollywood Stock Exchange

www.hsx.com

Visitors to HSX can buy and sell virtual shares in movies, celebrities, and musical artists with HSX's own currency—Hollywood Dollars. They can trade these hot entertainment commodities for free, build their portfolio, check out the latest news, chat with fellow entertainment buffs, and even win prizes.

Body Shop

www.bodyshop.com

It leverages the market for care with its focus on preserving the rain forests.

McDonald's

www.rmhc.com

It leverages the market for care with its Ronald McDonald House.

Abilizer Solutions

www.abilizer.com

It has attracted 70 companies with more than two million employees to use their Errand Portal, where workers can do everything from check stock quotes to plan family reunions and birthdays.

Connecting with the Customer

LEGO Mindstorms

www.legomindstorms.com

LEGO Mindstorms can be connected to a PC via an infrared signal to expand the toy's capability. At LEGO Mindstorms, owners of the toy are given free personalized accounts where they can upload creations and discuss building ideas thus creating a sense of community between the toy owners—that is, the LEGO customers.

EmWare

www.emware.com

They've created a lawn sprinkler system connected to the Net. The sprinkler itself is merely a platform for a range of upgraded services that can be integrated into the product. For a service fee, the sprinkler can be programmed to automatically contact the National Weather Service's Web site to check weather conditions and forecasts, and then turn the spray on and off accordingly.

PalmPower

www.palmpower.com

An online publication that carries advertising for your wireless product or service.

PalmUser

www.palmtop.co.uk/palmuser/index.htm

Another online publication that also carries advertising for your wireless product or service.

Pen Computing

www.pencomputing.com/palm/

Another online publication that also carries advertising for your wireless product or service.

Dynoform

dynoform.com

Lets you create personalized sweepstakes.

Sweepstakes Builder

sweepstakesbuilder.com

One of the largest sweepstakes sites in the world, this company can build, maintain, and promote your sweepstakes for you for a fee.

FreeShop.com

freeshop.com

A great place to list your incentive offer, free products and services, coupons, and other incentives.

Iq.com

www.iq.com

Thy have a product called Instant Action that is the digital equivalent of offline coupons. Using Instant Action, you can create any size teaser graphic that, when clicked, pops up an electronic coupon describing your offer.

ClickRewards

www.clickrewards.com

Offers ClickMiles—frequent flier miles—for shopping at your Web site.

MyPoints

www.mypoints.com

Offers shoppers reward points and offers a completely customizable private-label rewards program to e-businesses.

Creative Good

www.creativegood.com/survival

Offers a free report that shows how your e-business site can increase revenues by improving your customer experience. The report includes sections on strategies, tactics, and 31 e-commerce case studies on merchandising, email, navigation, search, checkout, and fulfillment.

EPage

www.homepage.com

The company's home page service offers a tool to e-businesses that personalizes customer Web pages to provide such customized information to the customer as product warranties, owner manuals, and purchase and customer service records—all part of on ongoing effort to keep customers informed and involved.

OrderTrust

www.ordertrust.com

This company's back-end loyalty program, called LoyalNet, is designed for easy use by online merchants, and the program is unthreatening and convenient for consumers worried about privacy and reluctant to carry even more frequent-purchase cards or to remember account codes.

Servicing the Customer

LivePerson

www.liveperson.com

Clicking a LivePerson link placed on a Web page launches a chat window where a customer service operator initiates a secure one-on-one text chat with the user. LivePerson requires no hardware or software installation on the part of your e-business.

eTetra.com

www.etetra.com

Web-based software enabling real-time, interactive communications with online customers.

HumanClick

www.HumanClick.com

Offers instant messaging chat service that connects Web site visitors with live sales people and customer service agents.

Live Assistance

www.liveassistance.com

A Web call center (in-house or outsourced) that offers communication through text chat.

Talk to a Person

www.talktoaperson.com

Allows a customer to chat instantly with sales and customer service staff.

Cahoots

www.cahoots.com

Puts Web surfers in touch with each other when visiting the same Web sites. Unlike instant messaging technology that lets people chat with others they know, Cahoots is designed to let strangers know about a site's content or products.

Webline Communications

www.webline.com

They offer an online chat window for customer service as well as a feature that allows two customers to link their browsers and shop together.

AOL Instant Messenger

www.aol.com/aim

Lets you chat with customers when they are online.

Jabber

www.jabber.com

A commercialized, open-source, XML-based instant messaging platform.

NetCall

www.netcall.com

Lets customers on the Net instantly connect to someone they can talk to whether from the Web, WAP, or digital TV, at any time, in real-time.

Global Online Telephone

www.globalonlinetelephone.com

Using Instant Call, the usual email promotion is sent but with the additional enhancement of an embedded link that gives recipients the option of receiving an immediate phone call from a sales or service representative.

HearMe

www.hearme.com

Their HearMe e-commerce solution provides both click-and-talk and phone callback capabilities, providing flexibility for both the customer and your customer service center.

Lipstream

www.lipstream.com

Lipstream has built a very simple, scalable voice service that enables people to talk to one another one-to-one or one-to-many, live on the Internet.

Vocalcommerce.com

www.vocalcommerce.com

Features voice over IP program. Adds Web-to-telephone functionality to Internet sites.

Instant Call

www.instantcall.com

Web callback service from USA Global Link. Customers click a button to instantly receive a free phone call. No software or hardware required.

Return Exchange

www.returnexchange.com

It provides a plug-in that allows e-tailers to make its service the 'Returns button' for their Web site. They manage the entire returns process.

Return View

www.returnview.com

Offers e-tailers a solution to managing returns including automated returns authorization, reporting, shipping, receiving, restoration, and resale.

Protecting Customer Privacy

Enonymous.com

www.enonymous.com

A Web-ratings firm that rates the privacy polices of Web sites.

Dash.com

www.dash.com

A comparison-shopping agent that looks over the shoulder of a consumer while he or she shops the Net. It compares the offers that a consumer is looking at with other online store offers in its database, showing better deals when available.

Persona

www.privaseek.com

Offers free software that gives Internet users control over how their personal information is used by the Persona-empowered sites they visit. By creating a Persona, consumers can provide only the types of personal information they would like to share with the sites they visit.

mValue.com

www.mvalue.com

It pays consumers cash to share their personal information with selected Web sites.

Advercast

www.surfsecret.com

Offers a software tool to consumers called SurfSecret, which blocks sites from tapping into the data stored on cookies in the user's browser.

TRUSTe

www.truste.org

TRUSTe has more than 1,300 companies participating in its privacy seal program, including names such as AOL, eToys, and myPoint.

Secure Assure

www.secureassure.org

It not only offers an audit program but requires members to adhere to a stringent privacy guideline stating that the e-business will never share a consumer's private information with a third party. It currently has almost 200 member sites.

ad click rate   Sometimes referred to as "click-through," this is the percentage of ad views that resulted in an ad click.

ad clicks   The number of times that users click on an ad banner.

ad views (impressions)   Number of times that an ad banner is downloaded and presumably seen by visitors.

affiliate   A Web site owner that earns a commission for referring clicks, leads, or sales to a merchant.

affiliate manager   The manager of an affiliate program who is responsible for creating a newsletter, establishing incentive programs, forecasting and budgeting, overseeing front-end marketing of the program, and monitoring the industry for news and trends.

affiliate program   A program that a Web site joins in which a merchant pays a commission to an affiliate for generating clicks, leads, or sales from a graphic or text link located on the affiliate's site.

affiliate program directory   A directory of affiliate programs, featuring information such as the commission rate, number of affiliates, and affiliate solution provider.

affiliate solution provider   A company that provides the network, software, and services needed to create and track an affiliate program.

affinity/point reward program   A program that rewards shoppers or visitors with predetermined rewards for purchases and other activity.

Asymmetrical Digital Subscriber Line (ADSL) The phone company's answer to cable modems. Unlike a cable modem, where many subscribers are on the same line, an ADSL circuit connects two specific locations and is much faster than a regular phone connection—it could be faster than a cable modem.

attention economy   A marketplace based on the idea that although information is essentially infinite, attention to it is limited. The term Attention Economy was coined by Michael H. Goldhaber in a paper presented at the conference on "Economics of Digital Information," in Cambridge, MA, January 23-26, 1997.

auto-responder   An email feature that sends an email message to anyone who sends it a blank message or a message with certain keywords.

bandwidth   The transmission capacity, usually measured in bits per second (bps), of a network connection. Video streaming and other multimedia applications require a high bandwidth.

banner   An electronic billboard or ad in the form of a graphic image that resides on a Web page, many of which are animated GIFs. The newer banners are interactive, with the capability to take an order through the banner ad.

baud   The baud rate refers to the speed of a modem. Common speed for modems today are 14.4K, 28.8K, 36.6K, and 56K. Cable modems and ASDL approach the speeds of a T1 telephone line.

bits per second (bps)   A measurement of how fast data is moved from one place to another, usually in thousands of bits per second (kilobits per second, Kbps) or millions of bits per second (megabits per second, Mbps). A 28.8 modem can transport 28,800 bits per second.

bot   A small piece of software that searches the Internet looking for sites or product pages (if it is a shopping bot).

brand   The commercial equivalent of a reputation.

browser   Software program such as Netscape or Internet Explorer that enables you to browse the World Wide Web and access the millions of pages that it contains.

cable modem   A modem connected to your local cable TV line. The bandwidth of a cable modem far exceeds the bandwidth of a 28.8Kbps modem and can be as fast at a T1 connection.

c-commerce   A subset of mobile commerce, or m-commerce. When transactions are made using a cellular phone, as opposed to any other Internet-enabled wireless device, this is called c-commerce.

chat room   You can "talk" in real time with other people in a chat room, but the words are typed instead of spoken.

click   Used in online advertising. A click is when someone follows a banner ad or link by clicking on it. The click rate is the number of clicks on an ad as a percentage of the number of times that the ad was downloaded with a Web page. A click rate of 1% means that 1% of the people who downloaded the page physically clicked on the ad.

client/server   The Internet is a client/server network. The client is the computer that requests a service or a piece of information from another computer system, or server, on the network. The PC that you use to access the Internet is the client. The Web server on which you store pages is the server.

commoditization   The process by which products become so easy to make or so plentiful that anybody can make or sell them, creating a highly competitive, price-sensitive marketplace.

concurrent dynamic pricing   The process of offering products for sale in more than one dynamic pricing method concurrently, such as auctions combined with a name-your-price strategy.

content-on-the-edges   A model in which information can be retrieved directly from PCs that are connected to the Internet without going through a central server.

convergence   The result of translating everything, from music to homework, into the digitized 1s and 0s of computer language and then making it all available anywhere in the world via the Internet on any type of wired or wireless Net appliance.

coopetition   Cooperation between competitors.

COPPA   The Children's Online Privacy Protection Act of 1998, put in place to protect the privacy of children on the Internet.

cracker   A person who breaks the security of computer systems to steal or destroy information. A nonmalicious cracker is called a hacker.

cyberspace   First coined by author William Gibson in his novel *Neuromancer*, cyberspace is used to describe the Internet.

data mining   Extracting knowledge from information. More than 95% of U.S. companies now use some form of data mining—this is often nothing more than mailing lists, but the collection of personal profiles is growing and upsets privacy advocates.

decentralization   Activities that are moved from the center of an organization or a process to the edges.

digital signatures   Like their pen-and-ink counterparts, these establish identity and can be used to establish legal responsibility.

disintermediation   The process of cutting out the middleman in the distribution channel from manufacturer to customer.

distributed selling   Selling through more than one technological distribution channel, such as through a Web site, a cell phone, a personal digital assistant (PDA), and an Internet-enabled appliance at that same time.

distribution channel   The means by which product is sold. Typical distribution channels include retail stores, catalogs, the Internet, and TV shopping.

dMail   The use of email for direct marketing.

domain name   A unique name that identifies an Internet site, such as mybusiness.com. A domain name always points to one specific server on the Internet where your Web site resides.

domain name server/domain name system (DNS)   A domain name server maps IP addresses to your URL on the Web. When someone types www.*your_business_name*.com into their browser, the DNS searches for your Web site's IP address, such as 208.56.111.00, and displays your Web page.

download   The transfer of data from a server on the Internet to your PC. You can use your browser or an FTP program to download files to your computer. When retrieving your email, you're downloading your email to your computer.

drop ship   Product shipped directly from the manufacturer typically without retailer inventory ownership.

e-cash (electronic cash)   A currency that can be exchanged over the Internet. It requires the buyer to purchase the electronic currency from a special bank via check, credit card, or debit card. The consumer then can use it to purchase goods from Internet vendors who accept e-cash.

e-CRM   Customer relationship marketing through electronic means.

email (electronic mail)   A message containing text or HTML sent over the Internet from one person to another or to a large number of email addresses using a mailing list.

email address   An electronic mailing address. Email addresses are in the form of `user@domain`, such as `frank@aol.com`.

email alias   Additional email addresses that point to another email address. All messages sent to an email alias are automatically forwarded to the specified "real" email address. This way, you can have more than one email address on an email account.

encryption   Procedure that encodes the contents of a file before sending it over the Internet. PGP (Pretty Good Privacy) is a commonly used encryption program. The recipient must have software to decrypt the file on their end.

FAQs (frequently asked questions)   A Web page that contains the most common questions and answers on a particular subject.

flame   The email equivalent of hate mail. Sometimes such hate messages are sent to the victim's email box tens and even hundreds of times.

FTP (file transfer protocol)   Used to download files from another computer, as well as to upload files from your computer to a remote computer. Through (regular) FTP, you can log in to another Internet site, but you must have a user ID and a password. Anonymous FTP servers don't require usernames or passwords.

gigabyte (GB)   One gigabyte equals approximately 1 billion bytes.

hacker   An expert programmer who uses his skills to break into computer systems or networks just for the fun of it or to expose security risks. Unlike a cracker, a real hacker doesn't want to harm anybody or anything.

hit   A single request from a browser to a server. All text on a Web page is a hit, and each individual graphic on a page is also counted as a hit. If a Web page consists of text and three graphics images, then one Web page would serve up four hits.

home page   The main page of a Web site. A Web site containing only one page is also called a home page.

ICQ ("I seek you")   A communications network on the Internet. If you want to know whether your friends are surfing the Web right now, ICQ does the searching for you, alerting you in real-time when your friends sign on. AOL Instant Messenger and Yahoo! Messenger are two other instant-messaging services.

impression   Each request from a user for a Web page on a particular server. Counting the impressions is a good way to measure the popularity of a Web site. If a user views three Web pages on your site, that counts as three impressions.

information technology   Tools for creating, sorting, storing, and moving data.

instant messaging   Sending messages directly to another individual in real-time. AOL Instant Messenger is an example. This can be used for instant customer service.

Integrated Services Digital Network (ISDN) Digital telephone system that can provide high-speed (up to 128Kbps) transmission of voice and data.

intellectual capital   The working knowledge that people carry in their heads—knowledge of products, customers, how to work together, and so on. This is a company's intellectual capital.

intellectual property   The legally protected ideas of an individual or company.

Internet   A network of computer networks. The Internet evolved from the ARPAnet (a U.S. military network) to an academic research network, to the current global commercial network. Other names for the Internet are the Net, cyberspace, and the information superhighway.

Internet service provider (ISP)   Company that provides Internet access to its members. Every time you log on, your ISP connects you to the Internet.

InterNIC (Internet Network Information Center)   The entity that keeps track of domain names. When you want to register a new domain name, you do it through InterNIC.

intranet   A private company network of computers using the same protocols as the Internet, but only for internal use.

IP address   A unique 32-bit Internet address consisting of four numbers separated by dots, such as 208.56.111.00. Every server connected to the Internet has a unique IP address.

IRL   Abbreviation for "in real life."

kilobits per second (Kbps)   Measure of data throughput. A 28.8Kbps modem transfers data at about 3.6KBps (kilobytes per second).

kilobyte (KB)   Approximately a thousand bytes (1,024 bytes).

Knowledge worker   Someone paid to think.

lifetime value of the customer   The amount of sales in dollars that a customer will spend with a company in his lifetime.

listserv   A mailing list. Similar to newsgroups but unlike newsgroups, listservs—a copyrighted type of mailing list software by Lsoft (www.listserv.net)—operate via email. When you send an email message to this group, your email is copied and sent to all subscribers.

location   Internet address as displayed on your browser. When you type the URL of a Web site into the location bar of your browser, your browser will take you to this page.

mail server   A server that handles incoming and outgoing email. This server is normally different from a Web server.

mass customization   A market of one person. Products and services customized for you.

megabits per second (Mbps)   Measure of data throughput in millions of bits per second.

m-commerce   Abbreviation for mobile commerce, selling products and services over a mobile device such as a cell phone or an Internet-enabled PDA.

meatspace   Cyberspeak for the real world—anything outside of cyberspace.

megabit   About one million bits. Exactly 1,048,576 bits.

megabyte (MB)   About one million bytes. Exactly 1,048,576 bytes, or 1,024KB.

mindshare   Brand awareness—and then some. Share of mind is much better than just share of market. Being talked about can be a very competitive advantage

Net   Abbreviation for the Internet.

netalog   A catalog companion to an e-commerce Web site. Products that are sold on the Web site are displayed and promoted in the printed catalog.

net-enabled devices   Any device that is connected to the Internet. This can be a cell phone, a PDA, a TV, or even a refrigerator or microwave oven.

netiquette (network etiquette)   Informal code of good manners on the Internet. One example is typing using both uppercase and lowercase letters because typing in all uppercase is considered shouting. Spamming is not good netiquette.

netizen   A responsible citizen of the Internet.

network   Group of computers or Internet-enabled devices that are connected so that they can share resources and exchange data.

newsgroup   Discussion group on Usenet among people who share a mutual interest. There are thousands of newsgroups covering almost every possible subject.

niche marketing   Meeting the needs of a particular buying audience. This involves, for instance, selling fitness equipment to health buffs, shock absorbers to auto manufacturers, or stock quotes to investors.

outsourcing   Contracting outside sources to fill your internal business needs.

page impression   A page impression occurs every time someone using the Internet displays a particular Web page.

PDA   Stands for Personal Digital Assistant. A Palm Pilot is an example of a PDA.

permission marketing   Gaining the permission of people before marketing to them. An opt-in email list is one form of permission marketing.

personalization   Directing a marketing message or providing a customized sales experience to a customer.

plug-in   Small piece of software, usually from a third-party developer, that adds new features to a Web browser.

posting   A single message posted to a newsgroup, bulletin board, or mailing list.

RA number   Return authorization number, required by a merchant to return a product.

rich media   An Internet advertising term for a Web page ad that uses advanced technology such as streaming video, downloaded applets (programs) that interact instantly with the user, and ads that change when the user's mouse passes over them.

screen scraper   A software application that lets users pull information from one Web site and deposit that information onto another Web site or into a database, even if the two sites are not connected.

search engine   An online database that enables Internet users to locate sites that have the information they need.

Secure Sockets Layer (SSL)   Protocol that enables you to send encrypted messages across the Internet. SSL uses public key encryption to pass data between your browser and a given server, such as when submitting credit card information. A URL that begins with `https` indicates that an SSL connection will be used.

server   A computer that has a permanent connection to the Internet. Web sites are stored on a Web server, and email is stored and sent through an email server.

shouting   Typing in all capital letters in a chat room or on a discussion board or newsgroup. This is deemed bad netiquette.

sig (signature file)   A small ASCII text file of four or five lines that is automatically attached to the end of an email message that includes additional information about the sender, such as name, address, phone numbers, and Web address (URL).

site-centric   A business model that consists of selling primarily from one's own Web site, accessible only from a computer.

spamming   Posting an unsolicited commercial message to a newsgroup or sending unsolicited email.

spider   Small piece of software, also known as a *bot*, used by some search engines to index Web sites.

streaming media (streaming audio/video)   Technology that enables you to play audio or video while it is still downloading.

T1   A telephone line that can transmit information at 1.544Mbps.

T3   A high-speed, high-bandwidth telephone line connection to the Internet. A T3 line can deliver information at 44.736Mbps—the equivalent of 28 T1 lines.

third-party customer service center   Outsourcing of customer service, including telephone center for handling orders and related customer service questions.

two-tier   Affiliate marketing model that allows affiliates to sign up additional affiliates below themselves so that when the second tier affiliates earn a commission, the affiliate above them also receives a commission.

URL (uniform resource locator) Address of any resource on the World Wide Web, such as your Web store's home page, for example `http://www.yourbusinessname.com`.

Usenet Worldwide decentralized distribution system of newsgroups. At least 15,000 newsgroups are available through the Internet.

viral marketing Any advertising that propagates itself the way viruses do. An example of this is Hotmail. When Hotmail users send emails, they promote the service to the recipients with a tagline at the bottom of their messages to get a Hotmail email address.

virtual private network (VPN) Either a private internal computer network commonly used by businesses, or a private external network such as America Online.

Web page One single document on the Web. A Web page can consist of text and graphics.

Web site A collection of Web pages that form a complete site.

Webmaster A person in charge of maintaining a Web site.

wetware Slang for the human brain.

World Wide Web An Internet client/server system to distribute information based upon the Hypertext Transfer Protocol (HTTP). Also known as WWW, W3, or the Web. It was created at CERN in Geneva, Switzerland, in 1991 by Dr. Tim Berners-Lee.

zine, e-zine Abbreviation for an online magazine. This is a good place to target-advertise your site.

A

shopping, 129

competition, 131-132

Dealtime, 130

Frictionless, 130

history of, 130

SmartShop, 130

Bottom Dollar

price comparisons, 108

Web site, 108

bounce-back emails, 178

brand reputation, protecting, 77-79

brands, scattering screen scrapers, 79-82

brick-and-mortar, 87

Internet success, 87

Broadband Content Delivery Forum, 135

brochureware, defined, 10

brokering

merchants

BizRate, 49

Customer Buying Cycle, 46, 49, 51

Frictionless Commerce, 49, 51

mySimon, 49-50

products (Customer Buying Cycle), 46, 48-49

Browse-it Web site, 81

building communities, 163

Bulletmail Web site, 178

business impact (Net Appliances), 19-21

business models

convergence, 17-19

site-centric, 115

defined, 116

dot-coms, 115-117

business-to-business. *See* **B2B**

business-to-consumer. *See* **B2C**

Buy.com Web site, 187

buying, aggregate, 149

Byrd, Lawrence, 217

C

c-commerce (cell commerce), 92

defined, 93

C2C (consumer-to-consumer) online auctions, 148

Cahoots Web site, 221

CallTheShots Web site, 80, 109

Campbell, Michael, *Nothing But 'Net*, **123**

Candor's Birthday and Anniversary Reminder Service Web site, 47

capital (intellectual)

New Economy, 28-29

retaining, 194

capturing

customer's attention, 13-15, 198-199, 202-206

share of customer, 200

share of market, 200

caring marketing, 192

catalogs (click-and-flip), 91

Sharper Image, 91

CCT (Concurrent Commerce Technologies), 151

cell commerce. *See* **c-commerce**

censorware, Cyber Patrol, 111

Centrata Web site, 137

centric strategies (e-business), 185

changing search profiles (consumers), 232

channels

contact, integrating, 16

marketing, 186-187

chargebacks, 74

chat rooms (interactive communities), 163-164

children, privacy, 236

Children's Online Privacy Protection Act. *See* **COPPA**

choice fair business practice, creating privacy policies, 238

choice fair information practice, 232

CinemaNow

streaming media, 135

Web site, 135

clearing transactions (AVS), 75

click-and-flip catalogs, 87-91

Sharper Image, 91

click-and-mortar, 87

click-to-chat

eTetra.com, 220

HumanClick, 220

International Business Systems, 220

LivePerson, 219-220

Talk To A Person, 220

ClickRewards Web site, 209

CNET Web site, 51

collecting customer information, 47-49

comments, monitoring customers, 78-79

commerce (online and offline), 88-91

DrugStore.com, 88

third-party privacy seals, 234

threats, 73

E-call Web site, 224

e-cash, 128, 139

eCount, 139

RocketCash, 139-140

e-commerce, 41

B2B, 52-53

bots, 129

content

informational, 159

education, 158-159

Customer Buying Cycle, 40

e-CRM. *See* **Electronic Customer Relationship Management**

e-tailers, 9

defined, 10

returns, 225-226

e-wallets, 139

eBay

C2C online auction, 148

dynamic pricing, 34

Web site, 34, 109, 148

eCollegeBid.org

price haggling, 147

Web site, 147

eCompare.com Web site, 188

economic, motivating consumers, 104

eCount

e-cash, 139

Web certificates, 89

Web site, 89, 139

education (content), e-commerce, 158-159

eduCommerce, defined, 159

eGroups Web site, 78

Electronic Customer Relationship Management, 214, 217

Electronic Information Center Web site, 239

electronic invitation services. *See* **invite sites**

Elron Software Web site, 76

email

affiliate marketing, 124-125

bounce-back, 178

direct, 179

messages, 179-180

rules, 180-181

text messages, 179

lists, opt-in, 177-178

marketing, 170-171

managing, 176

outsourcing, 170, 177-179

eMarketer

market intelligence research, 63

Web site, 63

Emblaze Creater 2.5

media technology, 134

Web site, 134

employees (New Economy intellectual capital), 28-29

emWare Web site, 201

Enderle, Rob, 222

Enliven

media firm, 135

Web site, 135

Enonymous.com Web site, 230

entertainment

consumers, motivating, 105

Napster, 105

EntryPoint

push marketing, 134

Web site, 134

ePage Web site, 209

ePinions.com Web site, 79

ePod

commerce-enabled content, 159

pop-ups, 123

Web site, 123, 159

escrow services

iEscrow, 140

Pay2Card, 140

PayPal, 140

ProPay.com, 140

TradeSafe, 140

eTetra.com

click-to-chat, 220

Web site, 220

European Data Protection Privacy Directive, 236

evaluating products (Customer Buying Cycle), 46, 51-52

events, staging, 192

Evoy, Ken, *Make Your Site Sell,* **123**

eWanted.com

price haggling, 146

Web site, 146

eWatch Web site, 79

Exchange flex pricing, 150

exchanges

industry

B2B, 54

PaperExchange, 54

services, creating value, 32

success (brick-and-mortar), 87

traffic

fiber, 185

wireless, 185

value, creating, 41

Internet Fraud Screen (CyberSource), 74-75

Internet service provider. *See* ISP

InternetPhone Web site, 27

investigations

federal (DoubleClick), 234

government, consumer information practices, 229-230

invite sites, 181-182

IP addresses, defined, 174

IPs

Information Packager, 42

Information Producer, 42

Information Provider, 42

Iq.com

Instant Action, 208

Web site, 123, 208

iShip

customer control, 51

Web site, 51

ISP (Internet service provider), 110

defined, 110

iSyndicate

content, 159

Web site, 159

J

Jabber

instant messaging, 222

Web site, 222

jack in, 190

Janel, Dan, *Dan Janel's Guide to Marketing on the Internet*, 209

Jeeves

B2BB2C (business-to-business business-to-customer), 55-56

Web site, 55-56

Jenson, Rolf, 191

Journal of Web Marketing, 64

Jupiter Communications, 223

industry analysts, 61

Web site, 61

K

keeping customer's attention, 208-212

keyboard's hot keys (RocketBoard), 118

killer apps, defined, 166

Kozmo.com

same-day delivery stores, 90

Web site, 90

L

L.L. Bean, 191

Lands End

chat interface, 164

customer relationships, 220

Web site, 164, 221

learning community, 162

leasing content, 160

LEGO, 201

LEGO Mindstorms Web site, 201

lifetime value, 199

defined, 200

Lightshare Web site, 138

links (banner), affiliate marketing, 121-122

LinkShare

affiliate solution provider, 120, 126

Web site, 126

Lipstream

live voice interaction, 223-224

Web site, 223-224

list management, outsourcing, 170

ListBot

discussion list service, 165

Web site, 165

Liszt

market intelligence (competitors), 65

Web site, 65

live voice interaction

customer service, 223

HearMe, 223-224

Instant Call, 224

Lipstream, 223-224

Net2Phone, 224

Vocalcommerce, 224

LivePerson

click-to-chat, 219-220

Web site, 218-220

LoCascio, Robert, 218, 221

locating Web sites, difficulties, 116

loss leaders, defined, 207

lotteries, promotions, 207

negotiating

    MobShop, 50

    ubid.com, 50

PricewaterhouseCoopers, 77

pricing

    dynamic, 35, 143-146

        Auto-By-Tel, 34

        concurrent, 150-153

        eBay, 34

        haggling, 146-147

        Mercata, 34

        MyGeek, 34

        online auctions, 147

        Priceline.com, 34

    flex (Exchange), 150

    personalized (Mercata), 143

privacy

    children, 236

    customers (e-businesses), 228-238

    government regulations, 230

    policies, creating, 237-239

    seals (third-party)

        Better Business Bureau, 235

        e-businesses, 234

        TRUSTe, 234

    statements (TRUSTe wizard), 127

private label manufacturing, 105

products

    consideration set, 46

    Customer Buying Cycle

        brokering, 46-49

        evaluating, 46, 51-52

        negotiating and purchasing, 46, 50-51

        servicing, 46, 51-52

    free, 201, 204-205

    Internet, 24

    suppliers (B2B), 53

promotions

    contests, 204

        Alternative Method of Entry, 207

        legal information, 206-207

    give-aways, 207

    lotteries, 207

    sweepstakes, 204-206

        Alternative Method of Entry (AMOE), 207

        legal information, 206-207

ProPay.com

    escrow service, 140

    Web site, 140

property (intellectual), threats, 76-77

protecting brand reputation, 77-79

providers (content), 161

Pumatach's Browse-it Web site, 81

purchasing products (Customer Buying Cycle), 46, 50-51

push marketing (EntryPoint), 134

push technology

    bandwidths, 134

    defined, 134

Q

QuickBrowse.com Web site, 109

Quitus Web site, 217

Quotron

    infomediary, 43

    Web site, 43

R

RadicalMail Web site, 132

Rangan, Venkat, 81

RBL (Realtime Blackhole List), 173

Real Audio Web site, 118

RealPublisher 5.0

    media technology, 134

    Web site, 134

Realtime Blackhole List. *See* **RBL**

Recommend It! Web site, 168

Recording Industry Association of America. *See* **RIAA**

Refer-it

    affiliate program directory, 122

    Web site, 122

registries (gifts), Your Registry, 47

REI Web site, 90-91

relationships

    bonding, 211

    customers, 198-202, 209-212

    management (customers), 214-225

    technologies, 199

Remarq

    market intelligence (competitors), 65

    Web site, 65

THE NEEDLES

A New Booke wher

Workes wrought with the

cut in Copper for the pleaf